World in Conflict, Mind in Transition

Interviews with Sam Vaknin

by

Sam Vaknin, Ph.D.

Professor of Psychology

Southern Federal University, Rostov-on-Don, Russian Federation and SIAS-CIAPS

Centre for International Advanced Professional Studies (SIAS Outreach)

The author is NOT a Mental Health Practitioner

The book is based on interviews since 1996 with 2000 people diagnosed with

Narcissistic and Antisocial Personality Disorders (narcissists and psychopaths)

and with thousands of family members, friends, therapists, and colleagues.

Editing and Design:

Lidija Rangelovska

A Narcissus Publications Imprint

Prague & Haifa 2023

Visit the Author's Web site	http://www.narcissistic-abuse.com
Facebook	http://www.facebook.com/samvaknin
	http://www.facebook.com/narcissismwithvaknin
YouTube channel	http://www.youtube.com/samvaknin
Instagram	https://www.instagram.com/vakninsamnarcissist/ (archive)
	https://www.instagram.com/narcissismwithvaknin/

Buy other books and video lectures about pathological narcissism and relationships with abusive narcissists and psychopaths here:

http://www.narcissistic-abuse.com/thebook.html

Buy Kindle books here:

http://www.amazon.com/s/ref=ntt_athr_dp_sr_1?_encoding=UTF8&field-author=Sam%20Vaknin&search-alias=digital-text&sort=relevancerank

CONTENTS

Throughout this book click on blue-lettered text to navigate to different chapters
or to access online resources

<u>Interview about Nothingness</u> (News Intervention)

Sam Vaknin (https://samvak.tripod.com/mediakit.html) is the author of Malignant Self-love: Narcissism Revisited as well as many other books and ebooks about topics in psychology, relationships, philosophy, economics, international affairs, and award-winning short fiction.

He is Visiting Professor of Psychology, Southern Federal University, Rostov-on-Don, Russia and Professor of Finance and Psychology in SIAS-CIAPS (Centre for International Advanced and Professional Studies).

Scott Douglas Jacobsen: Our focus today is the proposal of "nothingness" in a specific sense by you. To start in negation, what is not "nothingness," in your sense?

Professor Sam Vaknin:

Nothingness is not about being a nobody and doing nothing. It is not about self-negation, self-denial, idleness, fatalism, or surrender.

Jacobsen: Following from the previous question, what is nothingness?

Vaknin:

Nothingness is about choosing to be human, not a lobster. It is about putting firm boundaries between you and the world. It is about choosing happiness - not dominance. It is accomplishing from within, not from without. It is about not letting others regulate your emotions, moods, and thinking. It is about being an authentic YOU.

Jacobsen: How does this nothingness connect to Neo-Daoism and Buddhism?

Vaknin:

It would be best to watch this video: https://www.youtube.com/watch?v=C8ePaN70SyM&t=1s

Jacobsen: We live, as many know, in an era of narcissism. You brought this issue to light in 1995, particularly pathological narcissism. What are the roots of the ongoing rise in individual and collective narcissism?

Vaknin:

The need to be seen and noticed in an overcrowded and terrifyingly atomized world. Ironically, narcissism is a cry for help, a desperate attempt to reconnect. There is no such thing as an "individual": we are all the products of our interactions with others (object relations). But, increasingly, technology is rendering us self-sufficient and isolated. So, our social instincts metastasize into narcissism: dominance and hierarchy replace sharing and networking.

Jacobsen: How does one choose happiness over dominance, authenticity over being fake, and humanity rather than lobster-kind, with this form of nothingness?

Vaknin:

We need to choose happiness over dominance (be human, not a lobster); Choose Meaning over complexity; Choose fuzziness, incompleteness, imperfection, uncertainty, and unpredictability (in short: choose life) over illusory and fallacious order, structure, rules, and perfection imposed on reality (in short: death); Choose the path over any destination, the journey over any goal, the process over any outcome, the questions over any answers Be an authentic person with a single inner voice, proud of the internal, not the external.

Jacobsen: What is the importance of living a life worth remembering in the philosophy of nothingness?

Vaknin:

Identity depends on having a continuous memory of a life fully lived and actualized. At the end of it all, if your life were a movie, would you want to watch it from beginning to end? Nothingness consists of directing your life in accordance with an idiosyncratic autobiographical script: yours, no one else's. Being authentic means becoming the single story which only you can tell.

Jacobsen: What type of personality or person can accept nothingness in its fullest sense?

Vaknin:

Only those who are grandiose are incapable of Nothingness. Grandiosity is the illusion that one is godlike and, therefore, encompasses everything and everyone. Grandiosity, therefore, precludes authenticity because it outsources one's identity and renders it reliant on input from others (hive mind).

Jacobsen: How is nothingness an antidote to narcissism?

Vaknin:

Narcissism is ersatz, the only self is false, others are instrumentalized and used to regulate one's sense of faux cohering oneness. Nothingness is echt, harking back to the only true, authentic voice, eliminating all other introjects, not using others to regulate one's internal psychological landscape. Narcissism is alienation, it interpellates in a society of the spectacle. Nothingness gives rise to true intimacy.

Jacobsen: What is the ultimate wisdom in the philosophy of nothingness?

Vaknin:

Identify the only voice inside you that is truly you. Peel the onion until nothing is left behind but its smell. Rid yourself of introjected socialization. Become.

Jacobsen: Then, to conclude, what is the motto or catchphrase of nothingness in this sense?

Vaknin:

Do unto yourself what you want others to do to you.

Jacobsen: Thank you for the opportunity and your time, Professor Vaknin.

Vaknin: Much obliged for having me. Always a pleasure.

Return

<u>Interview about Narcissism</u> (News Intervention)

__Prof. Sam Vaknin__ is the author of <u>Malignant Self-love: Narcissism Revisited</u> *(*<u>Amazon</u>*) as well as many other* <u>books</u> *and* <u>ebooks</u> *about topics in psychology, relationships, philosophy, economics, international affairs, and award-winning short fiction. He is* <u>Visiting Professor of Psychology, Southern Federal University, Rostov-on-Don, Russia (September, 2017 to present) and Professor of Finance and Psychology in SIAS-CIAPS (Centre forInternational Advanced and Professional Studies) (April, 2012 to present)</u>*. Here we talk briefly about his work on narcissism, generally.*

Scott Douglas Jacobsen: Your *raison d'être* is narcissism. "Narcissism" is rooted in the Greek myth of Narcissus. Narcissus rejected a nymph, Echo. His punishment: eternal love with his reflection in water. Narcissists, as you state, love their reflection, not themselves. This raises the distinction between the False Self and the True Self. What distinguishes the False Self from the True Self?

Professor Sam Vaknin:

The True Self is the unconstellated (unintegrated) precursor to the Self. It includes introjected object-representation (voices and inner objects – "avatars" – which represent caregivers, such as parental figures).

Abuse during the formative years disrupts the integration of the True Self and its replacement by a False Self: a godlike construct that performs several functions.

1. It serves as a decoy, it "attracts the fire". It is a proxy for the True Self. It is tough as nails and can absorb any amount of pain, hurt and negative emotions. By inventing it, the child develops immunity to the indifference, manipulation, sadism, smothering, or exploitation – in short: to the abuse – inflicted on him by his parents (or by other Primary Objects in his life). It is a cloak, protecting him, rendering him invisible and omnipotent at the same time.

2. The False Self is misrepresented by the narcissist as his True Self. The narcissist is saying, in effect: "I am not who you think I am. I am someone else. I am this (False) Self. Therefore, I deserve a better, painless, more considerate treatment." The False Self, thus, is a contraption intended to alter other people's behaviour and attitude towards the narcissist.

In a full-fledged narcissist, the False Self imitates the True Self. To do so artfully, it deploys two mechanisms:

Re-Interpretation

It causes the narcissist to re-interpret certain emotions and reactions in a flattering, socially acceptable, light. The narcissist may, for instance, interpret fear as compassion. If the narcissist hurts someone he fears (e.g., an authority figure), he may feel bad afterwards and interpret his discomfort as empathy and compassion. To be afraid is humiliating – to be compassionate is commendable and earns the narcissist social commendation and understanding (narcissistic supply).

Emulation

The narcissist is possessed of an uncanny ability to psychologically penetrate others. Often, this gift is abused and put at the service of the narcissist's control freakery and sadism. The narcissist uses it liberally to annihilate the natural defences of his victims by faking empathy.

This capacity is coupled with the narcissist's eerie ability to imitate emotions and their attendant behaviours (affect). The narcissist possesses "emotional resonance tables". He keeps records of every action and reaction, every utterance and consequence, every datum provided by others regarding their state of mind and emotional make-up. From these, he then constructs a set of formulas, which often result in impeccably accurate renditions of emotional behaviour. This can be enormously deceiving.

Jacobsen: Why does the narcissist love their "reflected-Self," as in the myth of Narcissus, rather than their True Self?

Vaknin:

Because it provides all the above-mentioned functions. For the same reason that people love god. It is a proxy ideal parental figure and it renders the narcissist divine-by-association: omniscient, omnipotent, brilliant, perfect, infallible, and so on. Gradually, the narcissist comes to identify himself (or herself) with the False Self (which started off as a fantastic imaginary friend in a paracosm). Looking at it this way, narcissism is a private religion: the False Self is the deity, the narcissist is the worshipper, and the True Self is the human sacrifice.

Jacobsen: What differentiates the Ego, the Superego, and the Self? What is the nature of narcissism regarding these, in general?

Vaknin:

I regard the trilateral model as metaphorical, not as "real" or "objective" in any sense.

In the narcissist, the False Self usurps the role of the Ego and fulfils its functions: mediation between the individual and the world and a sense of personal continuity.

The False Self pretends to be the only self and denies the existence of a True Self. It is also extremely useful (adaptive). Rather than risking constant conflict, the narcissist opts for a solution of "disengagement".

The classical Ego, proposed by Freud, is partly conscious and partly preconscious and unconscious. The narcissist's Ego is completely submerged. The preconscious and conscious parts are detached from it by early traumas and form the False Ego.

The Superego in healthy people constantly compares the Ego to the Ego Ideal. The narcissist has a different psychodynamic. The narcissist's False Self serves as a buffer and as a shock absorber between the True Ego and the narcissist's sadistic, punishing, immature Superego. The narcissist aspires to become pure Ideal Ego.

The narcissist's Ego cannot develop because it is deprived of contact with the outside world and, therefore, endures no growth-inducing conflict. The False Self is rigid. The result is that the narcissist is unable to respond and to adapt to threats, illnesses, and to other life crises and circumstances. He is brittle and prone to be broken rather than bent by life's trials and tribulations.

The Ego remembers, evaluates, plans, responds to the world and acts in it and on it. It is the locus of the "executive functions" of the personality. It integrates the inner world with the outer world, the Id with the Superego. It acts under a "reality principle" rather than a "pleasure principle".

This means that the Ego is in charge of delaying gratification. It postpones pleasurable acts until they can be carried out both safely and successfully. The Ego is, therefore, in an ungrateful position. Unfulfilled desires produce unease and anxiety. Reckless fulfilment of desires is diametrically opposed to self-preservation. The Ego has to mediate these tensions.

In an effort to thwart anxiety, the Ego invents psychological defence mechanisms. On the one hand the Ego channels fundamental drives. It has to "speak their language". It must have a primitive, infantile, component. On the other hand, the Ego is in charge of negotiating with the outside world and of securing a realistic and optimal "bargains" for its "client", the Id. These intellectual and perceptual functions are supervised by the exceptionally strict court of the Superego.

Jacobsen: How do narcissists manage the balance between their sadistic superego and False Self?

Vaknin:

The irony is that narcissists are "self-less". The narcissist's True Self is introverted and utterly dysfunctional. In healthy people, Ego functions are generated from the inside, from the Ego. In narcissists, the Ego is dormant, comatose. The narcissist needs the input of and feedback from the outside world (from others) in order to perform the most basic Ego functions (e.g., "recognizing" of the world, setting boundaries, forming a self-definition or identity, differentiation, self-esteem, and regulating his sense of self-worth). This input or feedback is known as narcissistic supply" .Only the False Self gets in touch with the world. The True Self is isolated, repressed, unconscious, a shadow.

The False Self is, therefore, a kind of "hive self" or "swarm self". It is a collage of reflections, a patchwork of outsourced information, titbits garnered from the narcissist's interlocutors and laboriously cohered and assembled so as to uphold and buttress the narcissist's inflated, fantastic, and grandiose self-image. This discontinuity accounts for the dissociative nature of pathological narcissism as well as for the narcissist's seeming inability to learn from the errors of his ways.

In healthy, normal people ego functions are strictly internal processes. In the narcissist, ego functions are imported from the surroundings, they are thoroughly external. Consequently, the narcissist often confuses his inner mental-psychological landscape with the outside world. He tends to fuse and merge his mind and his milieu. He regards significant others and sources of supply as mere extensions of himself and he appropriates them because they fulfil crucial internal roles and, as a result, are perceived by him to be sheer internal objects, devoid of an objective, external, and autonomous existence.

The narcissist is an even more extreme case. His Ego is non-existent. The narcissist has a fake, substitute Ego. This is why his energy is drained. He spends most of it on maintaining, protecting and preserving the warped, unrealistic images of his (False) Self and of his (fake) world. The narcissist is a person exhausted by his own absence.

The healthy Ego preserves some sense of continuity and consistency. It serves as a point of reference. It relates events of the past to actions at present and to plans for the future. It incorporates memory, anticipation, imagination and intellect. It defines where the individual ends and the world begins. Though not coextensive with the body or with the personality, it is a close approximation.

In the narcissistic condition, all these functions are relegated to the False Ego. Its halo of confabulation rubs off on all of them. The narcissist is bound to develop false memories, conjure up false fantasies, anticipate the unrealistic and work his intellect to justify them.

The falsity of the False Self is dual: not only is it not "the real thing" – it also operates on false premises. It is a false and wrong gauge of the world. It falsely and inefficiently regulates the drives. It fails to thwart anxiety.

The False Self provides a false sense of continuity and of a "personal centre". It weaves an enchanted and grandiose fable as a substitute to reality. The narcissist gravitates out of his self and into a plot, a narrative, a story. He continuously feels that he is a character in a film, a fraudulent invention, or a con artist to be momentarily exposed and summarily socially excluded.

Moreover, the narcissist cannot be consistent or coherent. His False Self is preoccupied with the pursuit of Narcissistic Supply. The narcissist has no boundaries because his Ego is not sufficiently defined or fully differentiated. The only constancy is the narcissist's feelings of diffusion or annulment. This is especially true in life crises, when the False Ego ceases to function.

The narcissist's superego is comprised of infantile, harsh, sadistic introjects. It is frozen in time, in an early stage of personal development, devoid of reflective self-awareness. It is much closer to the Id and leverages its aggression against the self.

The narcissist is besieged and tormented by a sadistic Superego which sits in constant judgement. It is an amalgamation of negative evaluations, criticisms, angry or disappointed voices, and disparagement meted out in the narcissist's formative years and adolescence by parents, peers, role models, and authority figures.

These harsh and repeated comments reverberate throughout the narcissist's inner landscape, berating him for failing to conform to his unattainable ideals, fantastic goals, and grandiose or impractical plans. The narcissist's sense of self-worth is, therefore, catapulted from one pole to another: from an inflated view of himself (incommensurate with real life accomplishments) to utter despair and self-denigration.

Hence the narcissist's need for Narcissistic Supply to regulate this wild pendulum. People's adulation, admiration, affirmation, and attention restore the narcissist's self-esteem and self-confidence.

The narcissist's sadistic and uncompromising Superego affects three facets of his personality:

1. His sense of self-worth and worthiness (the deeply ingrained conviction that one deserves love, compassion, care, and empathy regardless of what one achieves). The narcissist feels worthless without Narcissistic Supply.

2. His self-esteem (self-knowledge, the deeply ingrained and realistic appraisal of one's capacities, skills, limitations, and shortcomings). The narcissist lacks clear boundaries and, therefore, is not sure of his abilities and weaknesses. Hence his grandiose fantasies.

3. His self-confidence (the deeply ingrained belief, based on lifelong experience, that one can set realistic goals and accomplish them). The narcissist knows that he is a fake and a fraud. He, therefore, does not trust his ability to manage his own affairs and to set practical aims and realize them.

By becoming a success (or at least by appearing to have become one) the narcissist hopes to quell the voices inside him that constantly question his veracity and aptitude. The narcissist's whole life is a two-fold attempt to both satisfy the inexorable demands of his inner tribunal and to prove wrong its harsh and merciless criticism.

It is this dual and self-contradictory mission, to conform to the edicts of his internal enemies and to prove their very judgement wrong, that is at the root of the narcissist's unresolved conflicts.

On the one hand, the narcissist accepts the authority of his introjected (internalised) critics and disregards the fact that they hate him and wish him dead. He sacrifices his life to them, hoping that his successes and accomplishments (real or perceived) will ameliorate their rage.

On the other hand, he confronts these very gods with proofs of their fallibility. "You claim that I am worthless and incapable" – he cries – "Well, guess what? You are dead wrong! Look how famous I am, look how rich, how revered, and accomplished!"

But then much rehearsed self-doubt sets in and the narcissist feels yet again compelled to falsify the claims of his trenchant and indefatigable detractors by conquering another woman, giving one more interview, taking over yet another firm, making an extra million, or getting re-elected one more time.

To no avail. The narcissist is his own worst foe. Ironically, it is only when incapacitated that the narcissist gains a modicum of peace of mind. When terminally ill, incarcerated, or inebriated the narcissist can shift the blame for his failures and predicaments to outside agents and objective forces over which he has no control. "It's not my fault" – he gleefully informs his mental tormentors – "There was nothing I could do about it! Now, go away and leave me be."

And then – with the narcissist defeated and broken – they do and he is free at last.

More generally:

In the patient with a personality disorder, the sadistic and disparaging inner voices that constitute the Superego (in Freud's parlance) are implacable. If the patient is successful these introjects, or inner representations (of narcissistic parents, for example), become virulently envious and punitive. If the patient fails in his endeavours, these internalized avatars feel vindicated, elated, euphoric and morally justified in their quest to inflict pain and castigation on the patient.

But why does the patient not resist? Why doesn't s/he rebel against these embedded tormentors, at least by doubting their omniscience, infallibility, and veracity? Because it feels good to satisfy them (it feels good to cater to mother's emotional needs and thereby to be a "good boy", for example). It is a masochistic Stockholm Syndrome, a shared psychosis (follies a plusieurs). The patient doesn't experiences these harsh juries sitting in judgement over him, his traits, skills, and actions as alien, but as an integral part of himself. Their gratification at his self-immolation is also his.

Jacobsen: What is the fundamental difference between individuals with low to moderate narcissistic tendencies and individuals with a formal diagnosis of Narcissistic Personality Disorder (NPD)?

Vaknin:

Len Sperry distinguished between narcissistic style and narcissist disorder. Millon contributed the mezzanine level: narcissistic personality. These are gradations. The differences between these three reflect a higher intensity, all-pervasiveness (effects on all realms of life) and the escalation of the effects of the various narcissistic behaviors and traits on the individual and on his human environment.

Jacobsen: Narcissism comes with internal processes and externalized behaviours, including abusive. What is the internal landscape, or matrix of cognitive and emotional processes, of a narcissist? What are the externalizing behaviours of narcissism, the signifiers?

Vaknin:

Both types of narcissists – overt and covert (fragile, shy, vulnerable, inverted) – are invested in extracting narcissistic supply to regulate their fluctuating sense of self-worth. They also lack empathy.

The fifth edition of the Diagnostic and Statistical Manual (DSM, 2013) includes a dimensional model of NPD.

The DSM V re-defines personality disorders thus:

"The essential features of a *personality disorder* ***are impairments in personality (self and interpersonal) functioning and the presence of*** *pathological personality* ***traits."***

According to the Alternative DSM V Model for Personality Disorders (p.767), the following criteria must be met to diagnose Narcissistic Personality Disorder (in parentheses my comments):

Moderate or greater impairment in **personality functioning** in either identity, or self-direction (should be: in both.)

Identity

The narcissist keeps referring to others excessively in order to regulate his self-esteem (really, sense of self-worth) and for "self-definition" (to define his identity.) His self-appraisal is exaggerated, whether it is inflated, deflated, or fluctuating between these two poles and his emotional regulation reflects these vacillations.

(Finally, the DSM V accepted what I have been saying for decades: that narcissists can have an "inferiority complex" and feel worthless and bad; that they go through cycles of ups and downs in their self-evaluation; and that this cycling influences their mood and affect).

Self-direction

The narcissist sets goals in order to gain approval from others (narcissistic supply; the DSM V ignores the fact that the narcissist finds disapproval equally rewarding as long as it places him firmly in the limelight.) The narcissist lacks self-awareness as far as his motivation goes (and as far as everything else besides.)

The narcissist's personal standards and benchmarks are either too high (which supports his grandiosity), or too low (buttresses his sense of entitlement, which is incommensurate with his real-life performance.)

Impairments in **interpersonal functioning** in either empathy or intimacy (should be: in both.)

Empathy

The narcissist finds it difficult to identify with the emotions and needs of others, but is very attuned to their reactions when they are relevant to himself (cold empathy.) Consequently, he overestimates the effect he has on others or underestimates it (the classic narcissist never underestimates the effect he has on others - but the inverted narcissist does.)

Intimacy

The narcissist's relationships are self-serving and, therefore shallow and superficial. They are centred around and geared at the regulation of his self-esteem (obtaining narcissistic supply for the regulation of his labile sense of self-worth.)

The narcissist is not "genuinely" interested in his intimate partner's experiences (implying that he does fake such interest convincingly.) The narcissist emphasizes his need for personal gain (by using the word "need", the DSM V acknowledges the compulsive and addictive nature of narcissistic supply). These twin fixtures of the narcissist's relationships render them one-sided: no mutuality or reciprocity (no intimacy).

Pathological personality traits

Antagonism characterized by **grandiosity and attention-seeking**

Grandiosity

The aforementioned feeling of entitlement. The DSM V adds that it can be either overt or covert (which corresponds to my taxonomy of classic and inverted narcissist.)

Grandiosity is characterized by self-centredness; a firmly-held conviction of superiority (arrogance or haughtiness); and condescending or patronizing attitudes.

Attention-seeking

The narcissist puts inordinate effort, time, and resources into attracting others (sources of narcissistic supply) and placing himself at the focus and centre of attention. He seeks admiration (the DSM V gets it completely wrong here: the narcissist does prefer to be admired and adulated, but, failing that, any kind of attention would do, even if it is negative.)

The diagnostic criteria end with disclaimers and differential diagnoses, which reflect years of accumulated research and newly-gained knowledge:

The above enumerated impairments should be ***"stable across time and consistent across situations ... not better understood as normative for the individual's developmental stage or socio-cultural environment ... are not solely due to the direct physiological effects of a substance (e.g., a drug of abuse, medication) or a general medical condition (e.g., severe head trauma)."***

It is important to note that the DSM is used mostly in North America. The rest of the world uses local variants of the ICD.

There is a revolutionary paradigm shift regarding personality disorders in the 11th edition of the ICD (International Statistical Classification of Diseases and Related Health Problems), published by the WHO (World Health Organization). Watch this video for more: https://www.youtube.com/watch?v=eZB0JE4mzaw

Jacobsen: Those externalized behaviours can be abusive, e.g., narcissistic abuse. What is narcissistic abuse?

Vaknin:

In 1995, I coined the phrase "narcissistic abuse" to describe a subtype of abusive behavior that was all-pervasive (across multiple areas of life) and involved a plethora of behaviors and manipulative or coercive techniques.

Narcissistic abuse differed from all other types of abuse in its range, sophistication, duration, versatility, and express and premeditated intention to negate and vitiate the victim's personal autonomy, agency, self-efficacy, and wellbeing.

The victims of narcissistic abuse appeared to present a clinical picture substantially different to victims of other, more pinpointed and goal-oriented types of abuse. They were more depressed and anxious, disoriented, aggressive (defiant reactance), dissociative, and trapped or hopeless owing to learned (intermittently reinforced or operant conditioned) helplessness. In short: they were in the throes of trauma bonding (Stockholm syndrome), a kind of cultish shared psychosis (folies a deux).

Repeated abuse has long lasting pernicious and traumatic effects such as panic attacks, hypervigilance, sleep disturbances, flashbacks (intrusive memories), suicidal ideation, and psychosomatic symptoms. The victims experience shame, depression, anxiety, embarrassment, guilt, humiliation, abandonment, and an enhanced sense of vulnerability.

C-PTSD (Complex PTSD) has been proposed as a new mental health diagnosis by Dr. Judith Herman of Harvard University to account for the impact of extended periods of trauma and abuse.

Jacobsen: For the most extreme cases of narcissism to the most minute, what are the principles for dealing with them if one cannot enact the no contact rule

Vaknin:

Here is a video that describes all the techniques I know: https://www.youtube.com/watch?v=euGhNMifaw8

Jacobsen: Thank you for the opportunity and your time, Professor Vaknin.

Vaknin:

Thank you again for your patience and perseverance!

Return

<u>Interview about Cold Therapy</u> (News Intervention)

Scott Douglas Jacobsen: Narcissism seems lifelong, immutable. You have commented, eloquently, about Narcissistic Personality Disorder and the lifetime 'devoured' by it, in an Instagram post (vakninsamnarcissist, 2020).[1] Yet, your intervention, Cold Therapy, is effective with Narcissism (and depression). What was the original insight into the first developments of Cold Therapy?

Prof. Sam Vaknin:

That, exactly like Borderline Personality Disorder, Narcissistic Personality Disorder is a post-traumatic condition, a form of complex trauma. So, Cold Therapy is based on two premises: (1) That narcissistic disorders are actually forms of CPTSD; and (2) That narcissists are the outcomes of arrested development and attachment dysfunctions. Consequently, Cold Therapy borrows techniques from child psychology and from treatment modalities which used to deal with PTSD.

Jacobsen: In "Cold Therapy and Narcissistic Disorders of the Self" (Vaknin, 2018), you list "four misconceptions about pathological narcissism."[2] Why have those been the misconceptions, in particular?

Vaknin:

Pathological narcissism is not merely a regression to an earlier childhood developmental phase, although such infantilization is a core psychodynamic of the disorder. There is so much more to it than that!

It is also not only a psychological defense, although narcissistic defenses and cognitive distortions play a key role in the pathology.

Narcissism is not simply an organizing principle or a schema, though, like every addiction (to narcissistic supply, in this case), it helps the addict to make sense of the world (is hermeneutic) and provides goal-orientation and direction. It comes replete with rituals, order, and structure (is an exoskeleton).

Finally, it is not strictly a personality disorder. The personality is intact and highly adaptive. Narcissism is a post-traumatic condition, amenable to trauma therapies. Like in every other form of complex trauma, emotions get dysregulated or repressed and cognitions get distorted.

Jacobsen: How are narcissistic disorders complex post-traumatic conditions, and forms of arrested development and attachment dysfunctions? How are both pampering and punishing a child, or an adolescent, forms of abuse in the creation of a narcissist?

Vaknin:

Pathological narcissism is a reaction to prolonged abuse and trauma in early childhood or early adolescence. The source of the abuse or trauma is immaterial - the perpetrators could be parents, teachers, other adults, or peers. Pampering, smothering, spoiling, and "engulfing" the child are also forms of abuse because they do not allow the child to separate from the parent and to confront reality as an agent of personal growth and development.

See these:

http://vaksam.tripod.com/narcissismglance.html

http://vaksam.tripod.com/npdglance.html

http://vaksam.tripod.com/journal42.html

https://web.archive.org/web/20161025014451/http://metapsychology.mentalhelp.net/poc/view_doc.php?type=de&id=419

Narcissistic and psychopathic parents and their children - click on the links:

https://groups.google.com/forum/#!topic/NARCISSISTIC-PERSONALITY-DISORDER/kA1vtsqWAiI

The Genetic Underpinnings of Narcissism

http://vaksam.tripod.com/journal43.html

The early childhood traumas of the narcissist prevent him (or her) from completing the process of separation-individuation. S/he is not permitted to develop boundaries and to become an individual. S/he freezes in time as a Puer Aeternus, a Peter Pan.

The narcissistic child reacts by avoiding the offending and hurtful parent, an insecure attachment style that becomes entrenched throughout the lifespan. He creates the False Self and outsources many Ego boundary functions, rendering him dependent on the appraising gaze of others to buttress his grandiose, inflated self-image. Gradually, he develops an addiction to confirmatory input (narcissistic supply) because he cannot regulate and stabilize his internal environment without it.

Jacobsen: What portions of the nervous system in early childhood and early adolescence seem most impacted by the long-term abuse and trauma to create Narcissism, if known?

Vaknin:

Not known. There are many studies about the neuroplastic effects of childhood abuse and trauma on the brain, but none of them is specific to NPD. There are studies about brain abnormalities in Borderline and Antisocial Personality Disorders (psychopathy).

Jacobsen: How are narcissistic disorders interpersonal disorders rather than disorders of the self?

Vaknin:

The concept of "individual" which regrettably permeates modern psychology is counterfactual. We are formed fully via relationships with others. To conceive of the Self as an outcome of narcissistic introversion (Jung) is disastrously mistaken.

Disorders of the personality are, therefore, problems in inter-relatedness (as the object theorists in the UK in the 1960s had postulated). Narcissism is no exception. The DSM V has adopted this stance in its Alternate Model of NPD (p. 767). I had been advocating it since 1997.

Jacobsen: What are the goals of Cold Therapy?

Vaknin:

The main two therapeutic goals are to render the False Self redundant and so drive it to atrophy ("use it or lose it") and to eliminate the need for narcissistic supply and the dysphorias that accompany its deficiencies.

In short: to get rid of the grandiosity dimension in Narcissistic Personality Disorder (NPD).

To process trauma via skilled reliving (owning the trauma and surviving retraumatization);

To foster more adaptive functioning that is not dependent on outsourced regulation, cognitive distortions (like grandiosity), and artificial constructs (like the False Self);

Replace negative coping (such as avoidance, withdrawal, defiance, or fantasy) with positive coping strategies;

To integrate distressing materials (thoughts, feelings, memories);

To lead to the internal resolution of dissonances, resulting in an equilibrium and homeostasis;

Help the client to evolve life skills such as resilience, empathy, and ego regulation.

Jacobsen: Why are no known, well-established therapies effective in the treatment of narcissistic disorders?

Vaknin:

Behavior Therapy

Replaces problem behaviors with constructive ones via conditioning and reinforcement

Cognitive Therapy

Changes negative automatic thoughts and schemas that lead to attributional and other biases as well as errors in order to alter problematic behaviors and dysfunctional feelings and behaviors.

CBT

Third wave of behavior therapy:

Primacy of therapeutic relationship, learning principles, analyze triggers and environmental cues, explore schemas and emotions, utilize modelling, homework, and imagery.

Dialectical Behavior Therapy (DBT)

Developed by Linehan in 1993 to treat BPD, but used with other personality disorders and disorders of mood, anxiety, eating, and substance abuse. It is deployed mainly with female patients in inpatient or residential settings.

Emphasizes emotional and affect regulation rather than cognitions.

Concerned with how were schemas formed via dialectic conflicts: seeks to connect affect and need to cognitive inference processes and belief systems so as to be reinterpreted with greater self-awareness

Identifies fixation or perseveration causes by early developmental deprivation and protective attentional constriction

Examines effects of negative reinforcement through emotional avoidance or inadequate coping skills rewarded through the partial reinforcement effect

Involves individual therapy, group skills training, phone contact, and therapist consultation. Focuses on using validation and problem solving to counter severe behavioral dyscontrol, issues of quiet desperation, problems of living, and reducing incompleteness.

Cognitive Behavior Analysis System of Psychotherapy (CBASP)

Developed by McCullough and adapted by Sperry. Not used with BPD.

Clients learn to analyze life situations and manage daily stressors. They evaluate which thoughts and behaviors prevent desired outcomes.

Elicitation and remediation: questions about the situation, the client's role and functioning in it, and the desired outcome lead to a revision of counterproductive behaviors and cognitions.

Replaces emotional reasoning with consequential one.

Mindfulness-based Cognitive Therapy (MBCT)

Developed by Teasdale.

Fosters aware focus on thoughts, feelings, and experiences in the present with an attitude of acceptance and without analysis or judgment.

Pattern-focused Psychotherapy

Developed by Sperry

Pattern: predictable, consistent, self-perpetuating style of thinking, feeling, acting, coping, and self-defense. Can be adaptive (competent) or maladaptive (inflexible, ineffective, inappropriate, cause symptoms, impair functioning and satisfaction).

Therapy consists of replacing hurtful maladaptive patterns (situational interpretations and behaviors) with helpful adaptive ones.

Schema Therapy

Developed by Young

Changes maladaptive schemas: 18 enduring and self-defeating ways of regarding oneself and others, arranged in 5 domains. Schemas are perpetuated through coping styles: schema maintenance, avoidance, and compensation.

Schemas can be reconstructed, modified, interpreted, or camouflaged.

TABLE 1.2 Maladaptive Schemas and Schema Domains

Disconnection and Rejection

• **Abandonment/Instability:** The belief that significant others will not or cannot provide reliable and stable support.

• **Mistrust/Abuse**: The belief that others will abuse, humiliate, cheat, lie, manipulate, or take advantage.

• **Emotional Deprivation**: The belief that one's desire for emotional support will not be met by others.

• **Defectiveness/Shame**: The belief that one is defective, bad, unwanted, or inferior in important respects.

• **Social Isolation/Alienation:** The belief that one is alienated, different from others, or not part of any group.

Impaired Autonomy and Performance

• **Dependence/Incompetence:** The belief that one is unable to competently meet everyday responsibilities without considerable help from others.

• **Vulnerability to Harm or Illness:** The exaggerated fear that imminent catastrophe will strike at any time and that one will be unable to prevent it.

• **Enmeshment/Undeveloped Self**: The belief that one must be emotionally close with others at the expense of full individuation or normal social development.

• **Failure:** The belief that one will inevitably fail or is fundamentally inadequate in achieving one's goals.

Impaired Limits

• **Entitlement/Grandiosity**: The belief that one is superior to others and not bound by the rules and norms that govern normal social interaction.

• **Insufficient Self-Control/Self-Discipline**: The belief that one is incapable of self-control and frustration tolerance.

Other-Directedness

• **Subjugation:** The belief that one's desires, needs, and feelings must be suppressed in order to meet the needs of others and avoid retaliation or criticism.

• **Self-Sacrifice:** The belief that one must meet the needs of others at the expense of one's own gratification.

• **Approval-Seeking/Recognition-Seeking**: The belief that one must constantly seek to belong and be accepted at the expense of developing a true sense of self.

Overvigilance and Inhibition

• **Negativity/Pessimism:** A pervasive, lifelong focus on the negative aspects of life while minimizing the positive and optimistic aspects.

• **Emotional inhibition:** The excessive inhibition of spontaneous action, feeling, or communication—usually to avoid disapproval by others, feelings of shame, or losing

control of one's impulses.

• **Unrelenting Standards/Hypercriticalness:** The belief that striving to meet unrealistically high standards of performance is essential to be accepted and to avoid

criticism.

• **Punitiveness.** The belief that others should be harshly punished for making errors.

Sperry, Len, "Handbook of Diagnosis and Treatment of DSM-5 Personality Disorders: Assessment, Case Conceptualization, and Treatment", 3rd Edition, 2016, Routledge

Transference-focused Psychotherapy

Developed by Kernberg

Infants form internal representations of self-others (objects) connected via affect. A personality disorder occurs when positive and negative representations fail to integrate later in life. Such splitting affects all relationships, including the therapeutic one.

Transference to the therapist exposes the faulty relationship template and allows for its empathic correction. Identity integration is accomplished as the patient experiences negative emotions in a safe environment.

Mentalization-based Treatment (MBT)

Developed by Bateman and Fonagy.

Experience secure attachment and enhancing impulse control by empathically and insightfully reflecting on and correctly labelling one's state of mind, especially one's powerful emotions, and cognitive errors. This leads to improves relational skills.

Developmental Therapy

Developed mainly by Blocher, Citright, and Sperry

Regards problems in personal growth and needs satisfaction on a dimensional continuum from disordered to adequate to optimal.

Cold Therapy

Developed by Vaknin

Jacobsen: What are the first steps in formal identification and opening treatments of a narcissist with Cold Therapy?

Vaknin:

The client present with a diagnosis of NPD by a clinician.

Cold Therapy consists of the re-traumatization of the narcissistic client in a hostile, non-holding environment which resembles the ambience of the original trauma. The adult patient successfully tackles this second round of hurt and thus resolves early childhood conflicts and achieves closure rendering his now maladaptive narcissistic defenses redundant, unnecessary, and obsolete.

Cold Therapy makes use of proprietary techniques such as erasure (suppressing the client's speech and free expression and gaining clinical information and insights from his reactions to being so stifled). Other techniques include: grandiosity reframing, guided imagery, negative iteration, other-scoring, happiness map, mirroring, escalation, role play, assimilative confabulation, hypervigilant referencing, and re-parenting. It is proving to be an effective treatment for major depressive episodes (see this article about the link between pathological narcissism and depression and this article about depression and regulatory narcissistic supply in narcissism).

More about the therapy:

https://www.scribd.com/document/349440458/Cold-Therapy-Seminar-Level-1-Lecture-Notes

http://www.opastonline.com/wp-content/uploads/2018/08/cold-therapy-and-narcissistic-disorders-of-the-self-jcrc-18.pdf

Jacobsen: Following from the previous question, as the series of therapy sessions conclude, and as the patient lives out life after Cold Therapy, what are the preliminary outcomes from your early research?

Vaknin:

We have been following up on 63 clients over the past 10 years. The results are promising (although the sample is way to small and self-selecting to provide any statistically significant validation to the treatment modality):

Major depression and anhedonia have vanished without a trace, with no remission;

The need for narcissistic supply had disappeared entirely;

and

The clients have altered their lifestyles radically, had re-established contact with estranged family and friends, and became much more gregarious.

Jacobsen: Thank you for the opportunity and your time, Professor Vaknin.

Vaknin: Thank you again for your interest in my work.

References

Vaknin, S. (2018). Cold Therapy and Narcissistic Disorders of the Self. *Journal of Clinical Review & Case Reports*, 3(6), 29-36. **https://doi.org/10.33140/JCRC/03/06/00005**

vakninsamnarcissist. (2020, January 31). [Prof. Vaknin reflects on life with NPD and the creation of Cold Therapy]. Instagram. **https://www.instagram.com/p/B7-0NCdgQxg/**.

Footnotes

[1] Vaknin's Instagram post (2020), in full, stated:

> *What a cruel irony it is that I have developed Cold Therapy - the first ever effective treatment (cure, really) for Narcissistic Personality Disorder (NPD) - too late to benefit from it myself.*
>
> *I am 59 years old, my health is failing. My mental illness had consumed my life - is still devouring it - as surely as the bush fires ravage homes in Australia, leaving only the ashes of Me behind.*
>
> *WARNING*
>
> *I will block anyone who gives me the feel good New Age crap about how it is never too late in life. Life has an expiry date beyond which it is all blood and tears and stools and wallowing in your own stench of decomposing physical and mental decrepitude. So back off with your American anodyne platitudes about how every age has its charms. Old age sucks 100%. We lie to ourselves about it in order to survive somehow in the face of our own vanishing dismemberment.*
>
> *NPD is the slowest invisible cancer - but of the soul and mind. It is spiritual AIDS with nothing to abet it. It is all-pervasive, relentless, and merciless. It starts at age 3. It causes people around the narcissist to hurt and torment him purposefully and profusely as a way of getting back at him for his egregious abuse. It is Inferno and I have been its Dante since 1995. No Beatrice can help me, no god, no healer. I have been doomed by my own progenitor to a life of itinerant, profound, debilitating hurt, unlovable, shunned like a leper, feared and loathed and mocked in equal measures.*

It is with impotent rage that I bequeath Cold Therapy to a world I care nothing for or about. Rage at the injustice of healing and aiding millions with my pioneering work since 1995 - except the only person who most deserved my love and my devotion and my succor: Sam.

See vakninsamnarcissist (2020).

[2] Vaknin, in "Cold Therapy and Narcissistic Disorders of the Self" (2018), stated:

   a. It is not only a regression to an earlier childhood developmental phase;

   b. It is not merely a psychological defense;

   c. It is not simply an organizing principle or a schema;

   d. It is not a personality disorder.

See Vaknin (2018).

Return

Interview on Giftedness and IQ (News Intervention)

Scott Douglas Jacobsen: You have been measured three times with a high IQ, an understatement.[1] An IQ between 180 and 190, between ages 9 and 35. You referred to this in some writings, in passing, including pages 2[2], 3[3], 4[4], 5[5], and 7[6], of epigrams, in an interview with Richard Grannon (2018), with _Smashwords_ (2014), and on a YouTube video answering viewer questions[7]. It has been mentioned in an article by Gavin Haynes (2016), too. With the IQ scores of 185 at age 9, 180 in the army at age 25, and 190 in prison at age 35 (vakninsamnarcissist, 2018; RICHARD GRANNON, 2018), presumably on a standard deviation of 15, what was the reaction of family, friends, peers, community, even the psychometricians or psychologists administering the tests each time?

Prof. Shmuel "Sam" Vaknin:

First, let me clarify than any result above 160 (some say, 140) is not normatively validated: it is rather arbitrary and meaningless because there are so few people to compare with (the sample is way too small). Matrix IQ tests are better at validating higher results, though.

Everyone always loathed me. I am a sadist, so from a very early age, I have leveraged my IQ to taunt people, hold them in contempt, and humiliate them. This did not endear obnoxious me to anyone. My own teachers sought to undermine my academic career, peers shunned or attempted to bully me (they failed), my mother detested me, my father pendulated between being awe-struck and being repelled by me. Both my parents beat me to an inch of my life every single day for 12 years.

Jacobsen: To you, as a scientific person, what defines intelligence?

Vaknin:

Anything that endows an individual with a comparative advantage at performing a complex task constitutes intelligence. In this sense, viruses reify intelligence, they are intelligent. Human intelligence, though, is versatile and the tasks are usually far more complex than anything a virus might need to tackle.

Jacobsen: What defines IQ or Intelligence Quotient?

Vaknin:

The ability to perform a set of mostly – but not only - analytical assignments corresponding to an age-appropriate average. So, if a 10 year old copes well with the tasks that are the bread and butter of an 18 years old, he scores 180 IQ.

IQ measures an exceedingly narrow set of skills and mental functions. There are many types of intelligence – for example: musical intelligence – not captured by any IQ test.

Jacobsen: What defines giftedness, to you? Even though, formal definitions exist.[8]

Vaknin:

Giftedness resembles autism very much: it is the ability to accomplish tasks inordinately well or fast by focusing on them to the exclusion of all else and by mobilizing all the mental resources at the disposal of the gifted person.

Obviously, people gravitate to what they do well. Gifted people have certain propensities and talents to start with and these probably reflect brain abnormalities of one kind or another.

Jacobsen: Inter-relating the previous three questions, what separates intelligence from IQ from giftedness, i.e., separates each from one another?

Vaknin:

IQ is a narrow measure of highly specific types of intelligence and is not necessarily related to giftedness. Gifted people invest themselves with a laser-focus to effect change in their environment conducive to the speedy completion of highly specific tasks.

Jacobsen: What defines genius?

Vaknin:

Genius is the ability to discern two things: 1. What is missing (lacunas) 2. Synoptic connections.

The genius surveys the world and completes it by conjuring up novelty (i.e., by creating). S/he also spots hidden relatedness between ostensibly disparate phenomena or data.

Jacobsen: How does genius differentiate from intelligence, IQ, and giftedness?

Vaknin:

A genius can have an average IQ or even not be analytically very intelligent (not be an intellectual). Some craftsmen are geniuses. Musicians, athletes, even politicians.

Jacobsen: What happens to most prodigies, or adults with exceptionally, profoundly, or unmeasurably high IQ?

Vaknin:

A majority of them end badly. IQ is a good predictor of academic accomplishments, but not much else. Character, upbringing, mental illness, genetics, nurture, the environment (including the physical environment), sexual and romantic history matter much more than IQ.

Many "geniuses" with a high IQ (Mensa types) are dysfunctional and deficient when it comes to life, intimacy, relationships, and social skills. Additionally, as Eysenck had correctly observed, creativity is often linked to psychoticism.

Jacobsen: What are the optimal things for raising gifted children and prodigies, and for resuscitating drifting adults with exceptionally, profoundly, or unmeasurably high IQ, if at all possible, to productive and healthy lives?

Vaknin:

All interventions are somewhat effective only during childhood and adolescence, up to age 21. Afterwards, it is an uphill battle.

The most crucial thing is to never remove the gifted child from his peer group (as was done to me). I am also dead set against academic shortcuts.

The gifted child should follow the same path as everybody else but feed his voracious mind with extracurricular enrichment programs and materials.

Jacobsen: Who seem like the greatest geniuses in history to you?

Vaknin:

The usual suspects: Einstein, Newton, Freud, da Vinci, other polymaths who had upended every discipline or field that they had turned their scintillating minds to.

Jacobsen: Thank you for the opportunity and your time, Professor Vaknin.

Vaknin: The opportunity is all mine.

References

Hayne, G. (2016, September 8). I Spent a Day Trying to Get to Know a Real-Life Narcissist. Vice. https://www.vice.com/en/article/nney4k/narcissism-interview-chosen-ones-gavin-haynes.

National Association for Gifted Children. (2019). *A Definition of Giftedness that Guides Best Practice*. https://www.nagc.org/sites/default/files/Position%20Statement/Definition%20of%2 0Giftedness%20%282019%29.pdf.

Prof. Sam Vaknin. (2020, September 19). *Narcissistic Buffet: Answering Your Questions (Well, Sort of)* [Video]. YouTube. https://www.youtube.com/watch?v=GiHeS8fMsoE.

RICHARD GRANNON. (2018, September 12). *THE SAM VAKNIN INTERVIEW - HOW NARCISSISM IS FORMED IN A CHILD GENIUS & THE HIVE MIND* [Video]. YouTube. https://www.youtube.com/watch?v=W89fG8220D8.

Smashwords. (2014, October 19). *Interview with Sam Vaknin*. https://www.smashwords.com/interview/samvaknin.

Vaknin, S. (n.d.a). Sam Vaknin's Instagram Epigrams – Page 2. samvaknin.tripod. https://samvak.tripod.com/instagramvaknin2.html.

Vaknin, S. (n.d.b). Sam Vaknin's Instagram Epigrams – Page 3. samvaknin.tripod. https://samvak.tripod.com/instagramvaknin3.html.

Vaknin, S. (n.d.c). Sam Vaknin's Instagram Epigrams – Page 4. samvaknin.tripod. https://samvak.tripod.com/instagramvaknin4.html.

Vaknin, S. (n.d.d). Sam Vaknin's Instagram Epigrams – Page 5. samvaknin.tripod. https://samvak.tripod.com/instagramvaknin5.html.

Vaknin, S. (n.d.e). Sam Vaknin's Instagram Epigrams – Page 7. samvaknin.tripod. https://samvak.tripod.com/instagramvaknin7.html.

vakninsamnarcissist. (2018, June 13). [Prof. Vaknin provides some biographical information on IQ test scores]. Instagram. https://www.instagram.com/p/Bj_r-KaAckn/?hl=en.

[1] Vaknin (2018) in Instagram stated, "My IQ was tested every time I got myself into serious trouble: at age 9 (result: 185), in the army (180), & in prison by an orthodox religious psychologist who made me his pet project (190). There are only 60 people in the world with IQ 185 & only 7 with IQ 190. It gets pretty lonely pretty fast. Being the sadistic asshole that I am, I am fond of saying that the gap in IQ between me & the average human is far bigger than the difference between that human & an orangutan (or a chimpanzee)." See vakninsamnarcissist (2018).

[2] "Sam Vaknin's Instagram Epigrams – Page 2" states:

> At the age of 9, I was sent to study in the Technion - Israel's leading technological university. I have been diagnosed with 180 IQ. It was my lowest score in 3 IQ tests I have taken over the decades. There started my love affair with physics...

> ...At a very early age I discovered that I lack the most basic life and social skills. I had only one thing going for me: my formidable intellect (there are only 6 other people in the whole wide world with my IQ). So, I deployed it to construct a shelter, a bubble, replete with its own rigid rules and defenses intended to shield me from the life-threatening hurt that the world was inflicting on me daily. This bubble was a self-constructed mental asylum with me as the sole inmate...

> ...Women also feel inferior & inadequate faced with my 190 IQ.

See Vaknin (n.d.a).

[3] "Sam Vaknin's Instagram Epigrams – Page 3" states:

> These are for lesser mortals with an IQ score inferior to my stratospheric 190.

See Vaknin (n.d.b).

[4] "Sam Vaknin's Instagram Epigrams – Page 4" states:

> There were two of us. I was not alone inside my body. Physiologically, I was supposed to be twins: I have two urethras, two sets of teeth, and, at an IQ of 185, probably double the brain. It's as though, denied their birth, this duo haunts me, an inbound, coupled poltergeist...

> ... My IQ - 190 - is literally off any known chart. There are only 8 people in the entire world with this level of intelligence and I am one of them.

> I used to be so proud of this fact. Now I realize that I am cursed. My IQ is a rare incurable disease...

See Vaknin (n.d.c).

[5] "Sam Vaknin's Instagram Epigrams – Page 5" states:

> I have 190 IQ and I make sure that my interlocutors are well appraised of this daunting fact...

See Vaknin (n.d.d).

[6] "Sam Vaknin's Instagram Epigrams – Page 7" states:

> So, I harnessed my formidable intellect - all 190 IQ points of it - to write my user's manual...

...After all, how does one succeed to not bore to tears someone with 190 IQ and encyclopedic knowledge?...

...They run away screaming to the waiting arms of the first man available because they find out that I am a reptile or a computer simulation or a robot with a brain who is about 10 times more potent than an average one (fact: I have 190 IQ). It is like being trapped in a futuristic sci-fi yarn with an alien life form, albeit carbon-based.

See Vaknin (n.d.e).

[7] See Prof. Sam Vaknin (2020).

[8] "A definition of Giftedness that Guides Best Practice" (2019) states:

Students with gifts and talents perform - or have the capability to perform - at higher levels compared to others of the same age, experience, and environment in one or more domains. They require modification(s) to their educational experience(s) to learn and realize their potential. Student with gifts and talents:

• Come from all racial, ethnic, and cultural populations, as well as all economic strata.

• Require sufficient access to appropriate learning opportunities to realize their potential.

• Can have learning and processing disorders that require specialized intervention and accommodation.

• Need support and guidance to develop socially and emotionally as well as in their areas of talent.

• Require varied services based on their changing needs.

See National Association for Gifted Children (2019).

<u>Return</u>

Interview on Religion and God (News Intervention)

Scott Douglas Jacobsen: Sorry for the delay, folks, and Prof. Vaknin, I had some equine (horsey) matters. For those who would like to see previous sessions with Prof. Vaknin, please see the links at the bottom of this session – 5th of 10 so far, the tedious sessions come in print with footnotes and references, so academic *accoutrement*; the more flowing, natural sessions come from readings by Prof. Vaknin on YouTube. He reads both interviewer and interviewee text, then interprets and interpolates for education and entertainment. Let's start on a general question, what defines faith and religion? Lots of extant definitions.[1]

Prof. Shmuel "Sam" Vaknin:

Religion is a sublimated (socially acceptable) form of delusional disorder whose contents include a supreme being or power which dictates a code of conduct and sanctions transgressors. Religion is the institutional manifestation of this mental illness, hijacked by psychopaths and narcissists for purposes of attaining power and riches.

Jacobsen: Why is the vast majority of the world beholden to religion or faith, attempts to connect with the so-called transcendent and metaphysical, trying to make their lives isomorphic with their 'holy' figures, and so on?

Vaknin:

The vast majority of people are in a constant state of anxiety. Religion, mysticism, the occult and affiliated derangements are anxiolytic (mitigate anxiety). They are also forms of escapism from unbearable reality via self-imposed psychotic delusions.

On a deeper level, people use religion and its institutions to constrain evil, antisocial behaviors, and negative affectivity (such as anger and envy). Religion is a pillar of communality and the status quo. Historically, when it had failed in this mission, religion had witnessed the rise of belligerent reformers such as Jesus and Martin Luther.

Jacobsen: Similar to the previous question, though on a different track of thought, what is, and is not, practically useful in religious scriptures, the purported biographies of the lives of religious leaders, and traditional rituals in faiths?

Vaknin:

Religion is a mental illness, both individual and collective. The content of its delusions had always been tailored by the elites to rein in the masses.

From the elites's point of view, religion is, therefore, a useful tool of social control.

From the viewpoint of the masses, it guarantees protections against social unrest, malevolent misconduct, arbitrary subjugation, and injustice. It ameliorates the anxiety and fear that these pernicious social phenomena evoke in individuals and in their collectives.

Religion is indeed "opium for the masses", but it has its utility in guaranteeing a structured order for all, founded on predictable and reliable ethics and codes of conduct.

Jacobsen: When metaphysicians, religious philosophers, and theologians opine about the existence and attributes of gods, what do these opinions, typically, state about their cognition and reality-testing abilities?

Vaknin:

Even renowned scientists, thinkers, and intellectuals can be or become delusional. But it is not as simple as that.

To start with, "religion" is an all-inclusive umbrella term, a big tent. Even among the Abrahamic monotheistic religion, there are vast hermeneutic differences.

The three major monotheistic religions of the world - Judaism, Christianity, and Islam - can be placed on the two arms of a cross. Judaism would constitute the horizontal arm: eye to eye with God. The Jew believes that God is an interlocutor with whom one can reason and plead, argue and disagree. Mankind is complementary to the Divinity and fulfills important functions. God is incomplete without human activities such as prayer and obeying the Commandments. Thus, God and Man are on the same plane, collaborators in maintaining the Universe.

The vertical arm of the cross would be limned by the upward-oriented Christianity and the downward-looking Muslim. Jewish synagogues are horizontal affairs with divine artifacts and believers occupying more or less the same surface. Not so Christian churches in which God (or his image) are placed high above the congregation, skyward, striving towards heaven or descending from it. Indeed, Judaism lacks the very concept of "heaven", or "paradise", or, for that matter, "hell". As opposed to both Islam and Christianity, Judaism is an earthly faith.

Islam posits a clear dichotomy between God and Man. The believer should minimize his physical presence by crumbling, forehead touching the ground, in a genuflection of subservience and acceptance ("islam") of God's greatness, omnipotence, omniscience, and just conduct. Thus, the Muslim, in his daily dealings with the divine, does not dare look up. The faithful's role is merely to interpret God's will (as communicated via Muhammad).

But the very concept of "god" – which is a narrative, an organizing principle, and an interpretative-explanatory tenet - is not necessarily incompatible with other dominant constructs, such as science. All human systems of thought rely on beliefs, implicit or explicit.

If neurons were capable of introspection and world-representation, would they have developed an idea of "Brain" (i.e., of God)? Would they have become aware that they are mere intertwined components of a larger whole? Would they have considered themselves agents of the Brain - or its masters? When a neuron fires, is it instructed to do so by the Brain or is the Brain an emergent phenomenon, the combined and rather accidental outcome of millions of individual neural actions and pathways?

There are many kinds of narratives and organizing principles. Science is driven by evidence gathered in experiments, and by the falsification of extant theories and their replacement with newer, asymptotically truer, ones. Other systems - religion, nationalism, paranoid ideation, or art - are based on personal experiences (faith, inspiration, paranoia, etc.).

Experiential narratives can and do interact with evidential narratives and vice versa.

For instance: belief in God inspires some scientists who regard science as a method to "sneak a peek at God's cards" and to get closer to Him. Another example: the pursuit of scientific endeavors enhances one's national pride and is motivated by it. Science is often corrupted in order to support nationalistic and racist claims.

The basic units of all narratives are known by their effects on the environment. God, in this sense, is no different from electrons, quarks, and black holes. All four constructs cannot be directly observed, but the fact of their existence is derived from their effects.

Granted, God's effects are discernible only in the social and psychological (or psychopathological) realms. But this observed constraint doesn't render Him less "real". The hypothesized existence of God parsimoniously explains a myriad ostensibly unrelated phenomena and, therefore, conforms to the rules governing the formulation of scientific theories.

The locus of God's hypothesized existence is, clearly and exclusively, in the minds of believers. But this again does not make Him less real. The contents of our minds are as real as anything "out there". Actually, the very distinction between epistemology and ontology is blurred.

But is God's existence "true" - or is He just a figment of our neediness and imagination?

Truth is the measure of the ability of our models to describe phenomena and predict them. God's existence (in people's minds) succeeds to do both. For instance, assuming that God exists allows us to predict many of the behaviors of people who profess to believe in Him. The existence of God is, therefore, undoubtedly true (in this formal and strict sense).

But does God exist outside people's minds? Is He an objective entity, independent of what people may or may not think about Him? After all, if all sentient beings were to perish in a horrible calamity, the Sun would still be there, revolving as it has done from time immemorial.

If all sentient beings were to perish in a horrible calamity, would God still exist? If all sentient beings, including all humans, stop believing that there is God - would He survive this renunciation? Does God "out there" inspire the belief in God in religious folks' minds?

Known things are independent of the existence of observers (although the Copenhagen interpretation of Quantum Mechanics disputes this). Believed things are dependent on the existence of believers.

We know that the Sun exists. We don't know that God exists. We believe that God exists - but we don't and cannot know it, in the scientific sense of the word.

We can design experiments to falsify (prove wrong) the existence of electrons, quarks, and black holes (and, thus, if all these experiments fail, prove that electrons, quarks, and black holes exist). We can also design experiments to prove that electrons, quarks, and black holes exist.

But we cannot design even one experiment to falsify the existence of a God who is outside the minds of believers (and, thus, if the experiment fails, prove that God exists "out there"). Additionally, we cannot design even one experiment to prove that God exists outside the minds of believers.

What about the "argument from design"? The universe is so complex and diverse that surely it entails the existence of a supreme intelligence, the world's designer and creator, known by some as "God". On the other hand, the world's richness and variety can be fully accounted for using modern scientific theories such as evolution and the big bang. There is no need to introduce God into the equations.

Still, it is possible that God is responsible for it all. The problem is that we cannot design even one experiment to falsify this theory, that God created the Universe (and, thus, if the experiment fails, prove that God is, indeed, the world's originator). Additionally, we cannot design even one experiment to prove that God created the world.

We can, however, design numerous experiments to falsify the scientific theories that explain the creation of the Universe (and, thus, if these experiments fail, lend these theories substantial support). We can also design experiments to prove the scientific theories that explain the creation of the Universe.

It does not mean that these theories are absolutely true and immutable. They are not. Our current scientific theories are partly true and are bound to change with new knowledge gained by experimentation. Our current scientific theories will be replaced by newer, truer theories. But any and all future scientific theories will be falsifiable and testable.

Knowledge and belief are like oil and water. They don't mix. Knowledge doesn't lead to belief and belief does not yield knowledge. Belief can yield conviction or strongly-felt opinions. But belief cannot result in knowledge.

Still, both known things and believed things exist. The former exist "out there" and the latter "in our minds" and only there. But they are no less real for that.

Jacobsen: Of the arguments for the existence of any god, what ones, in a principle of charity, seem the most reasonable? Of the arguments for the existence of any god, what ones, in ignoring the principle of charity, seem the most unreasonable?

Vaknin:

Could God have failed to exist (especially considering His omnipotence)? Could He have been a contingent being rather than a necessary one? Would the World have existed without Him and, more importantly, would it have existed in the same way? For instance: would it have allowed for the existence of human beings?

To say that God is a necessary being means to accept that He exists (with His attributes intact) in every possible world. It is not enough to say that He exists only in our world: this kind of claim will render Him contingent (present in some worlds - possibly in none! - and absent in others).

We cannot conceive of the World without numbers, relations, and properties, for instance. These are necessary entities because without them the World as we known and perceive it would not exist. Is this equally true when we contemplate God? Can we conceive of a God-less World?

Moreover: numbers, relations, and properties are abstracts. Yet, God is often thought of as a concrete being. Can a concrete being, regardless of the properties imputed to it, ever be necessary? Is there a single concrete being - God - without which the Universe would have perished, or not existed in the first place? If so, what makes God a privileged concrete entity?

Additionally, numbers, relations, and properties depend for their existence (and utility) on other beings, entities, and quantities. Relations subsist between objects; properties are attributes of things; numbers are invariably either preceded by other numbers or followed by them.

Does God depend for His existence on other beings, entities, quantities, properties, or on the World as a whole? If He is a dependent entity, is He also a derivative one? If He is dependent and derivative, in which sense is He necessary?

Many philosophers confuse the issue of existence with that of necessity. Kant and, to some extent, Frege, argued that existence is not even a logical predicate (or at least not a first-order logical predicate). But, far more crucially, that something exists does not make it a necessary being. Thus, contingent beings exist, but they are not necessary (hence their "contingency").

At best, ontological arguments deal with the question: does God necessarily exist? They fail to negotiate the more tricky: can God exist *only* as a Necessary Being (in all possible worlds)?

Modal ontological arguments even postulate as a premise that God is a necessary being and use that very assumption as a building block in proving that He exists! Even a rigorous logician like Gödel fell in this trap when he attempted to prove God's necessity. In his posthumous ontological argument, he adopted several dubious definitions and axioms:

(1) God's essential properties are all positive (Definition 1); (2) God necessarily exists if and only if every essence of His is necessarily exemplified (Definition 3); (3) The property of being God is positive (Axiom 3); (4) Necessary existence is positive (Axiom 5).

These led to highly-debatable outcomes:

(1) For God, the property of being God is essential (Theorem 2); (2) The property of being God is necessarily exemplified.

Gödel assumed that there is one universal closed set of essential positive properties, of which necessary existence is a member. He was wrong, of course. There may be many such sets (or none whatsoever) and necessary existence may not be a (positive) property (or a member of some of the sets) after all.

Worst of all, Gödel's "proof" falls apart if God does not exist (Axiom 3's veracity depends on the existence of a God-like creature). Plantinga has committed the very same error a decade earlier (1974). His ontological argument incredibly relies on the premise: "There is a possible world in which there is God!"

Veering away from these tautological forays, we can attempt to capture God's alleged necessity by formulating this *Axiom Number 1*:

"God is necessary (i.e. necessarily exists in every possible world) if there are objects or entities that would not have existed in any possible world in His absence."

We should complement Axiom 1 with *Axiom Number 2*:

"God is necessary (i.e. necessarily exists in every possible world) even if there are objects or entities that do not exist in any possible world (despite His existence)."

The reverse sentences would be:

Axiom Number 3: "God is *not* necessary (i.e. does not necessarily exist in every possible world) if there are objects or entities that exist in any possible world in His absence."

Axiom Number 4: "God is *not* necessary (i.e. does not necessarily exist in every possible world) if there are no objects or entities that exist in any possible world (despite His existence)."

Now consider this sentence:

Axiom Number 5: "Objects and entities are necessary (i.e. necessarily exist in every possible world) if they exist in every possible world even in God's absence."

Consider abstracta, such as numbers. Does their existence depend on God's? Not if we insist on the language above. Clearly, numbers are not dependent on the existence of God, let alone on His necessity.

Yet, because God is all-encompassing, surely it must incorporate all possible worlds as well as all *impossible* ones! What if we were to modify the language and recast the axioms thus:

Axiom Number 1:

"God is necessary (i.e. necessarily exists in every possible *and impossible* world) if there are objects or entities that would not have existed in any possible world in His absence."

We should complement Axiom 1 with *Axiom Number 2*:

"God is necessary (i.e. necessarily exists in every possible *and impossible* world) even if there are objects or entities that do not exist in any possible world (despite His existence)."

The reverse sentences would be:

Axiom Number 3: "God is *not* necessary (i.e. does not necessarily exist in every possible *and impossible* world) if there are objects or entities that exist in any possible world in His absence."

Axiom Number 4: "God is *not* necessary (i.e. does not necessarily exist in every possible *and impossible* world) if there are no objects or entities that exist in any possible world (despite His existence)."

Now consider this sentence:

Axiom Number 5: "Objects and entities are necessary (i.e. necessarily exist in every possible *and impossible* world) if they exist in every possible world even in God's absence."

According to the Vander Laan modification (2004) of the Lewis counterfactuals semantics, impossible worlds are worlds in which the number of propositions is maximal. Inevitably, in such worlds, propositions contradict each other (are inconsistent with each other). In impossible worlds, some counterpossibles (counterfactuals with a necessarily false antecedent) are true or non-trivially true. Put simply: with certain counterpossibles, even when the premise (the antecedent) is patently false, one can agree that the conditional is true because of the (true, formally correct) relationship between the antecedent and the consequent.

Thus, if we adopt an expansive view of God - one that covers all possibilities **and impossibilities** - we can argue that God's existence is necessary.

What about ontological arguments regarding God's existence?

As Lewis (In his book "Anselm and Actuality", 1970) and Sobel ("Logic and Theism", 2004) noted, philosophers and theologians who argued in favor of God's existence have traditionally proffered tautological (question-begging) arguments to support their contentious contention (or are formally invalid). Thus, St. Anselm proposed (in his much-celebrated "Proslogion", 1078) that since God is the Ultimate Being, it essentially and necessarily comprises all modes of perfection, including necessary existence (a form of perfection).

Anselm's was a prototypical ontological argument: God must exist because we can conceive of a being than which no greater can be conceived. It is an "end-of-the-line" God. Descartes concurred: it is contradictory to conceive of a Supreme Being and then to question its very existence.

That we do not **have** to conceive of such a being is irrelevant. First: clearly, we have conceived of Him repeatedly and second, our ability to conceive is sufficient. That we fail to realize a potential act does not vitiate its existence.

But, how do we know that the God we conceive of is even possible? Can we conceive of impossible entities? For instance, can we conceive of a two-dimensional triangle whose interior angles amount to less than 180 degrees? Is the concept of a God that comprises all compossible perfections at all possible? Leibnitz said that we cannot prove that such a God is impossible because perfections are not amenable to analysis. But that hardly amounts to any kind of proof!

Is God an external object - or an internal one? Is He a mere voice in our heads - or is He out there? Psychosis occurs when we confuse and conflate our inner world with outer reality. In this sense, all religious prophecy is psychotic and all religious faiths are manifestations of psychosis.

Julian Jaynes ("The Origins of Consciousness in the Breakdown of the Bicameral Mind", 1976) was the most forceful advocate of the idea of bicameralism and the bicameral mind: that supernatural revelation was merely how some people experienced a channel of communication between their cerebral hemispheres. Modern day ambient noise, information pollution, stress, and abnormal living conditions in cities served to suppress and extinguish this intracranial exchange, except in cases of schizophrenia. Instead, we developed compensatory introspection, self-awareness, and consciousness

There is, of course, the added problem of false prophecy: how to tell the ersatz from the echt. Most false prophets are not crooks: they sincerely believe in the authenticity of the provenance of their message and mission.

But does all this really matter? Whether these voices are mere hallucinatory neurological artifacts or the true Word of a god is immaterial as long as they affect the lives of millions, as they all too often do.

Jewish mysticism believes that humans have a major role: fixing the results of a cosmic catastrophe, the shattering of the divine vessels through which the infinite divine light poured forth to create our finite world. If Nature is determined to a predominant extent by its contained intelligences, then it may well be teleological.

Indeed, goal-orientated behaviour (or behavior that could be explained as goal-orientated) is Nature's hallmark. The question whether automatic or intelligent mechanisms are at work, really deals with an underlying issue, that of consciousness. Are these mechanisms self-aware, introspective? Is intelligence possible without such self-awareness, without the internalized understanding of what it is doing?

Kant's third and the fourth dynamic antinomies deal with this apparent duality: automatism versus intelligent acts.

The third thesis relates to causation which is the result of free will as opposed to causation which is the result of the laws of nature (nomic causation)

The antithesis is that freedom is an illusion and everything is pre-determined. So, the third antinomy is really about intelligence that is intrinsic to Nature (deterministic) versus intelligence that is extrinsic to it (free will)

The fourth thesis deals with a related subject: God, the ultimate intelligent creator. It states that there must exist, either as part of the world or as its cause a Necessary Being. There are compelling arguments to support both the theses and the antitheses of the antinomies.

Jacobsen: You have written on, or have been interviewed about, religion with references to atheism, anti-theism, and agnosticism.[2] In one interview[3], you identify as an agnostic. In an article, you identify as an anti-theist.[4] You defined atheism as a religion or another faith, too.[5] With agnosticism and anti-theism as self-identifications while atheism seen as another religion/faith, what is the current reasoning for agnosticism and anti-theism with more time passing from the words in the publications, if any?

Vaknin:

"If a man would follow, today, the teachings of the Old Testament, he would be a criminal. If he would strictly follow the teachings of the New, he would be insane"

(Robert Ingersoll)

In answer to your question, I would like to incorporate the full text of reference 4 in your question, amended to reflect my current views.

Is ours a post-religious world? Ask any born again Christian fundamentalist, militant Muslim, orthodox Jew, and nationalistic Hindu. Religion is on the rise, not on the wane. Eighteenth century enlightenment is besieged. Atheism, as a creed, is on the defensive.

First, we should get our terminology clear. Atheism is not the same as agnosticism which is not the same as anti-theism.

Atheism is a religion, yet another faith. It is founded on the improvable and unfalsifiable *belief* (universal negative) that there is no God. Agnosticism is about keeping an open mind: God may or may not exist. There is no convincing case either way.

Anti-theism is militant anti-clericalism. Anti-theists (such as myself) regard religion as an unmitigated evil that must be eradicated to make for a better world.

I am a **militant agnostic** when it comes to the question: "Does God exist?". I have reached the conclusion that there is no way anyone could ever answer this question. The query, as posed, is unresolvable in principle. There is no procedure or theorem that could ever lead to its resolution one way or another.

But God is NOT the same thing as religion. Religion consists of an ensemble of rituals and institutions with a social agenda. I am dead set against it. I am a **fundamentalist anti-theist**, therefore, not only a militant agnostic.

Authors like Tremblay and even Dawkins label religion a swindle and mental terrorism – befitting epithets, fully validated by its gory history. There seems to be an inextricable link between the belief in the afterlife and immorality, rather than morality.

Many authors castigate religion's intolerance coupled with its ever-shifting philosophical goalposts. Its dogmatism leads to a loss of experiential richness and to negative cognitive consequences to both the believer and his milieu.

Religion scams people with false promises of the hereafter, its texts are objectionable, it is unnatural, and it promotes falsities. In other words, it is a criminal enterprise.

Bogus arguments from design had been dealt with in the works of George Smith, Michael Martin, and Corey Washington: complexity and order do not a design make.

Still, we need to distinguish between established religions and cults or sects. Moreover, theocracy is not merely the rule of religion (lexically correct): in the real world, it is the misuse and abuse of religion by rulers and elites.

The purported existence of God has been scrutinized in a plethora of discoveries, theorems, hypotheses, and theories in the exact sciences and in formal logic.

Consider this example: it can be proven that God cannot and does not exist ("strong atheism") because having a God leads to either meaninglessness or to contradictions or to both. But this is precisely the Gödel theorem: formal logical systems can be either complete or consistent, but never both.

As Freud correctly noted a century ago, religion is a mental pathology. You cannot rationally argue with people whose judgment and reason are suspended. Distinctions between personal and objective beliefs are lost on delusional fanatics.

Religious people have faith in a god because it fulfills basic and entrenched (and unhealthy) emotional needs - not because its existence can or has been proven. We all - even atheists - hold irrational beliefs to some extent. Religion just happens to be a particularly virulent and insidious strain of irrationality.

Jacobsen: If you survey the landscape, not of the traditionally defined as religious but, of the anti-theists, atheists, agnostics, freethinkers, humanists, and the like, what seems like the status of them, e.g., growing and healthy, unhealthy and declining, on the assertive, on the defensive, etc.?

Vaknin:

There are emerging battle lines between the regrouping forces of reason and the resurging Dark Ages. This is the real Armageddon that is upon us.

But religion is only one penumbral force which combats rationality and the scientific method. Conspiracy theories; the occult; philosophical schools like deconstruction; political correctness and woke movements; truthism (fake news and misinformation online); the virulent rejection of authority, intellect, and expertise (malignant egalitarianism) – I regard all these as far bigger threats.

Jacobsen: Christianity, Islam, and Hinduism, comprise the most significant religious populations in the world, in absolute numbers. Yet, social ideologies and political philosophies seem to metastasize into dogmas, as well. What social ideologies and political philosophies seem as if dogmas akin to religions/faiths, and why? These could include political leaders as religious leaders as part of the examples. You have written on Islam and Liberalism, as two examples in comparisonand contrast.[6]

Vaknin:

All ideologies mutate into secular religions with their own churches, hagiography, and rituals. Religions are forms of victimhood movements (martyrology) and all social activism and woke movements tend to become dogmatic and exclusionary, with a claim on possessing a monopoly on the truth.

But there is an especially worrisome contemporary development: the confluence of narcissism, oligarchy, and religion.

I coined the neologism "theochlocracy" to describe the noxious mixture of theocracy and ochlocracy (mob-rule). Yet, as distinct from the former, in a theochlocracy, church and state are constitutionally separated. The power is not in the hands of the clergy, but, putatively, in the hands of the people and its representatives. Theochlocracies are often also democracies. Religion – in all its faux-manifestations – is imposed on non-believers and nonconformists by mobs and by populist collectives or organizations who claim to represent "public opinion".

These self-appointed tribunals seek to enforce mores and values they deem to be "universal" and indisputable (usually by virtue of their divine and epiphanic origins.) Such is the threat implicit in these proceedings that they often result in self-censorship and self-denial on the part of their targets and victims. Bible – or Qur'an – thumping give rise to terror and to the suppression of free speech and unmitigated self-expression. The penalties for transgressors range from ostracism to physical harm.

On the level of individuals, theochlocracy is a form of malignant narcissism.

The narcissist is prone to magical thinking. He regards himself in terms of "being chosen" or of "being destined for greatness". He believes that he has a "direct line" to God, even, perversely, that God "serves" him in certain junctions and conjunctures of his life, through divine intervention. He believes that his life is of such momentous importance, that it is micro-managed by God. The narcissist likes to play God to his human environment. In short, narcissism and religion go well together, because religion allows the narcissist to feel unique.

This is a private case of a more general phenomenon. The narcissist likes to belong to groups or to frameworks of allegiance. He derives easy and constantly available Narcissistic Supply from them. Within them and from their members he is certain to garner attention, to gain adulation, to be castigated or praised. His False Self is bound to be reflected by his colleagues, co-members, or fellows.

This is no mean feat and it cannot be guaranteed in other circumstances. Hence the narcissist's fanatic and proud emphasis of his membership. If a military man, he shows off his impressive array of medals, his impeccably pressed uniform, the status symbols of his rank. If a clergyman, he is overly devout and orthodox and places great emphasis on the proper conduct of rites, rituals and ceremonies.

The narcissist develops a reverse (benign) form of paranoia: he feels constantly watched over by senior members of his group or frame of reference, the subject of permanent (avuncular) criticism, the centre of attention. If a religious man, he calls it divine providence. This self-centred perception also caters to the narcissist's streak of grandiosity, proving that he is, indeed, worthy of such incessant and detailed attention, supervision and intervention.

From this mental junction, the way is short to entertaining the delusion that God (or the equivalent institutional authority) is an active participant in the narcissist's life in which constant intervention by Him is a key feature. God is subsumed in a larger picture, that of the narcissist's destiny and mission. God serves this cosmic plan by making it possible.

Indirectly, therefore, God is perceived by the narcissist to be at his service. Moreover, in a process of holographic appropriation, the narcissist views himself as a microcosm of his affiliation, of his group, or his frame of reference. The narcissist is likely to say that he *IS* the army, the nation, the people, the struggle, history, or (a part of) God.

As opposed to healthier people, the narcissist believes that he both represents and embodies his class, his people, his race, history, his God, his art – or anything else he feels a part of. This is why individual narcissists feel completely comfortable to assume roles usually reserved to groups of people or to some transcendental, divine (or other), authority.

This kind of "enlargement" or "inflation" also sits well with the narcissist's all-pervasive feelings of omnipotence, omnipresence, and omniscience. In playing God, for instance, the narcissist is completely convinced that he is merely being himself. The narcissist does not hesitate to put people's lives or fortunes at risk. He preserves his sense of infallibility in the face of mistakes and misjudgements by distorting the facts, by evoking mitigating or attenuating circumstances, by repressing memories, or by simply lying.

In the overall design of things, small setbacks and defeats matter little, says the narcissist. The narcissist is haunted by the feeling that he is possessed of a mission, of a destiny, that he is part of fate, of history. He is convinced that his uniqueness is purposeful, that he is meant to lead, to chart new ways, to innovate, to modernise, to reform, to set precedents, or to create from scratch.

Every act of the narcissist is perceived by him to be significant, every utterance of momentous consequence, every thought of revolutionary calibre. He feels part of a grand design, a world plan and the frame of affiliation, the group, of which he is a member, must be commensurately grand. Its proportions and properties must resonate with his. Its characteristics must justify his and its ideology must conform to his pre-conceived opinions and prejudices.

In short: the group must magnify the narcissist, echo and amplify his life, his views, his knowledge, and his personal history. This intertwining, this enmeshing of individual and collective, is what makes the narcissist the most devout and loyal of all its members.

The narcissist is always the most fanatical, the most extreme, the most dangerous adherent. At stake is never merely the preservation of his group – but his very own survival. As with other Narcissistic Supply Sources, once the group is no longer instrumental – the narcissist loses all interest in it, devalues it and ignores it.

In extreme cases, he might even wish to destroy it (as a punishment or revenge for its incompetence in securing his emotional needs). Narcissists switch groups and ideologies with ease (as they do partners, spouses and value systems). In this respect, narcissists are narcissists first and members of their groups only in the second place.

In short:

God is everything the narcissist ever wants to be: omnipotent, omniscient, omnipresent, admired, much discussed, and awe inspiring. God is the narcissist's wet dream, his ultimate grandiose fantasy. But God comes handy in other ways as well.

The narcissist alternately idealizes and devalues figures of authority.

In the idealization phase, he strives to emulate them, he admires them, imitate them (often ludicrously), and defends them. They cannot go wrong, or be wrong. The narcissist regards them as bigger than life, infallible, perfect, whole, and brilliant. But as the narcissist's unrealistic and inflated expectations are inevitably frustrated, he begins to devalue his former idols.

Now they are "human" (to the narcissist, a derogatory term). They are small, fragile, error-prone, pusillanimous, mean, dumb, and mediocre. The narcissist goes through the same cycle in his relationship with God, the quintessential authority figure.

But often, even when disillusionment and iconoclastic despair have set in - the narcissist continues to pretend to love God and follow Him. The narcissist maintains this deception because his continued proximity to God confers on him authority. Priests, leaders of the congregation, preachers, evangelists, cultists, politicians, intellectuals - all derive authority from their allegedly privileged relationship with God.

Religious authority allows the narcissist to indulge his sadistic urges and to exercise his misogynism freely and openly. Such a narcissist is likely to taunt and torment his followers, hector and chastise them, humiliate and berate them, abuse them spiritually, or even sexually. The narcissist whose source of authority is religious is looking for obedient and unquestioning slaves upon whom to exercise his capricious and wicked mastery. The narcissist transforms even the most innocuous and pure religious sentiments into a cultish ritual and a virulent hierarchy. He preys on the gullible. His flock become his hostages.

Religious authority also secures the narcissist's Narcissistic Supply. His coreligionists, members of his congregation, his parish, his constituency, his audience - are transformed into loyal and stable Sources of Narcissistic Supply. They obey his commands, heed his admonitions, follow his creed, admire his personality, applaud his personal traits, satisfy his needs (sometimes even his carnal desires), revere and idolize him.

Moreover, being a part of a "bigger thing" is very gratifying narcissistically. Being a particle of God, being immersed in His grandeur, experiencing His power and blessings first hand, communing with him - are all Sources of unending Narcissistic Supply. The narcissist becomes God by observing His commandments, following His instructions, loving Him, obeying Him, succumbing to Him, merging with Him, communicating with Him - or even by defying him (the bigger the narcissist's enemy - the more grandiosely important the narcissist feels).

Like everything else in the narcissist's life, he mutates God into a kind of inverted narcissist. God becomes his dominant Source of Supply. He forms a personal relationship with this overwhelming and overpowering entity - in order to overwhelm and overpower others. He becomes God vicariously, by the proxy of his relationship with Him. He idealizes God, then devalues Him, then abuses Him. This is the classic narcissistic pattern and even God himself cannot escape it.

In a narcissistic culture or civilization, these warped relationships - between individuals, their God, and their institutional affiliation - are magnified. Nowhere is this more true - and is theochlocracy more evident - than in the United States of America (USA).

Jacobsen: As you have written on religion a lot, what needs to happen to religion/faith in a self-centered era for survival of the species?

Vaknin:

Narcissism is the new religion. In an age of godlike technological self-sufficiency, everyone is rendered both a deity and a worshipper of themselves. This new religion is distributed: billions of equipotent divine nodes, one man or one woman cults and loci of worship.

Jacobsen: Thank you for the opportunity and your time, Professor Vaknin.

Vaknin: A pleasure as always.

References

Bishop, J. (2016, December 21). *Faith*. Stanford Encyclopedia of Philosophy. https://plato.stanford.edu/cgi-bin/encyclopedia/archinfo.cgi?entry=faith.

Psychology Today Staff. (2022). *Religion*. Psychology Today. https://www.psychologytoday.com/us/basics/religion

Smashwords. (2014, October 19). *Interview with Sam Vaknin*. https://www.smashwords.com/interview/samvaknin.

Taliaferro, C. (2021, December 21). *Philosophy of Religion*. Stanford Encyclopedia of Philosophy. https://plato.stanford.edu/cgi-bin/encyclopedia/archinfo.cgi?entry=philosophy-religion

The Editors of Encyclopaedia Britannica. (2017, June 16). *faith*. Encyclopedia Britannica. https://www.britannica.com/topic/faith

The Editors of Encyclopaedia Britannica (2021, February 2). *religion*. Encyclopedia Britannica. https://www.britannica.com/topic/religion

Vaknin, S. (n.d.a). *Atheism in a Post-Religious World: Book Review*. vaknin.tripod. https://samvak.tripod.com/atheism.html.

Vaknin, S. (2016, January 14). *Islam and Liberalism: Total Ideologies*. Medium. https://samvaknin.medium.com/islam-and-liberalism-total-ideologies-2eae7eaeb312

Vaknin, S. (n.d.b). *Sam Vaknin's Instagram Epigrams – Page 4*. samvak.tripod. https://samvak.tripod.com/instagramvaknin4.html

Footnotes

[1] "religion" states:

> **religion**, human beings' relation to that which they regard as holy, sacred, absolute, spiritual, divine, or worthy of especial reverence. It is also commonly regarded as consisting of the way people deal with ultimate concerns about their lives and their fate after death. In many traditions, this relation and these concerns are expressed in terms of one's relationship with or attitude toward gods or spirits; in more humanistic or naturalistic forms of religion, they are expressed in terms of one's relationship with or attitudes toward the broader human community or the natural world. In many religions, texts are deemed to have scriptural status, and people are esteemed to be invested with spiritual or moral authority. Believers and worshippers participate in and are often enjoined to perform devotional or contemplative practices such as prayer, meditation, or particular rituals. Worship, moral conduct, right belief, and participation in religious institutions are among the constituent elements of the religious life.

See Britannica, T. Editors of Encyclopaedia (2021).

"Religion" states:

> Since the earliest humans walked the earth, individuals have wondered where they came from, why they're here, and what it all means. Religion, by and large, represents society's attempts to answer those questions. While it isn't always able to achieve that goal, it often succeeds at providing followers with structure, a code of ethics, and a sense of purpose. The promise of an afterlife, a core tenet of most organized religions, is another key motivator for followers, as this belief serves an important psychological function.

See Psychology Today Staff (2022).

"Philosophy of Religion" states:

> Ideally, a guide to the nature and history of philosophy of religion would begin with an analysis or definition of religion. Unfortunately, there is no current consensus on a precise identification of the necessary and sufficient conditions of what counts as a religion. We therefore currently lack a decisive criterion that would enable clear rulings whether some movements should count as religions (e.g., Scientology or Cargo cults of the Pacific islands). But while consensus in precise details is elusive, the following general depiction of what counts as a religion may be helpful:
>
> > A religion involves a communal, transmittable body of teachings and prescribed practices about an ultimate, sacred reality or state of being that calls for reverence or awe, a body which guides its practitioners into what it describes as a saving, illuminating or emancipatory relationship to this reality through a personally transformative life of prayer, ritualized meditation,

and/or moral practices like repentance and personal regeneration. [This is a slightly modified definition of the one for "Religion" in the Dictionary of Philosophy of Religion, *Taliaferro & Marty 2010: 196–197; 2018, 240.]*

See Taliaferro (2021).

"Faith" states:

> *'Faith' is a broad term, appearing in locutions that express a range of different concepts. At its most general 'faith' means much the same as 'trust'. This entry is specifically concerned, however, with the notion of* religious *faith—or, rather (and this qualification is important),* the kind of faith exemplified in religious faith. *Philosophical accounts are almost exclusively about* theistic *religious faith—faith in God—and they generally, though not exclusively, deal with faith as understood within the Christian branch of the Abrahamic traditions. But, although the theistic religious context settles what kind of faith is of interest, the question arises whether faith* of that same general kind *also belongs to other, non-theistic, religious contexts, or to contexts not usually thought of as religious at all. Arguably, it may be apt to speak of the faith of a humanist, or even an atheist, using the same general sense of 'faith' as applies to the theist case.*

Bishop (2016).

"faith" states:

> **faith**, *inner attitude, <u>conviction</u>, or trust relating human beings to a supreme God or ultimate <u>salvation</u>. In religious traditions stressing divine <u>grace</u>, it is the inner certainty or attitude of love granted by God himself. In <u>Christian</u> <u>theology</u>, faith is the divinely inspired human response to God's historical <u>revelation</u> through <u>Jesus Christ</u> and, consequently, is of crucial significance.*

No definition allows for identification of "faith" with "religion." Some inner attitude has its part in all religious traditions, but it is not always of central significance. For example, words in <u>ancient Egypt</u> or Vedic India that can be roughly rendered by the general term "religion" do not allow for "faith" as a translation but rather connote cultic duties and acts. In <u>Hindu</u> and <u>Buddhist</u> <u>Yoga</u> traditions, inner attitudes recommended are primarily attitudes of trust in the guru, or spiritual preceptor, and not, or not primarily, in God. Hindu and Buddhist concepts of devotion (<u>Sanskrit</u> <u>bhakti</u>) and love or compassion (Sanskrit <u>karuna</u>) are more comparable to the Christian notions of love (<u>Greek</u> agapē, <u>Latin</u> caritas) than to faith. Devotional forms of <u>Mahayana</u> <u>Buddhism</u> and <u>Vaishnavism</u> show religious expressions not wholly dissimilar to faith in Christian and <u>Jewish</u> traditions.

The Editors of Encyclopaedia Britannica (2017).

[2] See Vaknin (n.d.a) about differentiation between the terms and personal anti-theism, Smashwords (2014) about family and himself, and Vaknin (n.d.b) about Ghandi's earlier life.

[3] "Interview with Sam Vaknin" (2014) states:

Q: What was your family's attitude toward religion?

A: My parents vacillated between ridicule and disdain and bouts of devoutness. On the average, we were a mildly traditionalist family: selectively observed a few religious commandments and rites. Two of my brothers flirt with fundamentalist Judaism (more charitably known as Orthodoxy). I am agnostic. I do not waste my time on questions the answers to which are, in principle, unknowable.

See Smashwords (2014).

[4] "Atheism in a Post-Religious World: Book Review" (n.d.) states:

Is ours a post-religious world? Ask any born again Christian fundamentalist, militant Muslim, orthodox Jew, and nationalistic Hindu. Religion is on the rise, not on the wane. Eighteenth century enlightenment is besieged. As the author himself often admits, atheism, as a creed, is on the defensive.

First, we should get our terminology clear. Atheism is not the same as agnosticism which is not the same as anti-theism.

*Atheism is a religion, yet another faith. It is founded on the improvable and unfalsifiable **belief** (universal negative) that there is no God. Agnosticism is about keeping an open mind: God may or may not exist. There is no convincing case either way.*

Anti-theism is militant anti-clericalism. Anti-theists (such as Tremblay and myself) regard religion as an unmitigated evil that must be eradicated to make for a better world. This treasure of a book - it is incredible how much the author squeezed into 50 pages! - is about anti-theism.

See Vaknin (n.d.a).

[5] See Ibid.

[6] "Islam and Liberalism: Total Ideologies" states:

Islam is not merely a religion. It is also — and perhaps, foremost — a state ideology. It is all-pervasive and missionary. It permeates every aspect of social cooperation and culture. It is an organizing principle, a narrative, a philosophy, a value system, and a vade mecum. In this it resembles Confucianism and, to some extent, Hinduism. Total ideologies are both prescriptive and proscriptive: by prohibiting certain kinds of activities and types of conduct, they cohere the pent-up energies ("libido") and underline narcissistic needs of their adherents and channel these forces towards predetermined goals, both constructive and disruptive (or destructive).

Judaism and its offspring, Christianity — though heavily involved in political affairs throughout the ages — have kept their dignified distance from such carnal matters. These are religions of "heaven" as opposed to Islam, a practical, pragmatic, hands-on, ubiquitous, "earthly" creed.

Secular religions — Democratic Liberalism, Communism, Fascism, Nazism, Socialism and other isms — are more akin to Islam than to, let's say, Buddhism. They are universal, prescriptive, and total. They provide recipes, rules, and norms regarding every aspect of existence — individual, social, cultural, moral, economic, political, military, and philosophical.

See Vaknin (2016).

Return

Interview about Science and Reality (News Intervention)

Prof. Shmuel "Sam" Vaknin (YouTube, Twitter, Instagram, Facebook, Amazon, LinkedIn, Google Scholar) is the author of Malignant Self-love: Narcissism Revisited *(Amazon) and* After the Rain: How the West Lost the East *(Amazon) as well as many other* books *and* ebooks *about* topics in psychology, relationships, philosophy, economics, international affairs, *and* award-winning short fiction*. He was Senior Business Correspondent for* United Press International *(February, 2001 - April, 2003), CEO of* Narcissus Publications *(April, 1997 - April 2013), Editor-in-Chief of Global Politician (January, 2011 -), a columnist for* PopMatters, *eBookWeb,* Bellaonline, *and* Central Europe Review, *an editor for* The Open Directory *and* Suite101 *(Categories: Mental Health and Central East Europe), and a contributor to* Middle East Times, *a contributing writer to The American Chronicle Media Group, Columnist and Analyst for* Nova Makedonija, Fokus, *and* Kapital, *Founding Analyst of The Analyst Network, former president of the Israeli chapter of the* Unification Church's Professors for World Peace Academy, *and served in the* Israeli Defense Forces *(1979-1982). He has been awarded Israel's Council of Culture and Art Prize for Maiden Prose (1997), The Rotary Club Award for Social Studies (1976), and the Bilateral Relations Studies Award of the American Embassy in Israel (1978), among other awards. He is Visiting Professor of Psychology,* Southern Federal University, Rostov-on-Don, Russia *(September, 2017 to present),* Professor of Finance and Psychology in SIAS-CIAPS (Centre for International Advanced and Professional Studies) (April, 2012 to present), *a Senior Correspondent for New York Daily Sun (January, 2015 - Present), and Columnist for Allied Newspapers Group (January, 2015 - Present). He lives in Skopje, North Macedonia with his wife,* Lidija Rangelovska. *Here we talk about science and reality.*

Scott Douglas Jacobsen: Reality - all that is, ever was, or ever will be, what defines it, to you?

Prof. Shmuel "Sam" Vaknin:

"Reality" is the name we give to our aggregate experiences, both of ourselves ("consciousness") and of not-ourselves (the "world out there").

We assume that a world exists independent of our perception of it or interaction with it because we maintain an intersubjective agreement with all other human beings.

The high correlation between the contents of our mind and the self-reports of others leads us to deduce that we must be sharing something distinct from our observations and experiences.

Of course, this commonly shared "theory of reality" is full of holes and easily refuted. But we tend to ignore this fact and impute "reality" even to simulated worlds - simply because they trigger reactions in our brains.

Jacobsen: What defines science?

Vaknin:

Scientific Theories

All theories - scientific or not - start with a problem. They aim to solve it by proving that what appears to be "problematic" is not. They re-state the conundrum, or introduce new data, new variables, a new classification, or new organizing principles. They incorporate the problem in a larger body of knowledge, or in a conjecture ("solution"). They explain why we thought we had an issue on our hands - and how it can be avoided, vitiated, or resolved.

Every scientific theory and many pillars of the scientific method are founded on metaphysical principles.

Evolution Theory hails from the metaphysical assumption that individual organisms as well as entire species aim or are geared to survive. Survival is the hermeneutic and organizing principle.

The Special Theory of Relativity is based on the Cartesian separation between observer and observed.

Popper's principle of Falsifiability is founded on a tautology (for a theory to be considered scientific, it must be falsifiable - but we can apply falsifiability only to scientific theories). Add to this the fact that the languages we use to communicate science - mathematics and geometry, for instance - are not neutral. They constrain in large measure what can and cannot be said, they shape content via context, and they provide language elements as theoretical entities.

There are two types of ideas: synoptic and prescriptive.

Synoptic ideas shed light on the interconnectedness of apparently disparate phenomena or concepts. These insights are titillating, fascinating, or even mind-boggling. But, with the exception of a few specialists and eggheads, they are usually of fleeting interest, akin to intellectual fireworks and pyrotechnics, a form of entertainment that fizzles out and is rendered tedious by repetition.

Synoptic ideas are deep and intertwined, so people tend to tune out and wander off (or fall asleep) in mid-sentence. Interdisciplinarity requires discipline and rigor that few have, not even the majority of scholars (witness the crowd dynamics in academic conferences).

In contradistinction, prescriptive ideas focus on proposed solutions based on cumulative data and experience or on theories and rules of derivation. They are highly relevant to their consumers because they aim to better their lives and resolve their problems. Religion, science, technology, and most of philosophy are prescriptive.

A public intellectual whose output is strictly synoptic won't remain public for very long: he will fall out of favor and be ignored and overlooked. Prescriptive thought leaders and change agents thrive and prosper the more anomic, disrupted, dysfunctional, and pathologized society is. The more lost, disoriented, anxious, and depressed people are, the more they seek prescription to extricate them from their predicament.

Scientific theories invite constant criticism and revision. They yield new problems. They are proven erroneous and are replaced by new models which offer better explanations and a more profound sense of understanding - often by solving these new problems. From time to time, the successor theories constitute a break with everything known and done till then. These seismic convulsions are known as "paradigm shifts".

It is interesting to note that paradigm-shifting work is often produced by non-specialist outsiders, gifted amateurs, and laymen (such as Da Vinci, Steno, Mandel, Freud, and, to some extent, Einstein). As Thomas Kuhn noted, run of the mill scientists are vested and invested in the status quo and normally generate paradigm-sustaining theories and discoveries.

Contrary to widespread opinion - even among scientists - science is not only about "facts". It is not merely about quantifying, measuring, describing, classifying, and organizing "things" (entities). It is not even concerned with finding out the "truth". Science is about providing us with concepts, explanations, and predictions (collectively known as "theories") and thus endowing us with a sense of understanding of our world.

Scientific theories are allegorical or metaphoric. They revolve around symbols and theoretical constructs, concepts and substantive assumptions, axioms and hypotheses - most of which can never, even in principle, be computed, observed, quantified, measured, or correlated with the world "out there". By appealing to our imagination, scientific theories reveal what David Deutsch calls "the fabric of reality".

Like any other system of knowledge, science has its fanatics, heretics, and deviants.

Instrumentalists, for instance, insist that scientific theories should be concerned exclusively with predicting the outcomes of appropriately designed experiments. Their explanatory powers are of no consequence. Positivists ascribe meaning only to statements that deal with observables and observations.

Instrumentalists and positivists ignore the fact that predictions are derived from models, narratives, and organizing principles. In short: it is the theory's explanatory dimensions that determine which experiments are relevant and which are not. Forecasts - and experiments - that are not embedded in an understanding of the world (in an explanation) do not constitute science.

Granted, predictions and experiments are crucial to the growth of scientific knowledge and the winnowing out of erroneous or inadequate theories. But they are not the only mechanisms of natural selection. There are other criteria that help us decide whether to adopt and place confidence in a scientific theory or not. Is the theory aesthetic (parsimonious), logical, does it provide a reasonable explanation and, thus, does it further our understanding of the world?

David Deutsch in "The Fabric of Reality" (p. 11):

"... (I)t is hard to give a precise definition of 'explanation' or 'understanding'. Roughly speaking, they are about 'why' rather than 'what'; about the inner workings of things; about how things really are, not just how they appear to be; about what must be so, rather

than what merely happens to be so; about laws of nature rather than rules of thumb. They are also about coherence, elegance, and simplicity, as opposed to arbitrariness and complexity ..."

Reductionists and emergentists ignore the existence of a hierarchy of scientific theories and meta-languages. They believe - and it is an article of faith, not of science - that complex phenomena (such as the human mind) can be reduced to simple ones (such as the physics and chemistry of the brain). Furthermore, to them the act of reduction is, in itself, an explanation and a form of pertinent understanding. Human thought, fantasy, imagination, and emotions *are* nothing but electric currents and spurts of chemicals in the brain, they say.

Holists, on the other hand, refuse to consider the possibility that some higher-level phenomena can, indeed, be fully reduced to base components and primitive interactions. They ignore the fact that reductionism sometimes does provide explanations and understanding. The properties of water, for instance, do spring forth from its chemical and physical composition and from the interactions between its constituent atoms and subatomic particles.

Still, there is a general agreement that scientific theories must be abstract (independent of specific time or place), intersubjectively explicit (contain detailed descriptions of the subject matter in unambiguous terms), logically rigorous (make use of logical systems shared and accepted by the practitioners in the field), empirically relevant (correspond to results of empirical research), useful (in describing and/or explaining the world), and provide typologies and predictions.

A scientific theory should resort to primitive (atomic) terminology and all its complex (derived) terms and concepts should be defined in these indivisible terms. It should offer a map unequivocally and consistently connecting operational definitions to theoretical concepts.

Operational definitions that connect to the same theoretical concept should not contradict each other (be negatively correlated). They should yield agreement on measurement conducted independently by trained experimenters. But investigation of the theory of its implication can proceed even without quantification.

Theoretical concepts need not necessarily be measurable or quantifiable or observable. But a scientific theory should afford at least four levels of quantification of its operational and theoretical definitions of concepts: nominal (labeling), ordinal (ranking), interval and ratio.

As we said, scientific theories are not confined to quantified definitions or to a classificatory apparatus. To qualify as scientific, they must contain statements about relationships (mostly causal) between concepts - empirically-supported laws and/or propositions (statements derived from axioms).

Philosophers like Carl Hempel and Ernest Nagel regard a theory as scientific if it is hypothetico-deductive. To them, scientific theories are sets of inter-related laws. We know that they are inter-related because a minimum number of axioms and hypotheses yield, in an inexorable deductive sequence, everything else known in the field the theory pertains to.

Explanation is about retrodiction - using the laws to show how things happened. Prediction is using the laws to show how things *will* happen. Understanding is explanation and prediction combined.

William Whewell augmented this somewhat simplistic point of view with his principle of "consilience of inductions". Often, he observed, inductive explanations of disparate phenomena are unexpectedly traced to one underlying cause. This is what scientific theorizing is about - finding the common source of the apparently separate.

This omnipotent view of the scientific endeavor competes with a more modest, semantic school of philosophy of science.

Many theories - especially ones with breadth, width, and profundity, such as Darwin's theory of evolution - are not deductively integrated and are very difficult to test (falsify) conclusively. Their predictions are either scant or ambiguous.

Scientific theories, goes the semantic view, are amalgams of models of reality. These are empirically meaningful only inasmuch as they are empirically (directly and therefore semantically) applicable to a limited area. A typical scientific theory is not constructed with explanatory and predictive aims in mind. Quite the opposite: the choice of models incorporated in it dictates its ultimate success in explaining the Universe and predicting the outcomes of experiments.

To qualify as meaningful and instrumental, a scientific explanation (or "theory") must be:

a. ***All-inclusive (anamnetic)*** – It must encompass, integrate and incorporate all the facts known.
a. ***Coherent*** – It must be chronological, structured and causal.
a. ***Consistent*** – Self-consistent (its sub-units cannot contradict one another or go against the grain of the main explication) and consistent with the observed phenomena (both those related to the event or subject and those pertaining to the rest of the universe).
a. ***Logically compatible*** – It must not violate the laws of logic both internally (the explanation must abide by some internally imposed logic) and externally (the Aristotelian logic which is applicable to the observable world).
a. ***Insightful*** – It must inspire a sense of awe and astonishment which is the result of seeing something familiar in a new light or the result of seeing a pattern emerging out of a big body of data. The insights must constitute the inevitable conclusion of the logic, the language, and of the unfolding of the explanation.
a. ***Aesthetic*** – The explanation must be both plausible and "right", beautiful, not cumbersome, not awkward, not discontinuous, smooth, parsimonious, simple, and so on.
a. ***Parsimonious*** – The explanation must employ the minimum numbers of assumptions and entities in order to satisfy all the above conditions.
a. ***Explanatory*** – The explanation must elucidate the behavior of other elements, including the subject's decisions and behavior and why events developed the way they did.
    i. ***Predictive (prognostic)*** – The explanation must possess the ability to predict future events, including the future behavior of the subject.
    j.

k.   *Elastic*– The explanation must possess the intrinsic abilities to self-organize, reorganize, give room to emerging order, accommodate new data comfortably, and react flexibly to attacks from within and from without.

Scientific theories must also be testable, verifiable, and refutable (falsifiable). The experiments that test their predictions must be repeatable and replicable in tightly controlled laboratory settings. All these elements are largely missing from creationist and intelligent design "theories" and explanations. No experiment could be designed to test the statements within such explanations, to establish their truth-value and, thus, to convert them to theorems or hypotheses in a theory.

This is mainly because of a problem known as ***the undergeneration of testable hypotheses:*** Creationism and intelligent Design do not generate a sufficient number of hypotheses, which can be subjected to scientific testing. This has to do with their fabulous (i.e., storytelling) nature and the resort to an untestable, omnipotent, omniscient, and omnipresent Supreme Being.

In a way, Creationism and Intelligent Design show affinity with some private languages. They are forms of <u>art</u> and, as such, are self-sufficient and self-contained. If structural, internal constraints are met, a statement is deemed true within the "canon" even if it does not satisfy external scientific requirements.

The Life Cycle of Scientific Theories

"There was a time when the newspapers said that only twelve men understood the theory of relativity. I do not believe that there ever was such a time... On the other hand, I think it is safe to say that no one understands quantum mechanics... Do not keep saying to yourself, if you can possibly avoid it, 'But how can it be like that?', because you will get 'down the drain' into a blind alley from which nobody has yet escaped. Nobody knows how it can be like that."
R. P. Feynman (1967)

"The first processes, therefore, in the effectual studies of the sciences, must be ones of simplification and reduction of the results of previous investigations to a form in which the mind can grasp them."
J. C. Maxwell, On Faraday's lines of force

" ...conventional formulations of quantum theory, and of quantum field theory in particular, are unprofessionally vague and ambiguous. Professional theoretical physicists ought to be able to do better. Bohm has shown us a way."
John S. Bell, Speakable and Unspeakable in Quantum Mechanics

"It would seem that the theory [quantum mechanics] is exclusively concerned about 'results of measurement', and has nothing to say about anything else. What exactly qualifies some physical systems to play the role of 'measurer'? Was the wavefunction of the world waiting to jump for thousands of millions of years until a single-celled living creature appeared? Or did it have to wait a little longer, for some better qualified system ... with a Ph.D.? If the theory is to apply to anything but highly idealized laboratory operations, are we not obliged to admit that more or less 'measurement-like' processes are

going on more or less all the time, more or less everywhere. Do we not have jumping then all the time?

The first charge against 'measurement', in the fundamental axioms of quantum mechanics, is that it anchors the shifty split of the world into 'system' and 'apparatus'. A second charge is that the word comes loaded with meaning from everyday life, meaning which is entirely inappropriate in the quantum context. When it is said that something is 'measured' it is difficult not to think of the result as referring to some pre-existing property of the object in question. This is to disregard Bohr's insistence that in quantum phenomena the apparatus as well as the system is essentially involved. If it were not so, how could we understand, for example, that 'measurement' of a component of 'angular momentum' ... in an arbitrarily chosen direction ... yields one of a discrete set of values? When one forgets the role of the apparatus, as the word 'measurement' makes all too likely, one despairs of ordinary logic ... hence 'quantum logic'. When one remembers the role of the apparatus, ordinary logic is just fine.

In other contexts, physicists have been able to take words from ordinary language and use them as technical terms with no great harm done. Take for example the 'strangeness', 'charm', and 'beauty' of elementary particle physics. No one is taken in by this 'baby talk'... Would that it were so with 'measurement'. But in fact the word has had such a damaging effect on the discussion, that I think it should now be banned altogether in quantum mechanics."
J. S. Bell, Against "Measurement"

"Is it not clear from the smallness of the scintillation on the screen that we have to do with a particle? And is it not clear, from the diffraction and interference patterns, that the motion of the particle is directed by a wave? De Broglie showed in detail how the motion of a particle, passing through just one of two holes in screen, could be influenced by waves propagating through both holes. And so influenced that the particle does not go where the waves cancel out, but is attracted to where they co-operate. This idea seems to me so natural and simple, to resolve the wave-particle dilemma in such a clear and ordinary way, that it is a great mystery to me that it was so generally ignored."
J. S. Bell, Speakable and Unspeakable in Quantum Mechanics

"...in physics the only observations we must consider are position observations, if only the positions of instrument pointers. It is a great merit of the de Broglie-Bohm picture to force us to consider this fact. If you make axioms, rather than definitions and theorems, about the "measurement" of anything else, then you commit redundancy and risk inconsistency."
J. S. Bell, Speakable and Unspeakable in Quantum Mechanics

"To outward appearance, the modern world was born of an anti-religious movement: man becoming self-sufficient and reason supplanting belief. Our generation and the two that preceded it have heard little of but talk of the conflict between science and faith; indeed it seemed at one moment a foregone conclusion that the former was destined to take the place of the latter... After close on two centuries of passionate struggles, neither science nor faith has succeeded in discrediting its adversary.
On the contrary, it becomes obvious that neither can develop normally without the other. And the reason is simple: the same life animates both. Neither in its impetus nor its achievements can science go to its limits without becoming tinged with mysticism and

I opened with lengthy quotations by John S. Bell, the main proponent of the Bohemian Mechanics interpretation of Quantum Mechanics (really, an alternative rather than an interpretation). The renowned physicist, David Bohm (in the 50s), basing himself on work done much earlier by de Broglie (the unwilling father of the wave-particle dualism), embedded the Schrödinger Equation (SE) in a deterministic physical theory which postulated a non-Newtonian motion of particles.

This is a fine example of the life cycle of scientific theories, comprised of three phases: Growth, Transitional Pathology, and Ossification.

Witchcraft, Religion, Alchemy and Science succeeded one another and each such transition was characterized by transitional pathologies reminiscent of psychotic disorders. The exceptions are (arguably) the disciplines of medicine and biology. A phenomenology of ossified bodies of knowledge would make a fascinating read.

Science is currently in its Ossification Phase. It is soon to be succeeded by another discipline or magisterium. Other explanations to the current dismal state of science should be rejected: that human knowledge is limited by its very nature; that the world is inherently incomprehensible; that methods of thought and understanding tend to self-organize to form closed mythic systems; and that there is a problem with the language which we employ to make our inquiries of the world describable and communicable.

Kuhn's approach to Scientific Revolutions is but one of many that deal with theory and paradigm shifts in scientific thought and its resulting evolution. Scientific theories seem to be subject to a process of natural selection every bit as organisms in nature are.

Animals could be thought of as theorems (with a positive truth value) in the logical system "Nature". But species become extinct because nature itself changes (not nature as a set of potentials - but the relevant natural phenomena to which the species are exposed). Could we say the same about scientific theories? Are they being selected and deselected partly due to a changing, shifting backdrop?

Indeed, the whole debate between "realists" and "anti-realists" in the philosophy of Science can be settled by adopting this single premise: that the Universe itself is not immutable. By contrasting the fixed subject of study ("The World") with the transient nature of Science anti-realists gained the upper hand.

Arguments such as the under-determination of theories by data and the pessimistic meta-inductions from past falsity (of scientific "knowledge") emphasize the transience and asymptotic nature of the fruits of the scientific endeavor. But such arguments rest on the implicit assumption that there is some universal, invariant, truth out there (which science strives to asymptotically approximate). This apparent problematic evaporates if we allow that both the observer and the observed, the theory and its subject, are alterable.

Science develops through reduction of miracles. Laws of nature are formulated. They are assumed to encompass all the (relevant) natural phenomena (that is, phenomena governed by natural forces and within nature). Ex definitio, nothing can exist outside nature: it is all-inclusive and all-pervasive, or omnipresent (formerly the attributes of the divine).

Supernatural forces, supernatural intervention, are contradictions in terms, oxymorons. If some thing or force exists, it is natural. That which is supernatural does not exist. Miracles do not only contravene (or violate) the laws of nature, they are impossible, not only physically, but also logically. That which is logically possible and can be experienced (observed), is physically possible.

But, again, we are faced with the assumption of a "fixed background". What if nature itself changes in ways that are bound to confound ever-truer knowledge? Then, the very shifts of nature as a whole, as a system, could be called "supernatural" or "miraculous".

In a way, this is how science evolves. A law of nature is proposed or accepted. An event occurs or an observation made which are not described or predicted by it. It is, by definition, a violation of the suggested or accepted law which is, thus, falsified. Subsequently and consequently, the laws of nature are modified, or re-written entirely, in order to reflect and encompass this extraordinary event. Result: Hume's comforting distinction between "extraordinary" and "miraculous" events is upheld (the latter being ruled out).

Extraordinary events can be compared to previous experience - miraculous events entail some supernatural interference with the normal course of things (a "wonder" in Biblical terms). It is by confronting the extraordinary and eliminating its "abnormal" or "supernatural" attributes that science progresses as a miraculous activity. This, of course, is not the view of the likes of David Deutsch (see his book, "The Fabric of Reality").

Back to the last phase of this Life Cycle, to Ossification. The discipline degenerates and, following the "psychotic" transitional phase, it sinks into a paralytic state which is characterized by the following:

All the practical and technological aspects of the dying discipline are preserved and continue to be utilized. Gradually the conceptual and theoretical underpinnings vanish or are replaced by the tenets and postulates of a new discipline - but the inventions, processes and practical know-how do not evaporate. They are incorporated into the new discipline and, in time, are erroneously attributed to it, marking it as the legitimate successor of the now defunct, preceding discipline.

The practitioners of the old discipline confine themselves to copying and replicating the various aspects of the old discipline, mainly its intellectual property (writings, inventions, other theoretical material). This replication does not lead to the creation of new knowledge or even to the dissemination of old one. It is a hermetic process, limited to the ever-decreasing circle of the initiated. Special institutions govern the rehashing of the materials related to the old discipline, their processing and copying. Institutions related to the dead discipline are often financed and supported by the state which is always an agent of conservation, preservation and conformity.

Thus, the creative-evolutionary dimension of the now-dead discipline is gone. No new paradigms or revolutions happen. The exegesis and replication of canonical writings become the predominant activities. Formalisms are not subjected to scrutiny and laws assume eternal, immutable, quality.

All the activities of the adherents of the old discipline become ritualized. The old discipline itself becomes a pillar of the extant power structures and, as such, is condoned and supported by them. The old discipline's practitioners synergistically collaborate with the powers that be: with the industrial base, the military complex, the political elite, the intellectual cliques in vogue. Institutionalization inevitably leads to the formation of a (mostly bureaucratic) hierarchy.

Emerging rituals serve the purpose of diverting attention from subversive, "forbidden" thinking. These rigid ceremonies are reminiscent of obsessive-compulsive disorders in individuals who engage in ritualistic behavior patterns to deflect "wrong" or "corrupt" thoughts.

Practitioners of the old discipline seek to cement the power of its "clergy". Rituals are a specialized form of knowledge which can be obtained only by initiation ("rites of passage"). One's status in the hierarchy of the dead discipline is not the result of objectively quantifiable variables or even of judgment of merit. It is the outcome of politics and other power-related interactions.

The need to ensure conformity leads to doctrinarian dogmatism and to the establishment of enforcement mechanisms. Dissidents are subjected to both social and economic sanctions. They find themselves ex-communicated, harassed, imprisoned, tortured, their works banished or not published, ridiculed and so on.

This is really the triumph of text over the human spirit. At this late stage in the Life Cycle, the members of the old discipline's community are oblivious to the original reasons and causes for their pursuits. Why was the discipline developed in the first place? What were the original riddles, questions, queries it faced and tackled? Long gone are the moving forces behind the old discipline. Its cold ashes are the texts and their preservation is an expression of longing and desire for things past.

The vacuum left by the absence of positive emotions is filled by negative ones. The discipline and its disciples become phobic, paranoid, defensive, and with a faulty reality test. Devoid of the ability to generate new, attractive content, the old discipline resorts to motivation by manipulation of negative emotions. People are frightened, threatened, herded, cajoled. The world is painted in an apocalyptic palette as ruled by irrationality, disorderly, chaotic, dangerous, or even lethal. Only the old discipline stands between its adherents and apocalypse.

New, emerging disciplines, are presented as heretic, fringe lunacies, inconsistent, reactionary and bound to regress humanity to some dark ages. This is the inter-disciplinary or inter-paradigm clash. It follows the Psychotic Phase. The old discipline resorts to some transcendental entity (God, Satan, or the conscious intelligent observer in the Copenhagen interpretation of the formalism of Quantum Mechanics). In this sense, the dying discipline is already psychotic and afoul of the test of reality. It develops messianic aspirations and is inspired by a missionary zeal and zest. The fight against new ideas and theories is bloody and ruthless and every possible device is employed.

But the very characteristics of the older nomenclature is in the old discipline's disfavor. It is closed, based on ritualistic initiation, and patronizing. It relies on intimidation. The numbers of the faithful dwindle the more the "church" needs them and the more it resorts to oppressive recruitment tactics. The emerging discipline wins by default. Even the initiated, who stand most to lose, finally abandon the old discipline. Their belief unravels when confronted with the truth value, explanatory and predictive powers, and the comprehensiveness of the emerging discipline.

This, indeed, is the main presenting symptom, the distinguishing hallmark, of paralytic old disciplines. They deny reality. They are rendered mere belief-systems, myths. They require the suspension of judgment and disbelief, the voluntary limitation of one's quest for truth and beauty, the agreement to leave swathes of the map in a state of "terra incognita". This reductionism, this schizoid avoidance, the resort to hermeticism and transcendental authority mark the beginning of the end.

Jacobsen: How are the mentally ill disconnected from reality in various ways?

Vaknin:

Mental illness is about opting out of the intersubjective agreement: disagreeing with most other people about what constitutes "reality". In various periods in history, the mentally ill were considered to be in possession of privileged or exceptional access to a more fundamental stratum of reality, beyond commonly shared experiences.

Is there a way to tell "objective" reality from dreams or mental illness? No, there isn't. To decide which version of reality is widely accepted, we use statistics (a polling of all the participants in any given worldline) or measures of efficacy (if it works, it must be real or it is based on a correct assessment of reality).

Jacobsen: Why is psychology not science, though following the forms?

Vaknin:

Are psychological theories scientific theories by any definition (prescriptive or descriptive)? Hardly.

First, we must distinguish between psychological theories and the way that some of them are applied (psychotherapy and psychological plots). Psychological plots are the narratives co-authored by the therapist and the patient during psychotherapy. These narratives are the outcomes of applying psychological theories and models to the patient's specific circumstances.

Psychological plots amount to storytelling - but they are still instances of the psychological theories used. The instances of theoretical concepts in concrete situations form part of every theory. Actually, the only way to test psychological theories - with their dearth of measurable entities and concepts - is by examining such instances (plots).

Storytelling has been with us since the days of campfire and besieging wild animals. It serves a number of important functions: amelioration of fears, communication of vital information (regarding survival tactics and the characteristics of animals, for instance), the satisfaction of a sense of order (predictability and justice), the development of the ability to hypothesize, predict and introduce new or additional theories and so on.

We are all endowed with a sense of wonder. The world around us in inexplicable, baffling in its diversity and myriad forms. We experience an urge to organize it, to "explain the wonder away", to order it so that we know what to expect next (predict). These are the essentials of survival. But while we have been successful at imposing our mind on the outside world – we have been much less successful when we tried to explain and comprehend our internal universe and our behavior.

Psychology is not an exact science, nor can it ever be. This is because its "raw material" (humans and their behavior as individuals and en masse) is not exact. It will never yield natural laws or universal constants (like in physics). Experimentation in the field is constrained by legal and ethical rules. Humans tend to be opinionated, develop resistance, and become self-conscious when observed.

The relationship between the structure and functioning of our (ephemeral) mind, the structure and modes of operation of our (physical) brain, and the structure and conduct of the outside world have been a matter for heated debate for millennia.

Broadly speaking, there are two schools of thought:

One camp identifies the substrate (brain) with its product (mind). Some of these scholars postulate the existence of a lattice of preconceived, born, categorical knowledge about the universe – the vessels into which we pour our experience and which mould it.

Others within this group regard the mind as a black box. While it is possible in principle to know its input and output, it is impossible, again in principle, to understand its internal functioning and management of information. To describe this input-output mechanism, Pavlov coined the word "conditioning", Watson adopted it and invented "behaviorism", Skinner came up with "reinforcement".

Epiphenomenalists (proponents of theories of emergent phenomena) regard the mind as the by-product of the complexity of the brain's "hardware" and "wiring". But all of them ignore the psychophysical question: what *IS* the mind and *HOW* is it linked to the brain?

The other camp assumes the airs of "scientific" and "positivist" thinking. It speculates that the mind (whether a physical entity, an epiphenomenon, a non-physical principle of organization, or the result of introspection) has a structure and a limited set of functions. It is argued that a "mind owner's manual" could be composed, replete with engineering and maintenance instructions. It proffers a dynamic of the psyche.

The most prominent of these "psychodynamists" was, of course, Freud. Though his disciples (Adler, Horney, the object-relations lot) diverged wildly from his initial theories, they all shared his belief in the need to "scientify" and objectify psychology.

Freud, a medical doctor by profession (neurologist) - preceded by another M.D., Josef Breuer – put forth a theory regarding the structure of the mind and its mechanics: (suppressed) energies and (reactive) forces. Flow charts were provided together with a method of analysis, a mathematical physics of the mind.

Many hold all psychodynamic theories to be a mirage. An essential part is missing, they observe: the ability to test the hypotheses, which derive from these "theories". Though very convincing and, surprisingly, possessed of great explanatory powers, being non-verifiable and non-falsifiable as they are – psychodynamic models of the mind cannot be deemed to possess the redeeming features of scientific theories.

Deciding between the two camps was and is a crucial matter. Consider the clash - however repressed - between psychiatry and psychology. The former regards "mental disorders" as euphemisms - it acknowledges only the reality of brain dysfunctions (such as biochemical or electric imbalances) and of hereditary factors. The latter (psychology) implicitly assumes that something exists (the "mind", the "psyche") which cannot be reduced to hardware or to wiring diagrams. Talk therapy is aimed at that something and supposedly interacts with it.

But perhaps the distinction is artificial. Perhaps the mind is simply the way we experience our brains. Endowed with the gift (or curse) of introspection, we experience a duality, a split, constantly being both observer and observed. Moreover, talk therapy involves *TALKING* - which is the transfer of energy from one brain to another through the air. This is a directed, specifically formed energy, intended to trigger certain circuits in the recipient brain. It should come as no surprise if it were to be discovered that talk therapy has clear physiological effects upon the brain of the patient (blood volume, electrical activity, discharge and absorption of hormones, etc.).

All this would be doubly true if the mind were, indeed, only an emergent phenomenon of the complex brain - two sides of the same coin.

Psychological theories of the mind are metaphors of the mind. They are fables and myths, narratives, stories, hypotheses, conjectures. They play (exceedingly) important roles in the psychotherapeutic setting – but not in the laboratory. Their form is artistic, not rigorous, not testable, less structured than theories in the natural sciences. The language used is polyvalent, rich, effusive, ambiguous, evocative, and fuzzy – in short, metaphorical. These theories are suffused with value judgments, preferences, fears, post facto and ad hoc constructions. None of this has methodological, systematic, analytic and predictive merits.

Still, the theories in psychology are powerful instruments, admirable constructs, and they satisfy important needs to explain and understand ourselves, our interactions with others, and with our environment.

The attainment of peace of mind is a need, which was neglected by Maslow in his famous hierarchy. People sometimes sacrifice material wealth and welfare, resist temptations, forgo opportunities, and risk their lives – in order to secure it. There is, in other words, a preference of inner equilibrium over homeostasis. It is the fulfillment of this overwhelming need that psychological theories cater to. In this, they are no different to other collective narratives (myths, for instance).

Still, psychology is desperately trying to maintain contact with reality and to be thought of as a scientific discipline. It employs observation and measurement and organizes the results, often presenting them in the language of mathematics. In some quarters, these practices lends it an air of credibility and rigorousness. Others snidely regard it as an elaborate camouflage and a sham. Psychology, they insist, is a pseudo-science. It has the trappings of science but not its substance.

Worse still, while historical narratives are rigid and immutable, the application of psychological theories (in the form of psychotherapy) is "tailored" and "customized" to the circumstances of each and every patient (client). The user or consumer is incorporated in the resulting narrative as the main hero (or anti-hero). This flexible "production line" seems to be the result of an age of increasing individualism.

True, the "language units" (large chunks of denotates and connotates) used in psychology and psychotherapy are one and the same, regardless of the identity of the patient and his therapist. In psychoanalysis, the analyst is likely to always employ the tripartite structure (Id, Ego, Superego). But these are merely the language elements and need not be confused with the idiosyncratic plots that are weaved in every encounter. Each client, each person, and his own, unique, irreplicable, plot.

To qualify as a "psychological" (both meaningful and instrumental) plot, the narrative, offered to the patient by the therapist, must be:

a. **_All-inclusive (anamnetic)_** – It must encompass, integrate and incorporate all the facts known about the protagonist.
a. **_Coherent_** – It must be chronological, structured and causal.
a. **_Consistent_** – Self-consistent (its subplots cannot contradict one another or go against the grain of the main plot) and consistent with the observed phenomena (both those related to the protagonist and those pertaining to the rest of the universe).
a. **_Logically compatible_** – It must not violate the laws of logic both internally (the plot must abide by some internally imposed logic) and externally (the Aristotelian logic which is applicable to the observable world).
a. **_Insightful (diagnostic)_** – It must inspire in the client a sense of awe and astonishment which is the result of seeing something familiar in a new light or the result of seeing a pattern emerging out of a big body of data. The insights must constitute the inevitable conclusion of the logic, the language, and of the unfolding of the plot.
a. **_Aesthetic_** – The plot must be both plausible and "right", beautiful, not cumbersome, not awkward, not discontinuous, smooth, parsimonious, simple, and so on.
a. **_Parsimonious_** – The plot must employ the minimum numbers of assumptions and entities in order to satisfy all the above conditions.
a. **_Explanatory_** – The plot must explain the behavior of other characters in the plot, the hero's decisions and behavior, why events developed the way they did.
a. **_Predictive (prognostic)_** – The plot must possess the ability to predict future events, the future behavior of the hero and of other meaningful figures and the inner emotional and cognitive dynamics.
a. **_Therapeutic_** – With the power to induce change, encourage functionality, make the patient happier and more content with himself (ego-syntony), with others, and with his circumstances.
a. **_Imposing_** – The plot must be regarded by the client as the preferable organizing principle of his life's events and a torch to guide him in the dark (vade mecum).
a. **_Elastic_** – The plot must possess the intrinsic abilities to self-organize, reorganize, give room to emerging order, accommodate new data comfortably, and react flexibly to attacks from within and from without.

In all these respects, a psychological plot is a theory in disguise. Scientific theories satisfy most of the above conditions as well. But this apparent identity is flawed. The important elements of testability, verifiability, refutability, falsifiability, and repeatability – are all largely missing from psychological theories and plots. No experiment could be designed to test the statements within the plot, to establish their truth-value and, thus, to convert them to theorems or hypotheses in a theory.

There are four reasons to account for this inability to test and prove (or falsify) psychological theories:

1. *Ethical* – Experiments would have to be conducted, involving the patient and others. To achieve the necessary result, the subjects will have to be ignorant of the reasons for the experiments and their aims. Sometimes even the very performance of an experiment will have to remain a secret (double blind experiments). Some experiments may involve unpleasant or even traumatic experiences. This is ethically unacceptable.
1. *The Psychological Uncertainty Principle* – The initial state of a human subject in an experiment is usually fully established. But both treatment and experimentation influence the subject and render this knowledge irrelevant. The very processes of measurement and observation influence the human subject and transform him or her - as do life's circumstances and vicissitudes.
1. *Uniqueness* – Psychological experiments are, therefore, bound to be unique, unrepeatable, cannot be replicated elsewhere and at other times even when they are conducted with the *SAME* subjects. This is because the subjects are never the same due to the aforementioned psychological uncertainty principle. Repeating the experiments with other subjects adversely affects the scientific value of the results.
1. *The undergeneration of testable hypotheses* – Psychology does not generate a sufficient number of hypotheses, which can be subjected to scientific testing. This has to do with the fabulous (=storytelling) nature of psychology. In a way, psychology has affinity with some private languages. It is a form of art and, as such, is self-sufficient and self-contained. If structural, internal constraints are met – a statement is deemed true even if it does not satisfy external scientific requirements.

So, what are psychological theories and plots good for? They are the instruments used in the procedures which induce peace of mind (even happiness) in the client. This is done with the help of a few embedded mechanisms:

a. *The Organizing Principle* – Psychological plots offer the client an organizing principle, a sense of order, meaningfulness, and justice, an inexorable drive toward well defined (though, perhaps, hidden) goals, the feeling of being part of a whole. They strive to answer the "why's" and "how's" of life. They are dialogic. The client asks: "why am I (suffering from a syndrome) and how (can I successfully tackle it)". Then, the plot is spun: "you are like this not because the world is whimsically cruel but because your parents mistreated you when you were very young, or because a person important to you died, or was taken away from you when you were still impressionable, or because you were sexually abused and so on". The client is becalmed by the very fact that there is an explanation to that which until now monstrously taunted and haunted him, that he is not the plaything of vicious Gods, that there is a culprit (focusing his diffuse anger). His belief in the existence of order and justice and their administration by some supreme, transcendental principle is restored. This sense of "law and order" is further enhanced when the plot yields predictions which come true (either because they are self-fulfilling or because some real, underlying "law" has been discovered).

b.   ***The Integrative Principle*** – The client is offered, through the plot, access to the innermost, hitherto inaccessible, recesses of his mind. He feels that he is being reintegrated, that "things fall into place". In psychodynamic terms, the energy is released to do productive and positive work, rather than to induce distorted and destructive forces.

c.   ***The Purgatory Principle*** – In most cases, the client feels sinful, debased, inhuman, decrepit, corrupting, guilty, punishable, hateful, alienated, strange, mocked and so on. The plot offers him absolution. The client's suffering expurgates, cleanses, absolves, and atones for his sins and handicaps. A feeling of hard won achievement accompanies a successful plot. The client sheds layers of functional, adaptive stratagems rendered dysfunctional and maladaptive. This is inordinately painful. The client feels dangerously naked, precariously exposed. He then assimilates the plot offered to him, thus enjoying the benefits emanating from the previous two principles and only then does he develop new mechanisms of coping. Therapy is a mental crucifixion and resurrection and atonement for the patient's sins. It is a religious experience. Psychological theories and plots are in the role of the scriptures from which solace and consolation can be always gleaned.

Jacobsen: If psychology is not a science, what are the ultimate odds of the development of a true taxonomy of mental illness (and mental health)?

Vaknin:

Taxonomy is not synonymous with science, nor does it have to rely on it. It could be descriptive-literary, for example.

The classificatory texts in psychology - such as the DSM and the ICD - are extensive and ample. They capture the gamut of manifested and observable human behaviors coupled with self-reported states of mind.

Jacobsen: How does science pierce the veil of reality, and give a modicum of comprehension and insight about reality?

Vaknin:

It is a common misconception that science is about "reality" (whatever this fuzzy concept may mean).

Science is about science. The texts of science provide self-referential allegories, metaphors, symbols, similes, and synecdoches. These texts build on each other in a hermetic loop of hermeneutics.

Ultimately, science is a methodology of constructing algorithmic narratives that enhance our efficacy in our environments through technologies. Good science is never teleological or tautological - and so, it is never explanatory.

Our uncanny ability to translate science to technology misleads us to believe that science endows us with a grasp of reality. It doesn't. Technology is merely the manipulation of symbols to yield "real life" outcomes. Science is the confluence of texts which often resolve into technology.

Jacobsen: Cranks, Creationism, cults, Intelligent Design advocates, non-falsifiable theoretical constructs, pseudoscience, religious fundamentalism, quack medicine, socio-political dogmatisms, the god concept, woo, and the like, are hindrances to a more full and robust comprehension of reality, by more people – an accurate view of the world. How does delusion play into science, as delusion plays into human psychology, as human psychology plays an implicit part in the scientific process?

Vaknin:

By far the most pernicious and hubristic delusion in science is the belief that it ultimately captures the "truth" or "reality" however incrementally or asymptotically.

The other, equally pervasive delusion, is the confusion between language and the scientific method. Many disciplines - most notably psychology and its close kin, economics - erroneously believe that the use of mathematics and statistics renders them "scientific".

Jacobsen: Will there ever be a true Grand Unified Theory (GUT), if not a Theory of Everything (ToE)?

Vaknin:

Elusive and tedious as the process may be, I have no doubt that we will end up having a TOE. Simply because both the mind and the universe are unitary. Eastern teachings are right: "reality" is nothing but illusory appearance. Underneath it all, there is a single engine of meaning.

How do I know that? Parsimony, Occam's razor. In all disciplines, even as we have been multiplying our knowledge, we have witnessed a massive reduction in the number of theoretical constructs and entities required to account for this ever proliferating cornucopia of observations.

Jacobsen: Will we need new principles of scientific methodology to construct a more comprehensive image of reality?

Vaknin:

No. The crowning achievement of the human mind is the scientific methodology as it stands today. I see no need to tinker with it.

We may, however, gain a new understanding of how to use it best. Popper's principle of falsification is an example of such an evolution in thinking.

We should also avoid all kinds of fads and fashions that masquerade as the scientific method or abuse it.

Finally, we should never confuse the use of language (maths) with the algorithmic nature of the scientific method (for example: the requirement that experiments be replicable).

There are no limits to the applicability of the scientific methodology. I wholeheartedly disagree with attempts to exclude any aspects of reality or existence from its remit.

Jacobsen: Is reality bound to full comprehension in principle or to asymptotic understanding while never reaching capital "T" Truth by some operators in the

universe (e.g., human beings)? Of course, we can include an apparent statistical phenomenon: Mean knowledge of all human beings oscillating within and between the epochs of human history.

Vaknin:

Though I accept that reality exists, albeit beyond our access, I reject the notion of "truth". The only measure is efficacy in any given environment. The kind of narrative that allows us to be efficacious and is conducive to survival is science. It has no truth value.

The extent of confusion that reigns when we discuss the concept of truth is evident in the film "The Invention of Lying". The movie takes place in a world where people are genetically unable to lie. When one of them, presumably an aberrant mutant (his son inherits his newfound ability), stumbles across the art of confabulation, his life is transformed overnight: he becomes rich, a celebrity, and marries the girl of his dreams (who scorned him before).

But, this clever piece of comedy is philosophically muddled. The denizens of this dystopian cosmos (yes, the truth hurts) not only respond veraciously when prompted – they actually and often sadistically share their innermost thoughts, opinions, and observations. The film fails to realize that volunteering the truth is not the same as being truthful.

What's worse, the characters in the movie take all statements about the future to be true. Yet, statements about the future can be and often are false even in a world where lying is unknown. As Aristotle has put it: nothing we say about the future has a truth value (can be confidently and rigorously determined to be true or false). We can lie only by making statements that we know with certainty to be false, but such certainty exists only with regard to the past and the present. We can make statements about the future that may be false, or that are probably false, or that we believe to be false – but we can never be sure that they are false. Therefore, we can never lie (or tell the truth!) about the future.

Still, it is not as simple as that. Truth must also be possible (there is no such thing as an impossible truth, though, of course, there are many improbable truths). Yet, the very concept of possibility has to do with the future. Moreover: only facts are possible. If something is not possible it is also not factual and nothing that is a fact is impossible.

Consider the following:

Thought experiments (Gedankenexperimenten) are "facts" in the sense that they have a "real life" correlate in the form of electrochemical activity in the brain. But it is quite obvious that they do not relate to facts "out there". They are not true statements.

But do they lack truth because they do not relate to facts? How are Truth and Fact interrelated?

One answer is that Truth pertains to the possibility that an event will occur. If true – it must occur and if false – it cannot occur. This is a binary world of extreme existential conditions. Must all possible events occur? Of course not. If they do not occur, would they still be true? Must a statement have a real-life correlate to be true?

Instinctively, the answer is yes. We cannot conceive of a thought divorced from brainwaves. A statement which remains a mere potential seems to exist only in the nether land between truth and falsity. It becomes true only by materializing, by occurring, by matching up with real life. If we could prove that it will never do so, we would have felt justified in classifying it as false. This is the outgrowth of millennia of concrete, Aristotelian logic. Logical statements talk about the world and, therefore, if a statement cannot be shown to relate directly to the world, it is not true.

This approach, however, is the outcome of some underlying assumptions:

First, that the world is finite and also close to its end. To say that something that did not happen cannot be true is to say that it will never happen (i.e., to say that time and space – the world – are finite and are about to end momentarily).

Second, truth and falsity are assumed to be mutually exclusive. Quantum and fuzzy logics have long laid this one to rest. There are real world situations that are both true and not-true. A particle can "be" in two places at the same time. This fuzzy logic is incompatible with our daily experiences but if there is anything that we have learnt from physics in the last seven decades it is that the world is incompatible with our daily experiences.

The third assumption is that the psychic realm is but a subset of the material one. We are membranes with a very particular hole-size. We filter through only well-defined types of experiences, are equipped with limited (and evolutionarily biased) senses, programmed in a way which tends to sustain us until we die. We are not neutral, objective observers. Actually, the very concept of observer is disputable – as modern physics, on the one hand and Eastern philosophy, on the other hand, have shown.

Imagine that a mad scientist has succeeded to infuse all the water in the world with a strong hallucinogen. At a given moment, all the people in the world see a huge flying saucer. What can we say about this saucer? Is it true? Is it "real"?

There is little doubt that the saucer does not exist. But who is to say so? If this statement is left unsaid – does it mean that it cannot exist and, therefore, is untrue? In this case (of the illusionary flying saucer), the statement that remains unsaid is a true statement – and the statement that is uttered by millions is patently false.

Still, the argument can be made that the flying saucer did exist – though only in the minds of those who drank the contaminated water. What is this form of existence? In which sense does a hallucination "exist"? The psychophysical problem is that no causal relationship can be established between a thought and its real-life correlate, the brainwaves that accompany it. Moreover, this leads to infinite regression. If the brainwaves created the thought – who created them, who made them happen? In other words: who is it (perhaps what is it) that thinks?

The subject is so convoluted that to say that the mental is a mere subset of the material is to speculate

It is, therefore, advisable to separate the ontological from the epistemological. But which is which? Facts are determined epistemologically and statistically by conscious and intelligent observers. Their "existence" rests on a sound epistemological footing. Yet we assume that in the absence of observers, facts will continue their existence, will not lose their "factuality", their real-life quality which is observer-independent and invariant.

What about truth? Surely, it rests on solid ontological foundations. Something is or is not true in reality and that is it. But then we saw that truth is determined psychically and, therefore, is vulnerable, for instance, to hallucinations. Moreover, the blurring of the lines in Quantum, non-Aristotelian, logics implies one of two: either that true and false are only "in our heads" (epistemological) – or that something is wrong with our interpretation of the world, with our exegetic mechanism (brain). If the latter case is true that the world does contain mutually exclusive true and false values – but the organ which identifies these entities (the brain) has gone awry. The paradox is that the second approach also assumes that at least the perception of true and false values is dependent on the existence of an epistemological detection device.

Can something be true and reality and false in our minds? Of course it can (remember "Rashomon"). Could the reverse be true? Yes, it can. This is what we call optical or sensory illusions. Even solidity is an illusion of our senses – there are no such things as solid objects (remember the physicist's desk which is 99.99999% vacuum with minute granules of matter floating about).

To reconcile these two concepts, we must let go of the old belief (probably vital to our sanity) that we can know the world. We probably cannot and this is the source of our confusion. The world may be inhabited by "true" things and "false" things. It may be true that truth is existence and falsity is non-existence. But we will never know because we are incapable of knowing anything about the world as it is.

We are, however, fully equipped to know about the mental events inside our heads. It is there that the representations of the real-world form. We are acquainted with these representations (concepts, images, symbols, language in general) – and mistake them for the world itself. Since we have no way of directly knowing the world (without the intervention of our interpretative mechanisms) we are unable to tell when a certain representation corresponds to an event which is observer-independent and invariant and when it corresponds to nothing of the kind. When we see an image – it could be the result of an interaction with light outside us (objectively "real"), or the result of a dream, a drug induced illusion, fatigue and any other number of brain events not correlated with the real world. These are observer-dependent phenomena and, subject to an agreement between a sufficient number of observers, they are judged to be true or "to have happened" (e.g., religious miracles).

To ask if something is true or not is not a meaningful question unless it relates to our internal world and to our capacity as observers. When we say "true" we mean "exists", or "existed", or "most definitely will exist" (the sun will rise tomorrow). But existence can only be ascertained in our minds. Truth, therefore, is nothing but a state of mind. Existence is determined by observing and comparing the two (the outside and the inside, the real and the mental). This yields a picture of the world which may be closely correlated to reality – and, yet again, may not.

Jacobsen: Thank you for the opportunity and your time, Professor Vaknin.

Vaknin: Thank you for giving me this space and for your excellent questions. Return

Interview about Gender Wars (News Intervention)

Scott Douglas Jacobsen: Sex and gender, you've done a decent amount of material on this subject matter. First, what is sex?

Prof. Shmuel "Sam" Vaknin: Sex is biological, albeit fluid. You are born with it, or at least with the corporeal propensity for it. It is a hardware issue.

Jacobsen: Second, what is gender?

Vaknin: Gender is performative, the outcome of socialization, an expression of dominance, and of a gendered personality. It is largely a sociocultural construct grounded in a specific history (see my response to your next question).

Jacobsen: Third, what are other pertinent terms within this context?

Vaknin: *"One is not born, but rather becomes, a woman.", Simone de Beauvoir, The Second Sex (1949)*

With same-sex marriage becoming a legal reality throughout the world, many more children are going to be raised by homosexual (gay and lesbian) parents, or even by transgendered or transsexual ones. How is this going to affect the child's masculinity or femininity?

Is being a gay man less manly than being a heterosexual one? Is a woman who is the outcome of a sex change operation less feminine than her natural-born sisters? In which sense is a "virile" lesbian less of a man than an effeminate heterosexual or homosexual man? And how should we classify and treat bisexuals and asexuals?

What about modern she-breadwinners? All those feminist women in traditional male positions who are as sexually aggressive as men and prone to the same varieties of misconduct (e.g., cheating on their spouses)? Are they less womanly? And are their stay-at-home-dad partners not men enough? How are sex preferences related to gender differentiation? And if one's sex and genitalia can be chosen and altered at will – why not one's gender, regardless of one's natural equipment? Can we decouple gender roles from sexual functions and endowments?

Aren't the feminist-liberal-emancipated woman and her responsive, transformed male partner as moulded by specific social norms and narratives as their more traditional and conservative counterparts? And when men adapted to the demands of the "new", post-modernist woman – were they not then rebuffed by that very same female as emasculated and unmanly? What is the source of this gender chaos? Why do people act "modern" while, at heart, they still hark back to erstwhile mores and ethos?

We assume erroneously that some roles are instinctual because, in nature, other species do it, too: parenting and mating come to mind. The discipline of sociobiology encourages us to counterfactually learn from animals about our social functioning.

But humans and their societies are so much more complex that there is little we can evince from lobsters, chimpanzees, or gorillas.

In nature, there is "male" and "female", not "man" and "woman" which are learned and acquired gender roles. There is no "mother" and "father", even among apes - just progenitors.

To fulfill any of these demanding and multifarious human functions, we must be exposed to good enough and working role models in childhood and then practice tirelessly through adulthood, constantly reframing and evolving as demands and expectations change with social mores and the times. Evolution in the human species is no longer predominantly genetic - but social and cultural.

So, many people simply don't know how to act as men or as women, as mothers or as fathers. Here, faking it never makes it.

In nature, male and female are distinct. She-elephants are gregarious, he-elephants solitary. Male zebra finches are loquacious - the females mute. Female green spoon worms are 200,000 times larger than their male mates. These striking differences are biological - yet they lead to differentiation in social roles and skill acquisition.

Alan Pease, author of a book titled "Why Men Don't Listen and Women Can't Read Maps", believes that women are spatially-challenged compared to men. The British firm, Admiral Insurance, conducted a study of half a million claims. They found that "women were almost twice as likely as men to have a collision in a car park, 23 percent more likely to hit a stationary car, and 15 percent more likely to reverse into another vehicle" (Reuters).

Yet gender "differences" are often the outcomes of bad scholarship. Consider Admiral Insurance's data. As Britain's Automobile Association (AA) correctly pointed out - women drivers tend to make more short journeys around towns and shopping centers and these involve frequent parking. Hence their ubiquity in certain kinds of claims. Regarding women's alleged spatial deficiency, in Britain, girls have been outperforming boys in scholastic aptitude tests - including geometry and maths - since 1988.

In an Op-Ed published by the New York Times on January 23, 2005, Olivia Judson cited this example:

"Beliefs that men are intrinsically better at this or that have repeatedly led to discrimination and prejudice, and then they've been proved to be nonsense. Women were thought not to be world-class musicians. But when American symphony orchestras introduced blind auditions in the 1970's - the musician plays behind a screen so that his or her gender is invisible to those listening - the number of women offered jobs in professional orchestras increased. Similarly, in science, studies of the ways that grant

applications are evaluated have shown that women are more likely to get financing when those reading the applications do not know the sex of the applicant."

On the other wing of the divide, Anthony Clare, a British psychiatrist and author of "On Men" wrote:

"At the beginning of the 21st century it is difficult to avoid the conclusion that men are in serious trouble. Throughout the world, developed and developing, antisocial behavior is essentially male. Violence, sexual abuse of children, illicit drug use, alcohol misuse, gambling, all are overwhelmingly male activities. The courts and prisons bulge with men. When it comes to aggression, delinquent behavior, risk taking and social mayhem, men win gold."

Men also mature later, die earlier, are more susceptible to infections and most types of cancer, are more likely to be dyslexic, to suffer from a host of mental health disorders, such as Attention Deficit Hyperactivity Disorder (ADHD), and to commit suicide.

In her book, "Stiffed: The Betrayal of the American Man", Susan Faludi describes a crisis of masculinity following the breakdown of manhood models and work and family structures in the last five decades. In the film "Boys don't Cry", a teenage girl binds her breasts and acts the male in a caricatured relish of stereotypes of virility. Being a man is merely a state of mind, the movie implies.

But what does it really mean to be a "male" or a "female"? Are gender identity and sexual preferences genetically determined? Can they be reduced to one's sex? Or are they amalgams of biological, social, and psychological factors in constant interaction? Are they immutable lifelong features or dynamically evolving frames of self-reference?

In rural northern Albania, until recently, in families with no male heir, women could choose to forego sex and childbearing, alter their external appearance and "become" men and the patriarchs of their clans, with all the attendant rights and obligations.

In the aforementioned New York Times Op-Ed, Olivia Judson opines:

"Many sex differences are not, therefore, the result of his having one gene while she has another. Rather, they are attributable to the way particular genes behave when they find themselves in him instead of her. The magnificent difference between male and female green spoon worms, for example, has nothing to do with their having different genes: each green spoon worm larva could go either way. Which sex it becomes depends on whether it meets a female during its first three weeks of life. If it meets a female, it becomes male and prepares to regurgitate; if it doesn't, it becomes female and settles into a crack on the sea floor."

Yet, certain traits attributed to one's sex are surely better accounted for by the demands of one's environment, by cultural factors, the process of socialization, gender roles, and what George Devereux called "ethnopsychiatry" in "Basic Problems of Ethnopsychiatry" (University of Chicago Press, 1980). He suggested to divide the unconscious into the id (the part that was always instinctual and unconscious) and the "ethnic unconscious" (repressed material that was once conscious). The latter is mostly molded by prevailing cultural mores and includes all our defense mechanisms and most of the superego.

So, how can we tell whether our sexual role is mostly in our blood or in our brains?

The scrutiny of borderline cases of human sexuality - notably the transgendered or intersexed - can yield clues as to the distribution and relative weights of biological, social, and psychological determinants of gender identity formation.

The results of a study conducted by Uwe Hartmann, Hinnerk Becker, and Claudia Rueffer-Hesse in 1997 and titled "Self and Gender: Narcissistic Pathology and Personality Factors in Gender Dysphoric Patients", published in the "International Journal of Transgenderism", "indicate significant psychopathological aspects and narcissistic dysregulation in a substantial proportion of patients." Are these "psychopathological aspects" merely reactions to underlying physiological realities and changes? Could social ostracism and labeling have induced them in the "patients"?

The authors conclude:

"The cumulative evidence of our study ... is consistent with the view that gender dysphoria is a disorder of the sense of self as has been proposed by Beitel (1985) or Pfäfflin (1993). The central problem in our patients is about identity and the self in general and the transsexual wish seems to be an attempt at reassuring and stabilizing the self-coherence which in turn can lead to a further destabilization if the self is already too fragile. In this view the body is instrumentalized to create a sense of identity and the splitting symbolized in the hiatus between the rejected body-self and other parts of the self is more between good and bad objects than between masculine and feminine."

Freud, Kraft-Ebbing, and Fliess suggested that we are all bisexual to a certain degree. As early as 1910, Dr. Magnus Hirschfeld argued, in Berlin, that absolute genders are "abstractions, invented extremes". The consensus today is that one's sexuality is, mostly, a psychological construct which reflects gender role orientation.

Joanne Meyerowitz, a professor of history at Indiana University and the editor of The Journal of American History observes, in her recently published tome, "How Sex Changed: A History of Transsexuality in the United States", that the very meaning of masculinity and femininity is in constant flux.

Transgender activists, says Meyerowitz, insist that gender and sexuality represent "distinct analytical categories". The New York Times wrote in its review of the book: "Some male-to-female transsexuals have sex with men and call themselves homosexuals. Some female-to-male transsexuals have sex with women and call themselves lesbians. Some transsexuals call themselves asexual."

So, it is all in the mind, you see.

This would be taking it too far. A large body of scientific evidence points to the genetic and biological underpinnings of sexual behavior and preferences.

The German science magazine, "Geo", reported recently that the males of the fruit fly "drosophila melanogaster" switched from heterosexuality to homosexuality as the temperature in the lab was increased from 19 to 30 degrees Celsius. They reverted to chasing females as it was lowered.

The brain structures of homosexual sheep are different to those of straight sheep, a study conducted recently by the Oregon Health & Science University and the U.S. Department of Agriculture Sheep Experiment Station in Dubois, Idaho, revealed. Similar differences were found between gay men and straight ones in 1995 in Holland and elsewhere. The preoptic area of the hypothalamus was larger in heterosexual men than in both homosexual men and straight women.

According an article, titled "When Sexual Development Goes Awry", by Suzanne Miller, published in the September 2000 issue of the "World and I", various medical conditions give rise to sexual ambiguity. Congenital adrenal hyperplasia (CAH), involving excessive androgen production by the adrenal cortex, results in mixed genitalia. A person with the complete androgen insensitivity syndrome (AIS) has a vagina, external female genitalia and functioning, androgen-producing, testes - but no uterus or fallopian tubes.

People with the rare 5-alpha reductase deficiency syndrome are born with ambiguous genitalia. They appear at first to be girls. At puberty, such a person develops testicles and his clitoris swells and becomes a penis. Hermaphrodites possess both ovaries and testicles (both, in most cases, rather undeveloped). Sometimes the ovaries and testicles are combined into a chimera called ovotestis.

Most of these individuals have the chromosomal composition of a woman together with traces of the Y, male, chromosome. All hermaphrodites have a sizable penis, though rarely generate sperm. Some hermaphrodites develop breasts during puberty and menstruate. Very few even get pregnant and give birth.

Anne Fausto-Sterling, a developmental geneticist, professor of medical science at Brown University, and author of "Sexing the Body", postulated, in 1993, a continuum of 5 sexes to supplant the current dimorphism: males, merms (male pseudohermaphrodites), herms (true hermaphrodites), ferms (female pseudohermaphrodites), and females.

Intersexuality (hermaphroditism) is a natural human state. We are all conceived with the potential to develop into either sex. The embryonic developmental default is female. A series of triggers during the first weeks of pregnancy places the fetus on the path to maleness.

In rare cases, some women have a male's genetic makeup (XY chromosomes) and vice versa. But, in the vast majority of cases, one of the sexes is clearly selected. Relics of the stifled sex remain, though. Women have the clitoris as a kind of symbolic penis. Men have breasts (mammary glands) and nipples.

The Encyclopaedia Britannica 2003 edition describes the formation of ovaries and testes thus:

"In the young embryo a pair of gonads develop that are indifferent or neutral, showing no indication whether they are destined to develop into testes or ovaries. There are also two different duct systems, one of which can develop into the female system of oviducts and related apparatus and the other into the male sperm duct system. As development of the embryo proceeds, either the male or the female reproductive tissue differentiates in the originally neutral gonad of the mammal."

Yet, sexual preferences, genitalia and even secondary sex characteristics, such as facial and pubic hair are first order phenomena. Can genetics and biology account for male and female behavior patterns and social interactions ("gender identity")? Can the multi-tiered complexity and richness of human masculinity and femininity arise from simpler, deterministic, building blocks?

Sociobiologists would have us think so.

For instance: the fact that we are mammals is astonishingly often overlooked. Most mammalian families are composed of mother and offspring. Males are peripatetic absentees. Arguably, high rates of divorce and birth out of wedlock coupled with rising promiscuity merely reinstate this natural "default mode", observes Lionel Tiger, a professor of anthropology at Rutgers University in New Jersey. That three quarters of all divorces are initiated by women tends to support this view.

Furthermore, gender identity is determined during gestation, claim some scholars.

Milton Diamond of the University of Hawaii and Dr. Keith Sigmundson, a practicing psychiatrist, studied the much-celebrated John/Joan case. An accidentally castrated normal male was surgically modified to look female, and raised as a girl but to no avail. He reverted to being a male at puberty.

His gender identity seems to have been inborn (assuming he was not subjected to conflicting cues from his human environment). The case is extensively described in John Colapinto's tome "As Nature Made Him: The Boy Who Was Raised as a Girl".

HealthScoutNews cited a study published in the November 2002 issue of "Child Development". The researchers, from City University of London, found that the level of maternal testosterone during pregnancy affects the behavior of neonatal girls and renders it more masculine. "High testosterone" girls "enjoy activities typically considered male behavior, like playing with trucks or guns". Boys' behavior remains unaltered, according to the study.

Yet, other scholars, like John Money, insist that newborns are a "blank slate" as far as their gender identity is concerned. This is also the prevailing view. Gender and sex-role identities, we are taught, are fully formed in a process of socialization which ends by the third year of life. The Encyclopaedia Britannica 2003 edition sums it up thus:

"Like an individual's concept of his or her sex role, gender identity develops by means of parental example, social reinforcement, and language. Parents teach sex-appropriate behavior to their children from an early age, and this behavior is reinforced as the child grows older and enters a wider social world. As the child acquires language, he also learns very early the distinction between "he" and "she" and understands which pertains to him- or herself."

So, which is it - nature or nurture? There is no disputing the fact that our sexual physiology and, in all probability, our sexual preferences are determined in the womb. Men and women are different - physiologically and, as a result, also psychologically.

Society, through its agents - foremost amongst which are family, peers, and teachers - represses or encourages these genetic propensities. It does so by propagating "gender roles" - gender-specific lists of alleged traits, permissible behavior patterns, and prescriptive morals and norms. Our "gender identity" or "sex role" is shorthand for the way we make use of our natural genotypic-phenotypic endowments in conformity with social-cultural "gender roles".

Inevitably as the composition and bias of these lists change, so does the meaning of being "male" or "female". Gender roles are constantly redefined by tectonic shifts in the definition and functioning of basic social units, such as the nuclear family and the workplace. The cross-fertilization of gender-related cultural memes renders "masculinity" and "femininity" fluid concepts.

One's sex equals one's bodily equipment, an objective, finite, and, usually, immutable inventory. But our endowments can be put to many uses, in different cognitive and affective contexts, and subject to varying exegetic frameworks. As opposed to "sex" - "gender" is, therefore, a socio-cultural narrative. Both heterosexual and homosexual men ejaculate. Both straight and lesbian women climax. What distinguishes them from each other are subjective introjects of socio-cultural conventions, not objective, immutable "facts".

In "The New Gender Wars", published in the November/December 2000 issue of "Psychology Today", Sarah Blustain sums up the "bio-social" model proposed by Mice Eagly, a professor of psychology at Northwestern University and a former student of his, Wendy Wood, now a professor at the Texas A&M University:

"Like (the evolutionary psychologists), Eagly and Wood reject social constructionist notions that all gender differences are created by culture. But to the question of where they come from, they answer differently: not our genes but our roles in society. This narrative focuses on how societies respond to the basic biological differences - men's strength and women's reproductive capabilities - and how they encourage men and women to follow certain patterns.

'If you're spending a lot of time nursing your kid', explains Wood, 'then you don't have the opportunity to devote large amounts of time to developing specialized skills and engaging tasks outside of the home'. And, adds Eagly, 'if women are charged with caring for infants, what happens is that women are more nurturing. Societies have to make the adult system work [so] socialization of girls is arranged to give them experience in nurturing'.

According to this interpretation, as the environment changes, so will the range and texture of gender differences. At a time in Western countries when female reproduction is extremely low, nursing is totally optional, childcare alternatives are many, and mechanization lessens the importance of male size and strength, women are no longer restricted as much by their smaller size and by child-bearing. That means, argue Eagly and Wood, that role structures for men and women will change and, not surprisingly, the way we socialize people in these new roles will change too. (Indeed, says Wood, 'sex differences seem to be reduced in societies where men and women have similar status,' she says. If you're looking to live in more gender-neutral environment, try Scandinavia.)"

Jacobsen: You wrote and spoke on the 'gender wars,' as such. What is the gender war, or are the gender wars?

Vaknin: The gender wars started 150 years ago, with the suffragettes and the first wave of feminism. Women acquired access to jobs, financial independence, and increasing political power. Men resented this relinquishment of traditionally male powers and the incursions on their turf. But the process of gaining equality and equity was inexorable.

Women are better educated than men and better suited for the modern, networked economy. They earn more than men do in some age groups. They are gaining ground in business (where one fifth of CEOs are female) and in politics.

Today, men are saying:

Women! You are too independent! I am terrified that you will no longer tolerate my abuse and my infantilism, you will decline to serve me, you will abandon me, and I will lose you. You are too well-educated. I feel inferior, inadequate, and outcompeted in the workplace. You sleep around with strangers and friends alike. It makes me feel like a statistic, a number, a mere conquest, objectified, not special, insecure, and unsafe. In short: you are too much like the men of yore!

It is actually a rational choice to not form a relationship with promiscuous people. They tend to be way more prone to serial cheating and to breakups or divorces.

Ask any man: women went too far. Too far not in terms of rights or equal pay, but in terms of militancy (zero sum game, men as the enemy); aggressiveness (reactance, defiance, in your face); usurpation of masculine traits, behaviors, norms, and roles; and raunch culture (gratuitous, "empowering" promiscuity).

Now, men are hitting back:

Domestic violence laws were abrogated in Russia; women are again confined to home under a male guardian in Afghanistan; Roe vs. Wade (the right to abortion) is being repealed in the USA; and toxic masculinity is spreading like wildfire, especially in online communities collectively known as the manosphere (MGTOW, incels, redpillers, dating coaches).

Men have one trump card left: intimate relationships, including physical intimacy (sex) where they are largely irreplaceable.

The "stalled revolution" means that when it comes to sexual mores, marriage, relationships, and family, men remain stuck in a Victorian England mindset while women have progressed into a feminist 21st century.

Confronted with this abyss, women face a stark choice:

1. They can give up on men altogether and go it alone while assuming masculine traits and roles; or

2. They can regress and subject themselves to male dominance and objectification in raunch culture and in supposedly "intimate" relationships.

There is no other alternative. Men won't budge. Men are fighting back. About one third of all men are celibate or lifelong singles.

As things stand now, most men are merely taking advantage of women's newfangled sex positivity and then walk away from casual sex, unscathed.

Women are paying the price of this male sexual opportunism in terms of heartbreak, bad sex, childlessness, loneliness, and career or financial damage.

Even as they make strides in the real world, when it comes to intimate relationships, women are more abused and disempowered than ever. And men just joyfully roam around, humping dozens of throwaway women in the promiscuous Disneyland of post-modernity.

Jacobsen: Does this antipathy, even outright hatred, signal a threat to the species in some ways? In that, if, traditionally speaking, couples can't negotiate the modern landscape of inter-relations for the creation of a safe and nurturing environment for the next generations, then the next generations may simply become an afterthought, something dismissed, if not outright discarded from individual life plans.

Vaknin:

In most industrial societies, so few couples are having children and they are having so few offspring that they fail to meet the replacement rate (the number of the dead exceeds the number of the newborns). Many modern men and women remain purposefully childless, prioritizing career, self-actualization, and fun way above procreation.

The gender wars are by far the greatest threat to the survival of the species, far greater than climate change.

Jacobsen: Natality rates globally have been declining for decades. Different regions of the world have different pressing concerns in regards to birth rates. In some regions, there are too many mouths to feed with too few resources to commit to them, sufficiently. In other regions, the rates of newborns are well below the proverbial replacement rate of 2.1 children per woman. In short, some regions need more children,

while others need fewer, for a balanced, sustainable growth pyramid generation after generation.

Vaknin: To sustain the global economic structure, we need to have more children. The population in the developed world is aging fast and safety nets such as pension schemes (social security) and healthcare are already technically insolvent. Immigration is only a partial solution because it strains the social fabric and results in conflicts.

The Black Death – an epidemic of bubonic plague in the 14th century – decimated between one third and one half of Europe's population, yet it was the best thing to have happened to Mankind in many centuries. The depleted number of survivors shared in the vast fortunes of the deceased, laying the foundation for modern, entrepreneurial capitalism; the added physical spaces and vacancies made available via the devastation of numerous households spurred urban renewal and magisterial architecture on an unprecedented scale; the crumbling authority of the Church and its minions led to reformist religious stirrings and the emergence of the Renaissance in arts and sciences; labourers and women saw their standing in society much improved as the scarcity of workforce rendered them much sought-after commodities.

Seven centuries later, an "inflation of humans" led to an ineluctable devaluation and may have erased at least the latter of these achievements: wage growth. Wages have stagnated in direct correlation with the explosion in global population. The social fabric itself has been rent by the mounting pressure of an annual net growth in population which exceeds the citizenry of Germany: interpersonal relationships, social organizational units, tolerant co-existence, peaceful multiculturalism and diversity have all crumbled worldwide.

So, is the solution to our global and escalating woes another pandemic?

The latest census in Ukraine revealed an apocalyptic drop of 10% in its population - from 52.5 million three decades ago to a mere 45.7 million a decade ago. Demographers predict a precipitous decline of one third in Russia's impoverished, inebriated, disillusioned, and ageing citizenry. Births in many countries in the rich, industrialized West are below the replacement rate. These bastions of conspicuous affluence are shriveling.

Scholars and decision-makers - once terrified by the Malthusian dystopia of a "population bomb" - are more sanguine now. Advances in agricultural technology eradicated hunger even in teeming places like India and China. And then there is the old idea of progress: birth rates tend to decline with higher education levels and growing incomes. Family planning has had resounding successes in places as diverse as Thailand, China, and western Africa.

Some intellectuals even regard the increase in the world's population as a form of "quantitative diversification": as technology homogenizes cultures, societies, and civilizations everywhere, the risks associated with such a monoculture grow. Homogeneous populations are less adaptable and, therefore, less fit for survival. The only defense lies in the sheer force of numbers. The greater the number of people, goes this strain of thinking, the more varied the human species, such variety and variation being the sole guarantors and generators of adaptability and, therefore, survival.

In the near past, fecundity used to compensate for infant mortality. As the latter declined - so did the former. Children are means of production in many destitute countries. Hence the inordinately large families of the past - a form of insurance against the economic outcomes of the inevitable demise of some of one's off-spring.

Yet, despite these trends, the world's populace is augmented by 130 million people annually. All of them are born to the younger inhabitants of the more penurious corners of the Earth. There were only 1 billion people alive in 1804. The number doubled a century later.

But our last billions - the sixth and the seventh - required only 19 fertile years. The entire population of Germany is added every half a decade to both India and China. Clearly, Mankind's growth is out of control, as affirmed in the 1994 Cairo International Conference on Population and Development.

Dozens of millions of people regularly starve - many of them to death. In only one corner of the Earth - southern Africa - food aid is the sole subsistence of entire countries. More than 18 million people in Zambia, Malawi, and Angola survived on charitable donations in 1992. More than 10 million expect the same this year, among them the emaciated denizens of erstwhile food exporter, Zimbabwe.

According to Medecins Sans Frontiere, AIDS kills 3 million people a year, Tuberculosis another 2 million. Malaria decimates 2 people every minute. More than 14 million people fall prey to parasitic and infectious diseases every year - 90% of them in the developing countries.

Millions emigrate every year in search of a better life. These massive shifts are facilitated by modern modes of transportation. But, despite these tectonic relocations - and despite famine, disease, and war, the classic Malthusian regulatory mechanisms - the depletion of natural resources - from arable land to water - is undeniable and gargantuan.

Our pressing environmental issues - global warming, water stress, salinization, desertification, deforestation, pollution, loss of biological diversity - and our ominous social ills - crime at the forefront - are traceable to one, politically incorrect, truth:

There are too many of us. We are way too numerous. The population load is unsustainable. We, the survivors, would be better off if others were to perish. Should population growth continue unabated - we are all doomed.

Doomed to what?

Numerous Cassandras and countless Jeremiads have been falsified by history. With proper governance, scientific research, education, affordable medicines, effective family planning, and economic growth, this planet can support even 10-12 billion people. We are not at risk of physical extinction and never have been.

What is hazarded is not our life - but our quality of life. As any insurance actuary will attest, we are governed by statistical datasets.

Consider this single fact:

About 1% of the population suffer from the perniciously debilitating and all-pervasive mental health disorder, schizophrenia. At the beginning of the 20th century, there were 16.5 million schizophrenics - nowadays there are 64 million. Their impact on friends, family, and colleagues is exponential - and incalculable. This is not a merely quantitative leap. It is a qualitative phase transition.

Or this:

Large populations lead to the emergence of high density urban centers. It is inefficient to cultivate ever smaller plots of land. Surplus manpower moves to centers of industrial production. A second wave of internal migrants caters to their needs, thus spawning a service sector. Network effects generate excess capital and a virtuous cycle of investment, employment, and consumption ensues.

But over-crowding breeds violence (as has been demonstrated in behavioral sink experiments with mice). The sheer numbers involved serve to magnify and amplify social anomies, deviate behaviour, and antisocial traits. In the city, there are more criminals, more perverts, more victims, more immigrants, and more racists per square mile.

Moreover, only a planned and orderly urbanization is desirable. The blights that pass for cities in most third world countries are the outgrowth of neither premeditation nor method. These mega-cities are infested with non-disposed of waste and prone to natural catastrophes and epidemics.

No one can vouchsafe for a "critical mass" of humans, a threshold beyond which the species will implode and vanish.

Jacobsen: What are the root dynamics of the gender wars in time, in global cultures, in collective psychologies in the early 21st century?

Vaknin:

The gender war is no different to any other conflict between erstwhile masters and their emancipated chattel or property. To this very day, whites are in pitched battles with blacks (their former slaves) and not only in the USA.

Women were domestic slaves. Then they leveraged the enlightenment and the age of revolutions to unshackle themselves in every way: sexually, politically, financially, and psychologically. Their former owners are incensed and are trying to turn back the wheel. Nothing new under the sun.

Jacobsen: What are the possible paths ahead for the genders and the sexes amid this conceptive whirlpool of personal and collective identities? What are the solutions? What are things to do *now* to rectify the bitterness, contempt, irascibility, and antagonisms for the sustainability of global culture reliant upon new generations of human beings? We all leave the stage, eventually. Even though, the play signifies nothing and is, indeed, written by an idiot.

Vaknin:

I see only two possible trajectories:

(a)   We renounce the contentious and adversarial organizing principles of gender and sex and allow for complete fluidity within a unigender; or

(b)   We revert to the 1950s in terms of more or less rigid gender roles and sexual scripts.

The most likely scenario is that some part of the population will opt for the former and others will adopt the latter. Whether these two camps could co-exist peacefully remains to be seen.

There is nothing much we can do but wait. The gender war is a part of a way more massive upheaval in human affairs. For the first time in human history, all social institutions and mores are crumbling simultaneously. Our hermeneutic narratives have been rendered useless.

When the dust settles, we will face a new world, based on the radical, technology-empowered self-sufficiency of the individual. Society and relationships – intimate or otherwise – may well be a thing of the past: redundant, obsolete, and burdensome.

Jacobsen: Thank you for the opportunity and your time, Professor Vaknin.

Vaknin: Thank you again for having me.

Return

Interview about Psychological Growth (News Intervention)

Scott Douglas Jacobsen: One fundamental aspect of life is change. All this begins with emotions and motivations. What are the basic emotions and motivations behind human action?

Prof. Shmuel "Sam" Vaknin:

Emotions are a subspecies of cognitions. Watch this video to learn more: https://www.youtube.com/watch?v=XMqT56189Ag

All emotions are directional (goal-oriented) and induce action. All actions result in change. Therefore, all emotions lead to change and are transformative.

Jacobsen: Why are emotions primary for action?

Vaknin:

Non-emotive cognitions are always subject to cognitive distortions and biases, are altered by the action of psychological defense mechanisms, and lead to a departure from reality (impaired reality testing). They are not helpful when it comes to survival. In a way, cognitions are a negative adaptation, from the point of view of evolution.

Emotions are more directly accessible to the mind in a non-intermediated way. They are less prone to mislabelling (in mentally healthy people). They are a more reliable guide and a trustworthy compass. Consequently, emotions are more intimately and immediately linked to action.

Jacobsen: What are the types of changes possible to the human nervous system now, whether introduced experientially, chemically, or otherwise?

Vaknin:

The human CNS (Central Nervous System) is largely neuroplastic. It is responsive to repeated identical stimuli and learning. It is closely integrated with all the elements of its dual environments: the internal (for example : the gastrointestonal system) as well as the external. Every single dimension and manifestation of the human experience can be reprogrammed efficaciously using chemical substances, foods, light, sound, words, and other inputs.

Jacobsen: How far could functional reliable manipulation of the structure of the nervous system be taken in this century?

Vaknin:

We are on the threshold of being able to create "designer CNS (nervous systems)" which will be responsive to idiosyncratic job descriptions and incorporate adaptations reactive to specific environments.

Simialry, soon we will learn to induce neural growth even in the brain and grow brains in a dish.

Finally, within a few decades, we will be routinely backing up our minds into external storage, the way we are doing with our smartphones today. Applications would be able to tap into these uploaded consciousnesses and data mining them both for commercial and medical purposes.

Jacobsen: There's a phrase in North America. "You can't change other people." Can these changes internally be facilitated by external sources to a reasonable degree, or is the common sense wisdom truly more wisdom than folly?

Vaknin:

After age 25, people rarely, if ever, change in fundamental ways. It is folly to try to transform your intimate partner, for example.

But, psychiatry and bioengineering are marching towards artificially engendered changes in personality, character, temperament, and mind. Neural implants, man-machine interfaces (cyborgs), tailored psychedelics and psychotropics, Immersive reality environments like the Metaverse – will all have irreversible impacts on the brains of willing (and unsuspecting) subjects.

Jacobsen: We've talked about religion and associated delusions. Some practices within religions induce real, lasting neurological change. If carving out the nonsense, and if keeping the practices, could these practices become part of robust, routine therapeutic techniques/modalities to create changes in patients'/clients' lives - probably already being done?

Vaknin:

Yes, it is already being done. Psychology is a brand of secular religion, of course, not a rigorous science by any stretch of the phrase. It makes use of many mind control and brainwashing techniques long deployed by institutional religions and sects. It leverages delusions and metaphors (ego, anyone ?) the same way the Church does.

Watch this : https://www.youtube.com/watch?v=IJqgR0VuUU8

Jacobsen: Even as a militant agnostic, you note the freethought movements more on the

defensive now. What happens to the central nervous systems of true believers in religions throughout life - or in religious conversion experiences - to make religion overwhelmingly enchanting, and reason and science non-starters, in general?

Vaknin:

Practice makes neural slaves. Religion, cunningly, insists on routines that consume the believers's lives and rewire their brains. It becomes literally hardwired. It is not a question of enchantment - more a type of verbal surgery. Faith is an alien implant that snatches the systems of body and mind. It is an infestation with adherence to delusions replacing critical thinking.

Jacobsen: What are the most evidenced means by which to create lasting psychological growth and positive neurological change in one's life for greater mental wellness in practices, in diets, in activities and hobbies, and the like?

Vaknin:

The secret is self-love. Not narcissism which is a compensation for self-loathing and an inferiority complex – but profound, all-pervasive self-love.

Self-love is a healthy self-regard and the pursuit of one's happiness and favorable outcomes. It rests on four pillars:

1. Self-awareness: an intimate, detailed and compassionate knowledge of oneself, a SWOT analysis: strengths, weaknesses, others's roles, and threats

2. Self-acceptance: the unconditional embrace of one's core identity, personality, character, temperament, relationships, experiences, and life circumstances.

3. Self-trust: the conviction that one has one's best interests in mind, is watching one's back, and has agency and autonomy: one is not controlled by or dependent upon others in a compromising fashion

4. Self-efficacy: the belief, gleaned from and honed by experience, that one is capable of setting rational, realistic, and beneficial goals and possesses the wherewithal to realize outcomes commensurate with one's aims.

Self love is the only reliable compass in life. Experience usually comes too late, when its lessons can no longer be implemented because of old age, lost opportunities, and changed circumstances. It is also pretty useless: no two people or situations are the same. But self-love is a rock: a stable, reliable, immovable, and immutable guide and the truest of loyal friends whose only concern in your welfare and contentment.

Jacobsen: What happens to one's capabilities to change one's mind throughout the lifespan?

Vaknin:

It diminishes dramatically and falls off a cliff after age 25 when the brain is fully formed. Confirmation bias sets in together with dozens of cognitive distortions (such as the Dunning-Kruger effect and the base rate fallcy). It is hopeless. The adult min dis an echo chamber, fortified behind the firewall of reality-reframing psychological defense mechanisms.

Jacobsen: When is it right or wrong to change one's mind?

Vaknin:

The only rational test is whether a change of mind enhances self-efficacy (is positively adaptive). It is all about survival. If altering your thinking enhances your chances to survive or thrive – you should, regardless of whether you find the transformation palatable or not.

Of course, many would disagree with such blatant utilitarianism. Parents sacrifice their lives for their children, for example. Soldiers and firemen and policemen do the same for the greater public good. On the face of it, these are irrational acts that beg for a seachange of mind.

Jacobsen: Thank you for the opportunity and your time, Professor Vaknin.

Vaknin: As usual, thank you for your thought-provoking questions.

Return

Interview about Structure, Function, Society, and Survival (News Intervention)

Scott Douglas Jacobsen: Embedment seems like a fundamental of reality described in a prior session, by you. Embedment of the intersubjective agreement and in the agreement upon the collective experiences ascertained as external, objective. Structures interact, functions follow. Internal objects and relations, external processes and dynamics, the mind and the universe structured in particular ways and the physics of the mind bound by the physics of the universe, in which it's embedded. What defines subjective experience, consciousness, the mind, and awareness?

Prof. Shmuel "Sam" Vaknin:

The source of the confusion that permeates the discourse regarding consciousness is the recursive conflation of introspection (an element of self-awareness) and its subject: the mind. The mind observing the mind. This leads, of course, to a vertiginous infinite regression.

To escape this sempiternal, dizzying tunnel, humans posit an arbitrary "self": the terminal station, where all phenomena converge and come to a halt. There is nothing beyond the self.

Introspection also objectifies the mind. It is as if the mind were an inert, immutable substrate (which, of course, it is not). This is why most people avoid true introspection: the experience is very much like death, like being pinned and mounted.

The physical world is founded on feedback loops very much like introspection. But presumably only humans are capable of meta-transcendence: being aware of their self-awareness. This leads to a feeling of a solipsistic, self-contained estrangement from the world, a kind of observer only mentality.

In a panicky attempt to reconnect, we institute the arbitrary and possibly counterfactual (non-falsifiable) intersubjective agreement. It is undergirded by two assumptions: (1) All human beings are the same; and (2) The physical world is only a part of human reality. The network of minds is the true Universe in which we operate and minds are somehow not fully physical (Cartesian dualism).

Such delusional defenses lead to the emergence of religion, culture, philosophy, and art. But they are counterfactual and brittle.

The truth is that humans and their minds are physical phenomena, subject to the laws of nature. Our complexity gives rise to emergent phenomena such as consciousness, mind, proprioception, and introspection. But we are still mere organisms. Monism is the only rigorous approach to reality.

Jacobsen: What is the relation of structure to function in the most general definition?

Vaknin:

Structure is merely the visible reification of function. It is dictated by it. Functions drive the evolution of structures inexorably. More broadly: environments dictate which functions will survive (will prove adaptive) and which will perish. So, structures are reactive to environmental pressures and data mediated via functions and meanings.

We cannot conceive of any process of production without the dubious aid of the Watchmaker's Metaphor: an artisan; a plan, or program, or procedure; raw materials, or inputs; and the finished product – all four elements distinct from one another. Yet, in nature, this division of labor is rarely true: in the vast majority of cases the raw materials and the program are one and the same and the artisan is missing altogether.

This discrepancy between our intuition and reality is so bothersome that even talented scientists, such as Rupert Sheldrake, were forced to resort to pseudoscience to reconcile it. His concept of "morphic fields" that dictate both the structure and functions of "morphic units" via a kind of "morphic resonance" and are formed by repetition of acts or thoughts is nothing short of mystic: it is unfalsifiable and, therefore, unscientific.

But dismissing Sheldrake's fields and Jung's "collective consciousness" leaves important questions unanswered: Why (not how) do stem cells and embryonic cells differentiate and grow into separate, highly-specific organs during the phases of embryogenesis or, later and in some animals, metamorphosis? How do animal colonies, flocks, and shoals form and function? Why and how do crystals "choose" to develop into specific forms rather than others, equally possible and "permissible" under the laws of physics? What is the organizing principle that guides the formation of neural networks and axon pathfinding (guidance)?

In other words: are Forms (and, by extension: functions) somehow predetermined, "out there", hylomorphically (as Plato, Aristotle, and, to some extent Leibniz suggested)? Are there potentials or "fields" that attract matter and energy and mold them into objects and processes (including mental processes)? And, if so, what decides in favour of certain forms (or "ideals" or "ideas") and not others? Discarding the religious response ("divine intervention") and the mystic solutions (such as the "Akashic records"), we find to our consternation that we are left with no answer at all.

To say, as science does, that the Laws of Nature yield "self-organization", or "self-assembly" is an embarrassing tautology (not to say teleology). To attribute pattern formation to regulatory or inhibitory molecular or chemical cues in the environment, to signalling, cell fates, or, in scientists' favourite phrase, to a "developmental induction cascade" is to confuse the "how" with the "why" and the "how come". Stating the obvious as did Adrian Bejan with his Constructal "Law" (which postulates that finite-size systems evolve to provide easier access to imposed currents that flow through them) does nothing to further our fundamental insight of the world.

Spontaneous order via stigmergy and sematectony, emergence (emergentism), connectionism, epiphenomenalism and, more generally, synergetics are even more circular and "magical" propositions: descriptive and phenomenological, they may well amount to mere language constructs. These approaches definitely add nothing to our understanding of the presumably causative chains underlying the sudden appearance of novel, coherent (or correlated), macro, dynamical, supervenient (the system supervenes its components), and ostensive patterns, behaviors, and properties.

We are supposed to believe that, somehow, the system – an abstract notion, wholly in the mind of its human promulgators - interacts with its environment and that context thus dictates the behavior at the micro level. Such models require a leap of faith and a suspension of scientific judgement. In defending them, Peter Corning was reduced to introducing a deus-ex-machina (the consciousness of chess players) through the back door to fully explicate emergence, for instance.

Clearly, to merely re-label and name the mystery does not make it go away. Nor can such fancy verbalizing disguise our fundamental ignorance regarding emergent order in phenomena as varied as bacteria cultures; swarm intelligence; the distribution of vegetation; foams, crystals, and flakes; and chemical and Turing patterns (e.g., the Belousov-Zhabotinsky reaction).

Instances of this propensity of modern thinkers to obscure rather than elucidate abound: Evolutionary Development's resurrected concept of morphogenetic fields (or units), or the incorporation of lattices in partial differential equations that describe dynamical evolving systems (e.g. in the Swift-Hohenberg equation) are only marginally more rigorous than Sheldrake's concept of morphic fields in that they fail to convincingly account for, respectively, *why* cells develop into specific organs even when they are mishandled and transplanted and why hysteresis arises in convection experiments.

What is it that tells cells to develop into a specific part of the organism and, equally important, to not develop into another? What is the source of their deterministic lack of "hesitation" and their directional "decisiveness"? And where does the path dependence spring from in certain physical systems?

Back to our initial question:

Is there anything *external* or extraneous involved in these mind-boggling processes of morphogenesis and differentiation (except the signalling biochemicals which constitute an integral part of the system?) Genes (DNA), morphogens, adhesion molecules, transcription proteins, the extracellular matrix, and hormones cannot by any stretch of the word be perceived as *outside* the largely autopoietic systems they control. Environmental chemicals and mechanical stresses are external, but it is difficult to understand why they trigger specific morphogenetic configurations and not others and, even so, they account for a minority of mutations and occurrences.

But isn't this whole self-contained unfolding reminiscent of a computer? After all: computers do run programs which are resident (internal). But here the parallels break: programs are written by programmers; chips are designed, manufactured, and assembled by armies of humans and machines; and input is provided yet again either by users or by other computing platforms. All these are external and independent agents.

To further complicate matters, "morphic units" (for want of a better term) such as cells or crystals comport themselves variably in identical circumstances. Consider axons for instance: their growth cones (which sense and react to gradients of biochemicals in the extracellular environment) respond differently in different times to the same cues, depending on previous exposure and habituation, timing, and physiological context. So, if there is a guiding principle, a matrix, field, template, lattice or structure "out there", it must be changing constantly to allow for these idiosyncratic reactions.

Why do we discern forms, patterns, and order everywhere? Because this ability to reorganize our perceptions of reality into predictable moulds and sequences bestows on us untold evolutionary advantages and has an immense survival value. Consequently, we compulsively read configurations and patterns even onto completely random sets of data. The way we perceive holes and other immaterial disruptions as structured entities attests to our "addiction to order and regularity" even where there is only nothing and nothingness.

Why do we all seem to spot essentially *the same* forms, patterns, and evolving order? Simply because we are possessed of largely identical hardware and software: wetware, our brains. We function well on the basis of these shared perceptions. Even so, the limitations of intersubjectivity mean that we can never *prove* that we experience the world in the same way: observers may perceive the colour red or the sensation of pain identically or differently. We simply don't know.

Moreover: beings equipped with other types of processing units, or even different eyes (with a much faster or slower blink rate, or an extended exposure to light), or creatures which use other segments of the electromagnetic spectrum for information gathering are bound to descry the world entirely differently with none of the forms, patterns, and order that we impose on it.

Yet, surely we can construct dictionaries to translate the observations of such alien beings and creatures and to reduce their perceptions, mathematics and physics, geometry, and biology into our own? Maybe so. There is no way to prove that all experiences are reducible and translatable to one another and that all perceptions and concepts can be mapped regardless of the qualities and parameters of the sensory organs that give rise to them in the first place.

Even if they were, the way we experience the Universe would still be vastly different to the subjective, inner landscape of beings or creatures with an unfathomably disparate sensorium, brain, and conceptual space: different to the point of being incommunicable. Even within our species, certain people – the mystics – resort to hermetic and hermeneutically-inaccessible private languages to describe their experiences. With such barriers afoot, we will never be able to ascertain that any translation, reduction, or mapping that we engage in is valid: the subjective dimensions or components of any complete knowledge of the world are as important as the objective ones. Absent operational intersubjectivity, we can never be sure that our knowledge of reality is the same as someone else's, let alone an extraterrestrial.

Churchfield commented astutely in 1994:

"Defining structure and detecting the emergence of complexity in nature are inherently subjective, though essential, scientific activities. Despite the difficulties, these problems can

be analysed in terms of how model-building observers infer from measurements the computational capabilities embedded in non-linear processes. An observer's notion of what is ordered, what is random, and what is complex in its environment depends directly on its computational resources: the amount of raw measurement data, of memory, and of time available for estimation and inference. The discovery of structure in an environment depends more critically and subtly, though, on how those resources are organized. The descriptive power of the observer's chosen (or implicit) computational model class, for example, can be an overwhelming determinant in finding regularity in data."

Still, regardless of **what** or **how** we perceive - is there some **thing** out there? Are we hallucinating when we refer to external entities, bodies, objects, events, and processes?

It is parsimonious to assume that there is an objective reality, independent of any and all observers. But, to account for all its manifestations and for our perceptions of it, such reality must be multifarious. We seem to **select** the forms and patterns that we see by collapsing a kind of superpositioned uber-wave function of all potential forms and patterns. Indeed, we **choose** the Universe, we do not observe it.

We do not **create** it, though (as the Copenhagen interpretation of Quantum Mechanics and some solipsistic epistemologies would have us believe): all the potential forms and patterns (one is almost tempted to say entelechies or monads had it not been for their teleological connotations) do really, independently, objectively and deterministically co-exist both spatially and temporally. The solutions to the wave function with the highest probabilities are the ones we encounter (select) most often. The less probable outcomes we call "mutations" (in biology) or "freak occurrences" (in statistics) or "exceptions" (to rules.)

It stands to reason that bifurcation (catastrophe), singularity, and chaos theories should be able to provide a precise account of the way that we dynamically affect our choices. Indeed, the entire Universe may be conceived as being in states of quenched, or (truer to reality) annealed order with the observers as its random variables. Alternatively, the Universe and the Observer can be viewed as states with differing topological orders and the collapse of the wave function as a phase transition from one to the other. It can be shown that this kind of description naturally gives rise to a Multiverse characterized by topological entropy.

Thus, we are back to where we started: there is no need for "morphic fields" or "morphic resonance" out there because forms and patterns are all "in our head", mere conventions, akin to Time. All forms and patterns co-exist as potentials and the observer determines which ones are best suited to his needs and predilections, biases and sensory equipment, processor and language (or meta-language).

The observer imposes his choices and selections by ignoring certain potentials (options) and by using the selected forms and patterns as organizing and exegetic principles. The history of science is full of paradigm shifts: collective transitions from one set of forms and patterns to another, adopted as the new preferred frame of reference. Not idealism, therefore ("reality is heavily dependent on our mental activity, perhaps to the point of not having an independent, absolute existence"), but some kind of a theory of filtering: the world is out there and we slice and dice and order it to fit our limitations.

We often see faces where there are none (pareidolia), discern spurious patterns and rules, hear hidden messages in vinyl records played backwards (backmasking), and, since time immemorial encounter shadow persons, spirits, fairies, demons, and ghosts.

Why do we discern forms, patterns, and order everywhere? Because this ability to reorganize our perceptions of reality into predictable moulds and sequences bestows on us untold evolutionary advantages and has an immense survival value. Consequently, we compulsively read configurations and patterns even onto completely random sets of data. The way we perceive holes and other immaterial disruptions as structured entities attests to our "addiction to order and regularity" even where there is only nothing and nothingness.

Why do we all seem to spot essentially the same forms, patterns, and evolving order? Simply because we are possessed of largely identical hardware and software: wetware, our brains. We function well on the basis of these shared perceptions. Even so, the limitations of intersubjectivity mean that we can never prove that we experience the world in the same way: observers may perceive the colour red or the sensation of pain identically or differently. We simply don't know.

Moreover: beings equipped with other types of processing units, or even different eyes (with a much faster or slower blink rate, or an extended exposure to light), or creatures which use other segments of the electromagnetic spectrum for information gathering are bound to descry the world entirely differently with none of the forms, patterns, and order that we impose on it.

Complexity arises spontaneously in nature through processes such as critical self-organization. Emergent phenomena are common as are emergent traits, not reducible to basic components, interactions, or properties.

Complexity does not, therefore, imply the existence of a designer or a design. Complexity does not imply the existence of intelligence and sentient beings. On the contrary, complexity usually points towards a natural source and a random origin. Complexity and artificiality are often incompatible.

Artificial designs and objects are found only in unexpected ("unnatural") contexts and environments. Natural objects are totally predictable and expected. Artificial creations are efficient and, therefore, simple and parsimonious. Natural objects and processes are not.

As Seth Shostak notes in his excellent essay, titled "SETI and Intelligent Design", evolution experiments with numerous dead ends before it yields a single adapted biological entity. DNA is far from optimized: it contains inordinate amounts of junk. Our bodies come replete with dysfunctional appendages and redundant organs. Lightning bolts emit energy all over the electromagnetic spectrum. Pulsars and interstellar gas clouds spew radiation over the entire radio spectrum. The energy of the Sun is ubiquitous over the entire optical and thermal range. No intelligent engineer - human or not - would be so wasteful.

Confusing artificiality with complexity is not the only terminological conundrum.

Complexity and simplicity are often, and intuitively, regarded as two extremes of the same continuum, or spectrum. Yet, this may be a simplistic view, indeed.

Simple procedures (codes, programs), in nature as well as in computing, often yield the most complex results. Where does the complexity reside, if not in the simple program that created it? A minimal number of primitive interactions occur in a primordial soup and, presto, life. Was life somehow embedded in the primordial soup all along? Or in the interactions? Or in the combination of substrate and interactions?

Complex processes yield simple products (think about products of thinking such as a newspaper article, or a poem, or manufactured goods such as a sewing thread). What happened to the complexity? Was it somehow reduced, "absorbed, digested, or assimilated"? Is it a general rule that, given sufficient time and resources, the simple can become complex and the complex reduced to the simple? Is it only a matter of computation?

We can resolve these apparent contradictions by closely examining the categories we use.

Perhaps simplicity and complexity are categorical illusions, the outcomes of limitations inherent in our system of symbols (in our language).

We label something "complex" when we use a great number of symbols to describe it. But, surely, the choices we make (regarding the number of symbols we use) teach us nothing about complexity, a real phenomenon!

A straight line can be described with three symbols (A, B, and the distance between them) - or with three billion symbols (a subset of the discrete points which make up the line and their inter-relatedness, their function). But whatever the number of symbols we choose to employ, however complex our level of description, it has nothing to do with the straight line or with its "real world" traits. The straight line is not rendered more (or less) complex or orderly by our choice of level of (meta) description and language elements.

The simple (and ordered) can be regarded as the tip of the complexity iceberg, or as part of a complex, interconnected whole, or hologramically, as encompassing the complex (the same way all particles are contained in all other particles). Still, these models merely reflect choices of descriptive language, with no bearing on reality.

Perhaps complexity and simplicity are not related at all, either quantitatively, or qualitatively. Perhaps complexity is not simply more simplicity. Perhaps there is no organizational principle tying them to one another. Complexity is often an emergent phenomenon, not reducible to simplicity.

The third possibility is that somehow, perhaps through human intervention, complexity yields simplicity and simplicity yields complexity (via pattern identification, the application of rules, classification, and other human pursuits). This dependence on human input would explain the convergence of the behaviors of all complex systems on to a tiny sliver of the state (or phase) space (sort of a mega attractor basin). According to this view, Man is the creator of simplicity and complexity alike but they do have a real and independent existence thereafter (the Copenhagen interpretation of a Quantum Mechanics).

Still, these twin notions of simplicity and complexity give rise to numerous theoretical and philosophical complications.

Consider life.

In human (artificial and intelligent) technology, every thing and every action has a function within a "scheme of things". Goals are set, plans made, designs help to implement the plans.

Not so with life. Living things seem to be prone to disorientated thoughts, or the absorption and processing of absolutely irrelevant and inconsequential data. Moreover, these laboriously accumulated databases vanish instantaneously with death. The organism is akin to a computer which processes data using elaborate software and then turns itself off after 15-80 years, erasing all its work.

Most of us believe that what appears to be meaningless and functionless supports the meaningful and functional and leads to them. The complex and the meaningless (or at least the incomprehensible) always seem to resolve to the simple and the meaningful. Thus, if the complex is meaningless and disordered then order must somehow be connected to meaning and to simplicity (through the principles of organization and interaction).

Moreover, complex systems are inseparable from their environment whose feedback induces their self-organization. Our discrete, observer-observed, approach to the Universe is, thus, deeply inadequate when applied to complex systems. These systems cannot be defined, described, or understood in isolation from their environment. They are one with their surroundings.

Many complex systems display emergent properties. These cannot be predicted even with perfect knowledge about said systems. We can say that the complex systems are creative and intuitive, even when not sentient, or intelligent. Must intuition and creativity be predicated on intelligence, consciousness, or sentience?

Thus, ultimately, complexity touches upon very essential questions of who we, what are we for, how we create, and how we evolve. It is not a simple matter, that...

Jacobsen: How do internal objects and relations of the mind integrate with subjective experience, consciousness, and awareness?

Vaknin:

Our subjective experience consists of the interplay between internal objects. Some of the information regarding these interactions makes it into our consciousness or awareness. The rest remains occult.

The experience is not entirely smooth. We are all capable to discerning different "voices" inside our mind (introjects). These dynamics often engender dissonance, even dysfunction.

"Objective" reality intrudes on this inner theatre and modifies its content. But even so, it is distinct from it. We appropriate the world "out there" and immediately convert it into representations and models in our mind in order to be able to manipulate it self-efficaciously.

This ability, to generate an ever-shifting simulation of the world in our minds, has enormous adaptive value. It is far easier to manipulate a symbol space than bulky, unwieldy objects. And the results always conform to reality almost entirely.

Jacobsen: How do the processes and dynamics of the universe operate?

Vaknin:

We know a lot about the language we use to describe the workings of the Universe: mathematics (and its implementations in physics and other disciplines). But we are barred from knowing the world itself fully and directly.

Everything is mediated – and therefore interpreted and transformed - via our senses and brain. Additionally, as both Godel and Heisenberg have famously observed, there are limitations in principle to what we can "know" about reality.

But why is mathematics so successful?

In earlier epochs, people used myths and religious narratives to encode all knowledge, even of a scientific and technological character. Words and sentences are still widely deployed in many branches of the Humanities, the encroachment of mathematical modeling and statistics notwithstanding. Yet, mathematics reigns supreme and unchallenged in the natural sciences. Why is that? What has catapulted mathematics (as distinct from traditional logic) to this august position within three centuries?

Mathematics is a language like no other. Still, it suffers from the drawbacks that afflict other languages. The structure of our language, its inter-relatedness with the world, and its inherent limitations dictate our worldview and determine how we understand, describe and explain Nature and our place in it. Granted, languages are living things and develop constantly (consider slang, or the emergence of infinite numbers theories in mathematics). But, they evolve within a formal grammar and syntax, a logic, a straitjacket that inhibits thinking "outside the box" and renders impossible the faithful perception of "objective" reality.

So, what made mathematics so different and so triumphant?

1. It is a universal, portable, immediately accessible language that requires no translation. Idealists would say that it is intersubjectively shared. This may be because, as Kant and others have suggested, mathematics somehow relates to or is derived from a-priori structures embedded in the human mind.

2. It provides high information density, akin to stenography. Just a few symbols arranged in formulas and equations account for a wealth of experiences and encapsulate numerous observations. Mathematical concepts and symbols do not correspond to material objects or cause them, nor do they alter reality or affect it in any way, shape, or form. One cannot map a mathematical structure or construct or number or concept into the observed universe. This is

because mathematics is not confined to describing what is, or what is necessarily so - it also limns what is possible, or provable.

3. Mathematics deals with patterns and laws. It can, therefore, yield predictions. Mathematics deals with forms and structures: some of these are in the material world, others merely in the mind of the mathematician.

4. Mathematics is a flexible, "open-source", responsive, and expandable language. Consider, for instance, how the introduction of the concept of the infinite and of infinite numbers was accommodated with relative ease despite the controversy and the threat this posed to the very foundations of traditional mathematics - or how mathematics ably progressed to deal with fuzziness and uncertainty.

5. Despite its aforementioned transigence, mathematics is invariant. A mathematical advance, regardless of how arcane or revolutionary, is instantly recognizable as such and can be flawlessly incorporated in the extant body of knowledge. Thus, the fluidity of mathematics does not come at the expense of its coherence and nature.

6. There is a widespread intuition or perception that mathematics is certain because it deals with a-priori knowledge and necessary truths (either objective and "out there", or mental, in the mind) and because it is aesthetic (like the mind of the Creator, the religious would add).

7. Finally, mathematics is useful: it works. It underlies modern science and technology unerringly and unfailingly. In time, all branches of mathematics, however obscure, prove to possess practical applications.

The octagonal Tower of the Winds in ancient Athens boasted eight sundials on its eight faces. From any given angle, only three of them were visible. Thus, the amount of information gleaned and its subsequent interpretation were determined by the physical limitations of the observer.

Imagine a being with the ability to "see" an infinite number of frames per second. Such a creature would lack the very concepts of motion and sequence. It would perceive both snapshots and video identically. The technology of motion pictures is adapted to our ocular restrictions.

But, would all observers, regardless of corporeal constraints, essentially come up with the same physics once subjected to mathematical transformations?

Imagine a being with an infinite mind (god-like.) Such an entity would never come up with the basic tenets of our perception of reality: time, space, motion, change, force, and identity. Lower down the hierarchy, a being able to perceive the entirety of creation bar one object would be forced to come up with the idea of time to account for his world: it is bound to relate to that one excluded object as **new,** set apart from the already-known rest of the universe. A being able to perceive only 90% of reality would likely introduce also space as an organizing principle. Finally, much more limited intelligences, such as ours, are bound to come up with a multiplicity of forces to describe their environment.

In <u>my work in physics</u>, I suggest that time and space as well as what we call "forces" (electromagnetic, weak, strong, and gravity) are really all emergent facets of the same underlying essence. While they can be formally described as mediated via particles (quantized) and interacting with each other, they do not exist in any objective sense of the word. They are completely interchangeable and convertible because, deep down, they are one and the same.

These conventions (spacetime and the forces) are mere witnesses to the structural and functional handicaps of our language, our sensory input, and our processing unit, the brain. After all, the Tower of Winds has facets because we can't perceive it all at once: its facets are mere conveniences, an accommodation of our finiteness, a way of organizing our sense. They are not objective, observer-independent entities.

Jacobsen: How are the physics of the mind – the physical interactions and information exchange through time of the Central Nervous System (C.N.S.) – limited by the processes and dynamics of the universe?

Vaknin:

The mind is a part and a manifestation of the Universe. It is subject to all its laws.

The tendency to posit Man as distinct from the world, a mere observer has its roots in religion.

The concept of "nature" is a romantic invention. It was spun by the likes of Jean-Jacques Rousseau in the 18th century as a confabulated utopian contrast to the dystopia of urbanization and Darwinian, ruthless materialism. The traces of this dewy-eyed conception of the "savage", his alleged harmony and resonance with nature, and his unmolested, unadulterated surroundings can be found in the more malignant forms of fundamentalist environmentalism and in pop-culture (the most recent example of which is the propaganda-laden cinematic extravaganza, "Avatar").

At the other extreme are religious literalists who regard Man as the crown of creation with complete dominion over nature and the right to exploit its resources unreservedly. Similar, veiled, sentiments can be found among scientists. The Anthropic Principle, for instance, promoted by many outstanding physicists, claims that the nature of the Universe is preordained to accommodate sentient beings - namely, us humans.

Industrialists, politicians and economists have only recently begun paying lip service to sustainable development and to the environmental costs of their policies. Thus, in a way, they bridge the abyss - at least verbally - between these two diametrically opposed forms of fundamentalism. Similarly, the denizens of the West continue to indulge in rampant consumption, but now it is suffused with environmental guilt rather than driven by unadulterated hedonism.

Still, essential dissimilarities between the schools notwithstanding, the dualism of Man vs. Nature is universally acknowledged.

Modern physics - notably the Copenhagen interpretation of quantum mechanics - has abandoned the classic split between (typically human) observer and (usually inanimate) observed. Environmentalists, in contrast, have embraced this discarded worldview wholeheartedly. To them, Man is the active agent operating upon a distinct reactive or passive substrate - i.e., Nature. But, though intuitively compelling, it is a false dichotomy.

Man is, by definition, a part of Nature. His tools are natural and so are his constructions, the built environment. Man interacts with the other elements of Nature and modifies it - but so do all other species. Arguably, bacteria and insects exert on Nature far more influence with farther reaching consequences than Man has ever done. Even an environmentalist like Bill McKibben of "End of Nature" fame, recognize this synergetic confluence. "To Think Like a Mountain" (Aldo Leopold) gradually came to be challenged by "To Think Like a Mall" (Steven Vogel). We should consider the entirety of our surroundings argues Vogel and seek to optimize our environment regardless of its origin: manmade or "natural".

The mind is a physical phenomenon. Period. There are only physical phenomena in existence.

Jacobsen: Human collectives - e.g., tribes, city centres, nation-states, and such - are composed of these same minds, in interaction, limited by the processes and dynamics of the universe. (Some newer modulations based on developments in digital information processing, e.g., the Internet.) The aforementioned intersubjective agreement becomes an emergent property from human collective arrangements. The human mind reflects a psychological structure with associated functions. The intersubjective agreement, in turn, reflects structures inter-related with emergent functions in collective psychology, and the prior associated functions in individual psychology. This may imply an embedment, where these minds in human collectives represent phenomena statistically interpretable as a singular entity. Not a literal entity, an abstraction for ease of comprehension. If so, these singular entities (phenomena statistically interpretable as such) may be contextualized in a manner similar to the physics of the mind. Even in the reverse direction, the neuronal networks, and associated support cells and structures, neurons, and so on, of the nervous system – and their outputs – become interpreted, contextualized, as a person with a mind. Back to the point, given the variation of human minds and the variants of human collectives, is it reasonable to make the connection of the limitations of human collectives as reflective of the limits in human psychology bound by the universe? A means by which to demarcate boundaries and draw a thread from individual narrative to mass psychology in scientific terms and referents, as seems, among educated people, accepted from parts of the nervous system in interaction to individual narrative. Even though, as you have noted elsewhere, notions of individuality, personality, and the like, are "misleading and counterfactual."

Vaknin:

The newly discovered phenomenon of entraining has taught us that minds literally meld, fuse, merge, and become one in response to regular or rhythmic stimuli (music). Speech may carry the same function in human collectives: to synchronize minds and foster a "hive" consciousness.

Human collectives display all the hallmarks and attributes of individual psychology, but some of these features are taken to the extreme, amplified as it were. For example: in a mob, individuals are far less inhibited and considerably more aggressive and paranoid.

Still, the limitations that apply in individual psychology are equally applicable to mass psychology. Crowds are nothing but individuals writ large.

In collectives, the executive functions of the individual's mind as well as the regulatory functions and ego boundary functions are relegated to the group. But this transfer does not alter them substantially.

Finally, individual pathologies clearly appear in masses of people. Collectives can be narcissistic or psychopathic, schizoid, paranoid, bipolar, or even borderline.

Jacobsen: How can a scientific approach to the arrangement of human collectives improve human flourishing, individually and collectively, with a fine understanding of human flaws?

Vaknin:

Human collectives are, first and foremost human. All our attempts at social engineering failed miserably and many of them resulted in incalculable catastrophes. I am adamantly set against such endeavours. I even consider psychology to be a grandiose pseudo-science.

Jacobsen: What are valid and reliable indices of healthy human collectives akin to individual self-love (not narcissism)?

Vaknin:

The secret of healthy, durable collectives is self-love. Not narcissism which is a compensation for self-loathing and an inferiority complex – but profound, all-pervasive self-love.

Self-love is a healthy self-regard and the pursuit of one's happiness and favorable outcomes. It rests on four pillars:

1. Self-awareness: an intimate, detailed and compassionate knowledge of oneself, a SWOT analysis: strengths, weaknesses, others's roles, and threats

2. Self-acceptance: the unconditional embrace of one's core identity, personality, character, temperament, relationships, experiences, and life circumstances.

3. Self-trust: the conviction that one has one's best interests in mind, is watching one's back, and has agency and autonomy: one is not controlled by or dependent upon others in a compromising fashion

4. Self-efficacy: the belief, gleaned from and honed by experience, that one is capable of setting rational, realistic, and beneficial goals and possesses the wherewithal to realize outcomes commensurate with one's aims.

Self love is the only reliable compass in life. Experience usually comes too late, when its lessons can no longer be implemented because of old age, lost opportunities, and changed circumstances. It is also pretty useless: no two people or situations are the same. But self-love is a rock: a stable, reliable, immovable, and immutable guide and the truest of loyal friends whose only concern in your welfare and contentment.

Jacobsen: Even if ignoring old ideas of flourishing, *eudaimonia*, and keeping to persistence, what needs to be considered for the survival of the species, human

collectives, and of the individual? What are the main threats to human collectives' survival now?

Vaknin:

Volitional Dissonance is when we act in ways which we perceive to be akratic, immoral, or antisocial, rather than phronetic. When we perceive our actions to have been the outcomes of akrasia (weak willed misbehavior contrary to our best judgment) and not of phronesis (good judgment, excellence of character, habits conducive to eudaimonia - a good life - and practical virtue).

So, we need to develop perseverance, determination, critical thinking, cooperation, and quest for excellence (but not superiority via relative positioning).

Regrettably, we are going in the opposite direction with blind alacrity. We are risk-averse to the point of effete timidity; we have microscopic attention spans; we are more gullible than ever (hence the pandemics of conspiracy theories and misinformation); we are atomized and self-sufficient; and we settle for alcohol-imbued entertainment-suffused mediocrity. This doesn't bode well to the survival of the species.

Jacobsen: Thank you for the opportunity and your time, Prof. Vaknin.

Vaknin: Thank you for showcasing some of my work.

Return

Interview about Chronon Field Theory and Time Asymmetry (News Intervention)

Scott Douglas Jacobsen: You earned a Ph.D. based on a dissertation entitled "Time Asymmetry Revisited" from California Miramar University (previously "Pacific Western University"). "Revisited" is a recurring term, whether on the physics of time or the psychology of narcissism. So, let's revisit the early 1980s, what was the inspiration or practical purpose of a doctorate in physics from 1982-83?

Prof. Shmuel "Sam" Vaknin:

In the 1970s, the second law of thermodynamics has emerged as a major explanation for the Time arrow: entropy inexorably increases and its unidirectional growth determines Time's exclusive trajectory, from past to future.

This tautology (after all: entropy increases in time!) dominated physics. It provided no insight into the nature of Time or reality (correlation is not causation or any other necessary linkage).

In 1982-3, I met Richard Feynman, the Nobel prize winning genius, in Geneva a few times for long evening reveries in a lakeside shed owned by a common friend (the late Dudley Wright).

One evening, Richard, tired of my diatribes, said: "You are insisting that Time is a nonreducible elementary theoretical entity. If it is so, surely you could derive all of physics from this one single underlying process or thing?"

And this is what I set out to do in my dissertation.

Recently, Eytan Suchard et al. took my work and ran with it and were able to derive every single theory and equation in all fields of physics from my original, way more primitive, thesis.

Jacobsen: Why study time in particular?

Vaknin:

Time is the only bridge between physical reality and the human mind. Many scholars – Einstein included - went as far as suggesting that Time is nothing but a mental artefact, a reflection of our inability, as finite creatures, to perceive reality in its totality. Others, starting with Newton, regarded time as ontic.

In my work, Time is the field of all potentials. Only the mind (a sentient intelligence) can witness the becoming of these potentials. This harks back to the observer in some interpretations of Quantum Mechanics.

Jacobsen: What were other research possibilities, in physics, of interest at the time?

Vaknin:

I did a lot of work in thermodynamics and quantum physics. But I became disenchanted with the latter as it began to resemble metaphysics.

Jacobsen: Why is time symmetric at one scale of existence and asymmetric at another one?

Vaknin:

A directional time does not feature in Newtonian mechanics, in electromagnetic theory, in quantum mechanics, in the equations which describe the world of elementary particles (with the exception of the kaon decay), and in some border astrophysical conditions, where there is time symmetry.

Yet, we perceive the world of the macro as time asymmetric and our cosmology and thermodynamics explicitly incorporate a time arrow, albeit one which is superimposed on the equations and not derived from them. The introduction of stochastic processes has somewhat mitigated this conundrum.

Time is, therefore, an epiphenomenon: it does not characterize the parts – though it emerges as a main property of the whole, as an extensive parameter of macro systems.

Jacobsen: What is the point at which time divides between asymmetric and symmetric, even if artificial and not truly real?

Vaknin:

No one knows. The emergence of time in macrosystems is one of the greatest mysteries of science.

Jacobsen: What are chronons?

In my doctoral dissertation (Ph.D. Thesis available from the Library of Congress), I postulates the existence of a particle (chronon). Time is the result of the interaction of chronons, very much as other forces in nature are "transferred" in such interactions.

The Chronon is a time "atom" (actually, an elementary particle, a time "quark"). We can postulate the existence of various time quarks (up, down, colors, etc.) whose properties cancel each other (in pairs, etc.) and thus derive the time arrow (time asymmetry).

My postulated particle (chronon) is not only an ideal clock, but also mediates time itself (same like the relationship between the Higgs boson and mass.) In other words: I propose that what we call "time" is the interaction between chronons in a field. The field *is* time itself. Chronons exchange a particle and thereby exert a force which we call time. Introducing time as a fifth force gives rise to a quasi-deterministic rendition of quantum theories and links inextricably time to other particle properties, such as mass.

"Events" are perturbations in the Time Field and they are distinct from chronon interactions. Chronon interactions (i.e. particle exchange) in the Time Field generate "time" (small t) and "time asymmetry" as we observe them.

My work is, therefore, a Field Theory of Time. The Universe is observing itself. It is the only privileged observer and frame of reference, which restores intuitive (Einsteinian) determinism to physics.

The idea of atomistic, discrete time has a long pedigree in physics (**Descartes, Gassendi, Torricelli**, among others). More recently, **Boltzmann, Mach**, and even **Poincare** all toyed with the concept. There was a brief flowering of various speculative and not very rigorous, almost metaphysical or numerological models immediately after the introduction of quantum mechanics in the 1920s and 1930s (**Palacios, Thomson** indirectly, **Levi** who coined the neologism "chronon", **Pokrowski, Gottfried Beck, Schames, Proca** with his "granular" time, **Ruark, Flint and Richardson, Glaser and Sitte**).

Oddly, luminaries such as **Pauli, de Broglie**, and especially **Schroedinger** were drawn into the fray, together with lesser lights like **Wataghin, Iwanenko, Ambarzumian, Silberstein, Landau, and Peierls**. By now, everyone was talking about minimal durations (somehow derived from or correlated to the mass or some other property of each type of elementary particle), not about time "atoms" or a lattice. This subtle conceptual transition between mutually-contradictory notions caused an almighty and enduring confusion. Is time itself somehow discrete/quantized/atomized – or are our measurements discontinuous?

Ever since the early 1960s and especially during the 1990s, there have been several attempts to build on the work of the likes of **H. S. Snyder** (Physical Review 71, (1) 1947, 38) to suggest a quantized spacetime or a Quantum Field Theory, **Tsung Dao Lee's** work being the most notable attempt. More recent work with relativistic stochastic models led inexorably to discrete time

P. Caldirola postulated the existence of a chronon (1955, 1980): ***"An elementary interval of time characterizing the variation of the particle's state under the action of external forces".*** He calculated chronons for several types of particles, most notably the electron, both classical and in (nonrelativistic) quantum mechanics.

In 1982-3, I proposed that chronons may be actual particles – more about my work HERE. A decade later, in 1992, **Kenneth J. Hsu** suggested the very same thing (though without reference to my work). He postulated sequencing cues delivered to particles by captured chronons. Like me, he hypothesized the existence of various types of chronons ("large" and small). Chronons, wrote Hsu are also involved in the catalysis of events. Finally, like me, Hsu also posited a field theory for the flow of chronons. In 1994, **C. Wolf** again suggested the existence of time atoms (Nuov. Cim. B 109 (3) 1994 213).

In 1993, **Arthur Charlesby** suggested that particles have an intrinsic discrete time property and that time (interval in the presence of relative motion) has a "quantized nature". This dispenses with the need for a wave concept as a mere mathematical expedient in the case of individual events (though still useful in contemplating continuous relative motion). This notion of "proprietary" or "individual" system-specific time as distinct from a "systemic", overall Time was further explored by **Alexander R. Karimov** in 2008.

In the same year (1993), **Sidney Golden** published a paper in which he claimed that *"quantum time-lapses are ... an essential feature of the changes undergone by the energy-eigenfunction-evaluated matrix elements of statistical operators that evolve in accordance with an intrinsic temporal discreteness characteristic of strictly irreversible behavior."*

A year later, in 1994, **A. P. Balachandran** and **L. Chandar** studied the quantized of time in discretized gravity models with multiple-valued Hamiltonians. **Ruy H. A. Farias** and **Erasmo Recami** (2010) applied a quantum of time to obtain startlingly impressive consequences regarding the treatment of electrons (and, more generally, leptons), the free particle, the harmonic oscillator, and the hydrogen atom in both classical and quantum physics, in effect proffering a discretized and surprisingly powerful and useful quantum mechanics. Strangely, their work had very little resonance.

Quantized time has been used to suggest solutions to a panoply of riddles in physics, including the K-meson decay, the Klein-Gordon equation, and the application of Kerr-Newman black holes to electron theory, q-deformations and stochastic subordination ("quantum subordination"), among others (**R. Hakim**, Journal of Mathematical Physics 9 1968, 1805; **B. G. Sidharth**, 2000, **Alexander R. Karimov**,2008; **Claudio Albanese and Stephan Lawi**).

Vaknin:

Jacobsen: With the interactions between the chronons in a field creating perturbations for the creation of the idea of the Time Field, the argument implies the 4-dimensionality of space as space-time comes from the perturbations in the Time Field based on the interactions of the chronons in the field exerting a force. So, in a sense, chronons' interactions in the Time Field produce the temporal dimension, where without the chronons' interactions in the Time Field; time would not pass because time would not exist in the first place. What is the apparent time asymmetry in this context?

Vaknin:

Timespace can be regarded as a wave function with observer-mediated collapse. All the chronons are entangled at the exact "moment" of the Big Bang. This yields a relativistic QFT with chronons as its Field Quanta (excited states.) The integration is achieved via the quantum superpositions.

Another way to look at it is that the metric expansion of time is implied if time is a fourth dimension of space. Time may even be described as a PHONON of the metric itself.

A more productive approach may involve Perturbative QFT. Time from the Big Bang is mediated by chronons and this leads to expansion (including in the number of chronons.) In this case, there are no bound states.

Chronons as excitation states (stochastic perturbations, vibrations) tie in nicely with superstring theories, but without the baggage of extra dimensions and without the metaphysical nonsense of "music of the spheres". Perturbations also yield General Relativity: cumulative, "emerging" perturbations amount to a distortion (curvature) of time-space. Both superstring theories and GRT are, therefore, private cases of a Chronon Field Theory.

Jacobsen: Have there been other advancements on these ideas since 1983?

Vaknin:

Eytan H. Suchard's Work

Interacting particles with non-gravitational fields can be seen as clocks whose trajectory is not Minkowsky geodesic.

A field in which a small enough clock is not geodesic can be described by a scalar field of time whose gradient has non-zero curvature. The scalar field is either real which describes acceleration of neutral clocks made of charged matter or imaginary, which describes acceleration of clocks made of Majorana type matter.

This way the scalar field adds information to space-time, which is not anticipated by the metric tensor alone. The scalar field can't be realized as a coordinate because it can be measured from a reference sub-manifold along different curves.

In a "Big Bang" manifold, the field is simply an upper limit on measurable time by interacting clocks, backwards from each event to the big bang singularity as a limit only.

In De Sitter / Anti De Sitter space-time, reference sub-manifolds from which such time is measured along integral curves are described as all the events in which the scalar field is zero. The solution need not be unique but the representation of the acceleration field by an anti-symmetric matrix is unique up to $SU(2) \times U(1)$ degrees of freedom.

Matter in Einstein-Grossmann equation is replaced by the action of the acceleration field, i.e. by a geometric action which is not anticipated by the metric alone. This idea leads to a new formalism of matter that replaces the conventional stress-energy-momentum-tensor. The formalism will be mainly developed for classical but also for quantum physics. The result is that a positive charge manifests small attracting gravity and a stronger but small repelling acceleration field that repels even uncharged particles that measure proper time, i.e. have rest mass.

The negative charge manifests a repelling anti-gravity but also a stronger acceleration field that attracts even uncharged particles that measure proper time, i.e. have rest mass.

The theory leads to causal sets. Spacetime exists only where a chronon wave-function collapses. Work still to be done is to replace particles by strings of collapse events. The theory in its quantum form is of events and not of particles.

The theory has technological repercussions and implications regarding "Dark Matter" and "Dark Energy".

Jacobsen: Have there been any experimental results supporting the theoretical framework, even the basic claim of the existence of chronons?

Vaknin:

None. The theoretical framework emerged less than 5 years ago. But there are some technological implications and even an application for a patent in the USA (https://pdfaiw.uspto.gov/.aiw?PageNum=0&docid=20200130870&IDKey=58760C759BBB)

Jacobsen: As a Field Theory of Time, as the field itself *is* time or events in spacetime equate to perturbations in this field of time, if true, what does this leave - *a la* Feynman – for future paths of the development of time asymmetry, chronons, temporal field theoretic considerations, and integrations of the Field Theory of Time into a GUT (Grand Unified Theory) and a ToE (Theory of Everything, which you consider inevitable or have "no doubt" about its arrival - eventually)?

Vaknin:

Chronon Field Theory is a GUT/TOE. It is parsimonious (Time is the only entity and also the only principle of action). Watch this: https://www.youtube.com/watch?v=8AEEwYcWUuc

Every potential in the field, once observed ("collapsed"), is an aspect of physics: mass, momentum, force, particles, symmetry, energy, field coefficients, fine structure constant, gravity, etc.

The theory predicts new particles (for example between muons and bottom quarks); a new, fifth force of nature; a natural connection between electromagnetism and gravity; and many other goodies which can be leveraged into futuristic technologies.

Jacobsen: Thank you for the opportunity and your time, Prof. Vaknin.

Vaknin: Much appreciated.

Return

Interview about Genius and Insanity (News Intervention)

Scott Douglas Jacobsen: Delusions remain ubiquitous. Delusions in conspiracy theories found in 5G, backmasking, Big Pharma, chemtrails, free energy suppression, Holocaust denial, New World Order-ism, QAnon, and so on. Delusions formalized in cults. Delusions in religious discourse, organization, and practice. Delusions promoted in quack 'medicine' with acupuncture, alternative 'medicine,' anti-GMO movements, anti-vaccination activism, aromatherapy, chiropractory, conversion therapy, faith healing, homeopathy, naturopathy, psychic surgery, Reiki, reflexology, traditional Chinese medicine, and such. Delusions in anti-intellectualism with creation 'science' (e.g., the variants of Creationism and Intelligent Design), global warming denialism or even alarmism in some respects, God of the gaps-ism, 'holy' text literalism, homeschooling, paranormalism, quantum woo, _und so weiter_. Delusions in bigotries and prejudices including anti-Semitism, or racist ideologies bound to politics or religion (e.g., white supremacist KKK, black supremacist Nation of Islam, and the like). Delusions in social and political cure-alls for societies' ills - panaceas, e.g., American commitments to the idea of every problem having a solution. Then there are those who took a permanent lift-off from _terra firma_ and detached from reality altogether, e.g., or a case study, the person running the "Sam Vaknin Scum Antichrist" YouTube channel – an apparent idiotic crazy (read: demented screwball) person. You know the deal. We're on the same page in the identical book here. There's a thin line, as has been observed before, between true genius and real insanity. What factors set the distinctions between insanity, on the one hand, and genius, on the other?

Prof. Shmuel "Sam" Vaknin:

The problem is that both madness and genius involve the ability to reframe reality in an unexpected way (i.e., provide insight) either by gaining a synoptic or interdisciplinary vantage point – or by radically departing from hidden underlying assumptions.

The scientific method is designed to tell the two apart by applying the test of falsifiable predictions. Both madness and genius are theories of the world and of the mind and, like every other type of theory, they yield predictions which can then be tested and falsified.

Most of the predictions yielded by insanity are easily and instantly falsifiable. Most of the predictions garnered by genius hold water for long stretches of time and, even when falsified, it is only in private cases or in extreme conditions. Thus, the theories of relativity falsify Newtonian prediction only on vast scales with incredible energies.

Jacobsen: What are the easiest means by which to distinguish a genius from an insane person?

Vaknin:

Psychopathology is rigid. It is unyielding, not amenable to learning, nauseatingly repetitive, constricting, and divorced from reality (impaired reality testing). The genius is immersed in the world even if he is a recluse, he learns and evolves all the time, his mind is kaleidoscopic and vibrant, ever expanding. Insanity is mummified, genius is life reified.

Jacobsen: Is high intelligence required for true genius?

Vaknin:

If by intelligence you mean IQ then the answer is a resounding no. The adage about perspiration and inspiration applies. But, more importantly, genius is the ability to see familiar things in a fresh, unprecedented way. Imagination, intuition, and the ability to tell apart the critical from the tangential are the core constituents of genius – not intelligence.

What intelligence does contribute to genius is alacrity. It is a catalyst. It speeds up both the processes of theorizing and of discovery.

Jacobsen: What happens to an insane person who happens to have high intelligence too?

Vaknin:

He is likely to construct theories that will pass for genius, especially among laymen. The intelligence of the gifted madman serves to camouflage the lack of rigor and the delusional, counterfactual content of his creations. Rather than catalyze disruptive discoveries, his intellect works overtime at the service of aggressively defending a manifestly risible sleight of hand. It is not open to any modificatory feedback from the environment. The madman's intellect is solipsistic and moribund.

Jacobsen: What happens in the mind of a genius who slowly deteriorates into an insane person?

Vaknin:

He visibly transitions from cognitive flexibility to defensive and hypervigilant rigidity (confirmation bias). His work becomes way more easily falsifiable, sometimes even with mere Gedankenexperiments. He repeats himself ad nauseam. He becomes grandiose (cognitively distorts reality to buttress an inflated and fantastic self-image).

Jacobsen: How do fake geniuses cover for their lack of insight, ingenuity, intelligence, etc.?

Vaknin:

They copy and plagiarize. They imitate a real genius's structured thinking and work. They are good at promoting themselves and getting credit where none is due. Most of these frauds are actually intelligent, but dark personalities (subclinical narcissists, subsclinical psychopa

Jacobsen: Is true genius more inborn, innate, native to the individual or more honed, refined, developed extrinsically?

Vaknin:

We know that IQ is responsive to environmental stimuli. The analytic kind genius (IQ above 140 or 160) is by far the most studied because it is the most facilely measurable. There are no studies that rigorously link it to heredity. On balance, anecdotal evidence clearly suggests that genius is acquired and can be inculcated at an early age if the child is subjected to rigorous training and a regime of positive and negative reinforcements.

It would behoove us to make a distinction between polymath or synoptic genius and "idiot savant" type of one-track mental acuity (think "Rain Man"). The latter form definitely is neurological and, probably, with a pronounced genetic contribution.

Jacobsen: Some mental disorders, including schizophrenia, appear mostly heritable. Is it the same for various states of insanity in general?

Vaknin:

We don't know enough, not by a long shot. Certain mental illnesses present with structural and functional abnormalities of the brain that are very likely to be genetically coded for: schizophrenia or Bipolar Disorder. Other mental health issues run in families, so a genetic component is indicated: Borderline Personality Disorder and psychopathy, for instance.

Jacobsen: Which five individuals seem like true geniuses in the modern world to you? I do not mean rich, famous, well-cited, and the like; even though, they may be rich, famous, or well-cited, etc., as a consequence of successful implementation of aspects of their genius.

Vaknin:

Versatile polymaths included Einstein (of course), Richard Feynman (see my interview on Chronon Field Theory), Noam Chomsky, George Steiner (whom I had the pleasure of knowing), and Adolf Hitler (who regrettably turned his considerable gifts to the dark side).

Jacobsen: Do you consider yourself a genius?

Vaknin: Yes.

Shoshannim: Thank you, once again, for your time and the opportunity, Prof. Vaknin.

Vaknin: OK, Shoshanim!

Return

Interview about Freedom of Expression (News Intervention)

Scott Douglas Jacobsen: Freedom of expression is a paper right in most places of the world. It is listed in international rights documents and in national constitutions. Yet, one could ask, "What is the 'free' part of freedom of expression?" It depends on the society and the culture, and the person. So, to open this session, what is a proper framing of rights, responsibilities, obligations, and privileges in societies, i.e., an accurate frame or definition to ground practice of free expression?

Prof. Shmuel "Sam" Vaknin:

Freedom of expression, including freedom of speech and freedom of the press, is a feature of individualistic societies. Where collectivism reigns, this amalgam of rights is subordinated to the greater good.

Ironically, utilitarianism inexorably leads to limitations on these freedoms intended to protect the majority against the incursions of disruptive or even destructive minorities.

Yet, even in anarchic polities, freedom of expression cannot be abused to spread panic (crying fire in a crowded theatre), life threatening misinformation (re: the COVID-19 pandemic), or to threaten the wellbeing and lives of others (e.g., virulent racism, or calls for eugenic culling, or victimization). Only anomic civilizations in decadent decline countenance such toxic speech acts.

Jacobsen: Which countries and parts of the world seem the freest regarding freedom of expression?

Vaknin:

It is a surprisingly mixed bag including perennials like Denmark and Finland, but also surprises like Argentina and Slovakia.

But freedom – all freedoms – are on the decline everywhere, besieged by populism, profound mistrust of authority and of expertise, anti-intellectualism, anti-elitism, anti-liberalism (anti-"progressivism"), and the dominance of rapid dissemination technologies such as social media.

Ochlocracies (mob rule) are regaining ground all over the world, led by authoritarian, proudly ignorant, and defiantly contumacious and reactant narcissistic-psychopathic leaders.

Jacobsen: Which nations and regions of the world seem the least free regarding freedom of expression?

Vaknin:

Again, the rankings are counterintuitive. Canada, for example, is less free than Uruguay and the USA is languishing with Peru somewhere at the bottom of the upper third.

Jacobsen: How did (and does) the internet change freedom of expression or the access to free exchange of words, ideas, and philosophies, or simply disjointed randomly emoted thoughts?

Vaknin:

In the internet age, the distinction between raw information and knowledge (structured data) is lost. The internet is a huge dumping ground for half-baked truths, rank nonsense, misinformation, propaganda, hate speech, speculation, and outright derangement. Even where vetted and reliable information is available, it is unprocessed and out of context.

No single technology has harmed free expression more than the internet. It has created a problem of discoverability (locating quality content in a sempiternal tsunami of trash) and allowed mobs to form and to ominously suppress speech by sheer force of numbers (the cancel culture is the latest example of such transgressions).

All semblance of civilized, informed speech is now lost even in academe. Social media were deliberately constructed by engineers and turncoat psychologists to polarize aggressive speech and cement confirmation bias (silos of like-minded people in echo chambers).

Jacobsen: Following from the previous question, is this net good or net bad?

Vaknin:

Bad by a long shot.

https://videotranscripts.dk/ (Transcripts)

https://www.youtube.com/watch?v=wpvv_ooqJik **(The True Toxicity of Social Media)**

https://www.youtube.com/watch?v=QY79nDYjW94 **(Malignant Egalitarianism)**

https://www.youtube.com/watch?v=jvuRmP3KP1g **(The Need to Be Seen)**

https://www.youtube.com/watch?v=WgjOH0kDErw **(A-social Media: Fracking Mankind)**

https://www.youtube.com/watch?v=jVprI6_P8GE **(Plugged-in Documentary)**

https://www.youtube.com/watch?v=w2rKrWNWkS0 **(How to Fix Social Media)**

https://www.youtube.com/watch?v=fIElARjRGTo **(Social Media as the Big Eye)**

https://www.youtube.com/watch?v=5NTwxAJDMTo **(Metaverse: Conspiracy or Heaven?**

Jacobsen: One camp will claim complete freedom of expression in social media will be a net good because the liars and defamers will be overwhelmed by more reasonable voices and evidence. Another camp thinks there should be sharp restrictions on particular types of speech, electronic communication, and so on. Those are two big ones. A third believes in outlawing social media altogether, so stringently binding or making illegal social media for some people if not most or all. It'd be similar to acquisition of a firearm in much of the world, getting a driver's license, qualifying as a surgeon or an accountant, and such. You have commented on this. With social media, what should be done for or against freedom of expression, if anything?

Vaknin:

Social media are utilities and should be subjected to the same regulatory oversights that other media and monopolistic utilities are under.

Additionally, owing to the addictive nature of social media, laws should be passed to restrict their use and to monitor the content posted on them.

Self-regulation is a myth on Wall Street as it is in tech valleys around the globe. Where money rears its head, morality and restraint and the public interest go out of the window.

Crowdsourced regulation is the dumbest idea ever. Majorities are forever silent and conflict-averse. Ask the misnamed Mensheviks who were actually the overwhelming majority and yielded to the equally mislabeled Bolsheviks who were more ruthless and vociferous and better mobilized.

Jacobsen: What does social media and internet use do in mild use and in chronic use to the mental health of individuals and groups?

Vaknin:

The evidence is unequivocal (see the studies by Twenge et al.): the more extensive the exposure to screens, the longer the screentime, the higher the prevalence and incidence of anxiety and depressive disorders, especially among the young (under 25) and among seniors over 65. There is no such thing as "mild" or "moderate" use: the effects commence at the first moment of use.

Jacobsen: What do trends of expression and outcomes among users of social media tell us about individual psychology and mass psychology, and social media in general?

Vaknin:

By far the biggest problem social media use has fostered is what I call "malignant egalitarianism".

Malignant egalitarianism is threatening our existence as a species. Until about 10 years ago, people - even narcissists - had role models they sought to learn from and emulate and ideals which they aspired to.

Today, everyone - never mind how unintelligent, ignorant, or unaccomplished - claim superiority or at least equality to everyone else.

Armed with egalitarian equal access technology like social media, everyone virulently detest and seek to destroy or reduce to their level their betters and that which they cannot attain or equal.

Pathological envy (egged on by instruments of relative positioning such as "likes") had fully substituted for learning and self-improvement. Experts, scholars, and intellectuals are scorned and threatened. Everyone is an instant polymath and an ersatz da Vinci.

But, this is just one of many vile side effects and byproducts of social media. Watch my videos on the topic (see links above).

Jacobsen: How will the Metaverse, and associated developments, in the 2030s affect relations between people?

Vaknin:

Is the Metaverse the ultimate dystopia, an escape from reality, or the promised technological heaven? I summarized my views in this interview: https://www.youtube.com/watch?v=5NTwxAJDMTo

Jacobsen: If the goal is mental health for most people most of the time, what are the most efficacious policies and laws for governments to enact, and for individuals and families to practice, regarding social media and the right to freedom of expression?

Vaknin:

Limit usage time (clocks embedded in the app will terminate use after 2 hours);

Only real life friends and acquaintances would be allowed to become online friends;

Identity verification would be mandatory for various types of content;

Introduce an accreditation system for experts, gurus, and coaches online;

ScholarTube for vetted, evidence-based knowledge provided by real-life academics or experts;

Curation of most content prior to its release (the contemporary Wikipedia model as distinct from the original crowdsourcing mess).

More here: https://www.youtube.com/watch?v=w2rKrWNWkS0 **(How to Fix Social Media)**

Shoshannim: Thank you, Dr. Shmuel.

Vaknin: You are always welcome, shoshanim!

Return

Interview about Misogyny and Misandry (News Intervention)

Scott Douglas Jacobsen: Misogyny and misandry, what defines them?

Prof. Shmuel "Sam" Vaknin:

Misogyny and misandry are forms of inverted gender dysphoria, actually. It is hatred, resentment, and revulsion brought on by the opposite sex. It encompasses all aspects and dimensions of the hate figure and in this sense, it is akin to racism.

Jacobsen: Historically, how have misogyny and misandry manifested in partnerships, in individual social settings, and in cultures at large?

Vaknin:

Misogyny has been the patriarchal organizing principles of all societies from the agricultural revolution to this very day. It permeated all institutions, from the family to the Church to the state.

Misogyny was mainly intended to restrict the freedoms of women in order to prevent them from procreating extradyadically and thus secure the intergenerational transfer of wealth to the male's rightful offspring.

Misandry is the reaction of some waves of feminism in the past 150 years or so. It is visceral and bitter, but not nearly as organized and institutionalized as misogyny.

Recently both are on the increase.

Jacobsen: As you note in several productions, there are obvious cases of a 'rollback' of women's rights in the United States through murmurings of repeals of *Roe v Wade* and in state legislatures, in Russia with the (re-)legalization – in a manner of speaking – of domestic abuse, in Afghanistan with women confined to the home, in Ethiopia with sexual violence (by Ethiopian and Eritrean forces), in Turkey via withdrawal from the *Istanbul Convention*, and in online hate groups comprised of resentful, bitter, anomic, hopeless, potentially mentally ill, batches of men in MGTOW (Men Going Their Own Way), Black Pillers, Red Pillers, Incels (Involuntary Celibates), generic male supremacists, PUAs (Pick Up Artists), MRM men (Men's Rights Movement), TFLers (True Forced Loners), and so on. These men, young and old alike, seem composed of anomie, despair, and porcelain, transmogrified into contempt for the Other. Do these seem like a disunified variegated 'wave' of anti-women sentiments and acts by men online and offline around the world?

Vaknin:

Some men are fighting back against what they perceive to be the ominous usurpation of rights and powers by women. They are also aghast at the way women have appropriated stereotypical male behaviors, such as promiscuity.

The counter-movement started off in disparate groups but now has coalesced into an agenda that is promoted by lawmakers all over the world. The backlash is fierce. Men are still the gatekeepers in most countries in the world. This doesn't bode well for women. Legal rights and access to services such as healthcare and educations are being rolled back and freedoms are curtailed.

Women are bound to be radicalized by such counter-reform. They are likely to become way more militant and masculinized. They are shunning men in growing numbers and resorting to male substitutes even when it comes to procreation: donor sperm and IVF.

Jacobsen: What seems like the psychology of the men with the authority to impose these 'rollbacks' in legislation and socio-cultural life?

Vaknin:

This is a state of panic, both moral and operational. Inter-gender morality was imposed by men in order to preserve the "purity" of women and their role as domestic comforters-in-chief. As power shifted from men to women, this ideal has been shattered.

Moreover, women emulate aggressive, ambitious men. In multiple studies, women described themselves in exclusively masculine terms. They have been taking away men's jobs for well over a hundred years now. They are way more educated than men so men feel absolutely threatened, very much like a species going extinct.

Men who react adversely to the ascendance of women and the emergence of a unigender world via legislation and politics are anxious, sociosexually restricted, narcissistic (but not psychopathic), insecure, and, in some cases, with a conflicted sexual and gender identity.

Jacobsen: What seems like the psychology of the men in these international, disparate online groups, who even create their own lingo, patois?

Vaknin:

These are rabid misogynists who have created an ideology around their deep-seated, irrational, and pathological hatred. They have primitive defenses, are highly narcissistic and even psychopathic, and tend to externalize aggression. They tend to hold grudges and grievances, ruminate and fixate, and be vengeful and hypervigilant.

Jacobsen: You agree with First Wave Feminism and Second Wave Feminism, and disagree with Third Wave Feminism and Fourth Wave Feminism. What defines them?

Vaknin:

First and second wave feminisms (in plural: there are many schools) were focused on leveling the playing field and fighting abusive and exploitative practices such as prostitution and pornography.

Starting with the suffragettes, they focused on the franchise (the right to vote), equal wages, access (to healthcare, education, the workplace, daycare), revising the dress code ("rational dress"), the right to own and dispose of property, and converting marriage from indentured bondage to an intimate, hopefully lifelong equal partnership.

The third wave was a psychopathic outgrowth. While claiming to be inclusive and permissive, it was a defiant and reckless attempt to "empower" women by eliminating all boundaries, conventions, and mores of any kind in all fields of life.

What women have garnered from the confluence of the three waves is that they should make their careers the pivot of their lives, avoid meaningful, committed relationships with men, and pursue sex as a pastime with any man.

Ironically, the third wave played right into the hands of predatory men ("players") who took advantage of the newfangled promiscuity while assiduously avoiding any hint of commitment or investment. Third wave feminists internalized the male gaze ("internalized oppression") and pride themselves on being "sluts".

The fourth wave of feminism is focused on real problems such as sexual harassment, rape, and body shaming as well as intersectionality (discrimination of women who belong to more than one minority). In many ways, it is an offshoot of second wave feminism.

Jacobsen: Even within these four waves of feminism, what seem like the most laudable portions and the most contemptible parts of each?

Vaknin:

First, second, and fourth wave feminisms are legitimate movements which have improved and strengthened societies around the world by integrating women in the social and economic fabrics of their milieus.

The third wave was utterly destructive. It hijacked the feminist message and precipitated the gender wars which are threatening to undo the accomplishments of the first and second waves.

Moreover: corporate interested coopted the messaging of the third wave to encourage women to remain single and promiscuous in order to encourage their participation in the labor force and thus convert them into consumers.

Jacobsen: Since history cannot be rewritten in actuality, though can be erased and rewritten in records, what might Fifth Wave Feminism incorporate as lessons from the previous four to correct course from the clear antipathy between the sexes – maintaining the proper equalitarian victories and jettisoning the improper inegalitarian losses?

Vaknin:

Feminism needs to fight the patriarchy and its discriminatory practices – not men. It needs to recognize that men and women are equal, but not identical. It needs to encourage women to adopt boundaried sexuality and the formation of intimate partnerships, cohabitation households, and families with men (or women, if they are so inclined). It needs to expose the way business and the third wave end up disempowering women like never before.

Jacobsen: How can science on sex and gender clarify the fact from the fiction, as the sea floor of these waves – so to speak? Something to set limits on conversation based on reality in contrast to discourses entirely in the realm of fantasy.

Vaknin:

I dealt with this at length in the interview I gave you about gender wars https://www.newsintervention.com/prof-sam-vaknin-on-the-gender-wars/

Jacobsen: How might such a fifth wave grounded in science inform international human rights discourse, national legislation, sociocultural lives, families, and individual self-identification?

Vaknin:

Women are not a minority. Numerically, they are a majority. Their situation is reminiscent of apartheid in South Africa and needs to be tackled with the same tools: nonviolent resistance; truth and reconciliation; a peaceful and consensual transfer of power; an integrated society with no discrimination or subterfuge; equal rights and obligations while recognizing the uniqueness of each constituency.

Shoshanim: Thanks much, Prof. Samuel.

Vaknin: You are very welcome. May we both live to see the day men and women love each other the way they should.

Return

Interview about Victimization, Victims, and Victim Identity Movements (News Intervention)

Scott Douglas Jacobsen: What defines victimization? What defines a real victim in contrast to a fake victim?

Prof. Shmuel "Sam" Vaknin: Victimization involves the denial of the self-determination, identity, self-actualization, rights, and boundaries of a person without their express consent and collaboration.

Jacobsen: What makes victim identity movements, in fact, movements?

Vaknin: When victimhood becomes an organizing and explanatory (hermeneutic) principle, a determinant of the victim's identity, and a socially binding force centred around grievances; prosocial or communal grandiosity; entitlement; conspiracism (paranoid or persecutory delusions); aggressive engagement or, on the other end of the spectrum, schizoid withdrawal; dysempathy; defiance (reactance); and contumaciousness (rejection of expertise and authority) – we have on our hands a victim identity movement.

No one is a victim. We may end up being victimized – but it doesn't render us victims for life, it doesn't brand us.

Jacobsen: Some studies in British Columbia, as you have noted, found some victimhood movements have been hijacked by narcissists and psychopaths. How does this muddy the waters of the real justice movements and make them ineffectual?

Vaknin: This was not the only study to have unearthed this very disconcerting undertow. We are beginning to wake up to the reality of what Gabay et al. call (2020) Tendency for Interpersonal Victimhood, TIV). "professional" or "career" victims with emphasized narcissistic and psychopathic tendencies find new homes ("pathological narcissistic spaces") in these social justice upswells.

It makes it difficult to tell apart legitimate evidence-based grievances from entitlement-fueled manipulative and counterfactual claims.

One helpful way to distinguish the two is by noting that narcissists and psychopaths are destructive, not solutions-oriented. They thrive on negative affects such as anger and envy and are loth to invest in the routine and tedious chores attendant upon rectifying wrongs and building a better world.

More here: Victimhood Movements Hijacked by Narcissists and Psychopaths
https://www.youtube.com/watch?v=lBpxFxMAztA

Jacobsen: What have been extreme historical cases of this going awry, as this phenomenon has been historically cyclical, including one close to 'home' in 2004?

Vaknin: Nazism is a victimhood movement gone awful. And, to a lesser degree the white man's grievance movement implausibly headed by Trump is a more recent example of such subversive dynamics.

Jacobsen: What is the typical arc of development of victim movements?

Vaknin:

The sociologist Bradley Campbell suggested that we have transitioned from a culture centred around dignity to one based on victimhood.

Learn more by reading Habermas, Fukuyama, and Foucault. All justice-seeking movements start with grievances (injustices). They decry and seek to remedy and reverse individual transgressions (eg, the narcissistic abuse online movement) or societal and cultural biases (implicit and explicit), discrimination, and suppression.

The victims organize themselves around exclusionary identity politics and intersectionality and this orientation results in grandiosity and entitlement, in other words: in growing narcissism. Increasingly more aggressive, these movements often become psychopathic (defiant and contumacious) and demonize the Other.

Left-leaning victimhood movements centre around entitlement and reparations claims on the majority, on social institutions, and on history. Right-wing movements are conspiracy-minded and avoidant, but also more violent.

Narcissists and psychopaths gravitate to such movements in order to obtain narcissistic supply, money, power, and sex. They become the public faces and the media darlings on these hapless victims, having hijacked their legitimate complaints and demands.

Jacobsen: How much of the online content on narcissism and psychopathy is garbage (worthless or worse) now?

Vaknin: About 90%. It is not only worthless (wrong), it is dangerously misleading and entrenches a lifelong self-defeating and self-aggrandizing victimhood stance even as it demonizes and mythologizes abusers.

Jacobsen: What is the Tendency for Interpersonal Victimhood (TIV)?

Vaknin:

A series of two studies by Israeli scholar Gabay and others, published in 2020. The authors provided this abstract:

"In the present research, we introduce a conceptualization of the Tendency for Interpersonal Victimhood (TIV), which we define as an enduring feeling that the self is a victim across different kinds of interpersonal relationships. Then, in a comprehensive set of eight studies, we develop a measure for this novel personality trait, TIV, and examine its correlates, as well as its affective, cognitive, and behavioral consequences. In Part 1 (Studies 1A-1C) we establish the construct of TIV, with its four dimensions; i.e., need for recognition, moral elitism, lack of empathy, and rumination, and then assess TIV's internal consistency, stability over time, and its effect on the interpretation of ambiguous situations. In Part 2 (Studies 2A-2C) we examine TIV's convergent and discriminant validities, using several personality dimensions, and the role of attachment styles as conceptual antecedents. In Part 3 (Studies 3–4) we explore the cognitive and behavioral consequences of TIV. Specifically, we examine the relationships between TIV, negative attribution and recall biases, and the desire for revenge (Study 3), and the effects of TIV on behavioral revenge (Study 4). The findings highlight the importance of understanding, conceptualizing, and empirically testing TIV, and suggest that victimhood is a stable and meaningful personality tendency."

Read an analysis of these studies here: "The Tendency for Interpersonal Victimhood: The Personality Construct and its Consequences" (https://www.sciencedirect.com/science/article/abs/pii/S0191886920303238):

https://www.psypost.org/2020/12/researchers-identify-a-new-personality-construct-that-describes-the-tendency-to-see-oneself-as-a-victim-58753

Another interesting study:

"New research provides evidence that narcissism, psychopathy, and Machiavellianism — maladaptive personality traits known as the "Dark Triad" — are associated with overt displays of virtue and victimhood. The study suggests that people with dark personalities use these signals of "virtuous victimhood" to deceptively extract resources from others."

("Signaling Virtuous Victimhood as Indicators of Dark Triad Personalities", was authored by Ekin Ok, Yi Qian, Brendan Strejcek, and Karl Aquino, Journal of Personality and Social Psychology, American Psychological Association, May 2020).

Jacobsen: What are the primary signifiers of narcissists and psychopaths who have or might hijack legitimate victimhood or justice movements looking for money, power, and sex?

Vaknin:

Ironically, these usually are prosocial or communal narcissists. They often "control from the bottom" (emotionally blackmail by being self-sacrificial). So, the infestation of victimhood activism by narcissists and psychopaths is the tip of a submerged iceberg of ersatz altruism.

Some narcissists are ostentatiously generous: they dedicate time and other resources to social justice movements and to activism, they donate to charity, lavish gifts on their closest, abundantly provide for their nearest and dearest, and, in general, are open-handed and unstintingly benevolent. It is a form of virtue signalling. How can this be reconciled with the pronounced lack of empathy and with the pernicious self-preoccupation that is so typical of narcissists?

The act of giving enhances the narcissist's sense of omnipotence, his fantastic grandiosity, and the contempt he holds for others. It is easy to feel superior to the supplicating recipients of one's largesse. Narcissistic altruism is about exerting control and maintaining it by fostering dependence in the beneficiaries.

But narcissists give for other reasons as well.

The narcissist flaunts his charitable nature as a bait. He impresses others with his selflessness and kindness and thus lures them into his lair, entraps them, and manipulates and brainwashes them into subservient compliance and obsequious collaboration. People are attracted to the narcissist's larger than life posture – only to discover his true personality traits when it is far too late. "Give a little to take a lot" – is the narcissist's creed.

This does not prevent the narcissist from assuming the role of the exploited victim. Narcissists always complain that life and people are unfair to them and that they invest far more than their "share of the profit". The narcissist feels that he is the sacrificial lamb, the scapegoat, and that his relationships are asymmetric and imbalanced. "She gets out of our marriage far more than I do" – is a common refrain. Or: "I do all the work around here – and they get all the perks and benefits!"

Some narcissists are compulsive givers.

To all appearances, the compulsive giver is an altruistic, empathic, and caring person. Actually, he or she is a people-pleaser and a codependent. The compulsive giver is trapped in a narrative of his own confabulation: how his nearest and dearest need him because they are poor, young, inexperienced, lacking in intelligence or good looks, and are otherwise inferior to him. Compulsive giving, therefore, involves pathological narcissism. In reality, it is the compulsive giver who coerces, cajoles, and tempts people around him to avail themselves of his services or money. He forces himself on the recipients of his ostentatious largesse and the beneficiaries of his generosity or magnanimity. He is unable to deny anyone their wishes or a requests, even when these are not explicit or expressed and are mere figments of his own neediness and grandiose imagination.

Some narcissists are ostentatiously generous -- they donate to charity, lavish gifts on their closest, abundantly provide for their nearest and dearest, and, in general, are open-handed and unstintingly benevolent. How can this be reconciled with the pronounced lack of empathy and with the pernicious self-preoccupation that is so typical of narcissists? The act of giving enhances the narcissist's sense of omnipotence, his fantastic grandiosity, and the contempt he holds for others. It is easy to feel superior to the supplicating recipients of one's largesse. Narcissistic altruism is about exerting control and maintaining it by fostering dependence in the beneficiaries.

The People-pleasers

People-pleasers dread conflicts and wish to avoid them (they are conflict-averse) - hence their need to believe that they are universally liked. Always pleasant, well-mannered, and civil, the conflict-averse people-pleaser is also evasive and vague, hard to pin down, sometimes obsequious and, generally, a spineless "non-entity". These qualities are self-defeating as they tend to antagonize people rather than please them.

But conflict-aversion is only one of several psychodynamic backgrounds for the behavior known as "people-pleasing":

1.   Some people-pleasers cater to the needs and demands of others as a form of penance, or self-sacrifice;

2.   Many people-pleasers are codependents and strive to gratify their nearest and dearest in order to allay their own abandonment anxiety and the ensuing intense – and, at times, life-threatening - dysphoria ("if I am nice to him, he won't break up with me", "if I cater to her needs, she won't leave me");

3.   A few people-pleasers are narcissistic: pleasing people enhances their sense of omnipotence (grandiosity). They seek to control and disempower their "charges" ("she so depends on and looks up to me"). Even their pity is a form of self-aggrandizement ("only I can make her life so much better, she needs me, without me her life would be hell."). They are misanthropic altruists and compulsive givers.

All people-pleasers use these common coping strategies:

1.   Dishonesty (to avoid conflicts and unpleasant situations);

2.   Manipulation (to ensure desired outcomes, such as an intimate partner's continued presence);

3.   Fostering dependence: codependent people-pleasers leverage their ostentatious helplessness and manifest weaknesses to elicit the kind of behaviours and solicit the benefits that they angle for, while narcissistic people-pleasers aim to habituate their targets by bribing them with gifts, monopolizing their time, and isolating them socially;

4.   Infantilization: displaying childish behaviours to gratify the emotional needs of over-protective, possessive, paranoid, narcissistic, and codependent individuals in the people-pleaser's milieu;

5.   Self-punishment, self-defeat, and self-sacrifice to signal self-annulment in the pursuit of people-pleasing.

Jacobsen: What, historically speaking, can be done to combat these Cluster B bad behaviours connected to some social movements?

Vaknin:

As the grievances of these movements are addressed, they become a part of the establishment. This is when the hard work begins: the labors of writing laws, regulatory oversight, politics, negotiations and compromise, and the tedium of perseverance and routine.

These newfangled demands on the psychological and logistical resources of the movement and its adherents drive narcissists and psychopaths away: they are unaccustomed to and reject the hard slog and the often Sisyphean undertakings of public policy.

Shoshanim: Thanks so much for the time and opportunity, Prof. V.

Shoshanim's Shoshanim: V for Victim or V for Vaknin? Just kidding. Thank you for suffering me yet again!

Interview about Gut Feelings and Intuition (News Intervention)

Scott Douglas Jacobsen: What differentiates intuitions from gut feelings if at all?

Prof. Shmuel "Sam" Vaknin: Gut feeling is immediate and nebulous. Intuition takes longer to form and feels more precise, incisive, and certain.

Jacobsen: How much of knowledge is filtered, processed, and prefabricated non-consciously and then presented to a conscious arena/awareness for decision-making?

Vaknin:

There are three types of intuition.

Eidetic Intuitions

Intuition is supposed to be a form of direct access. Yet, direct access to what? Does it access directly "intuitions" (abstract objects, akin to numbers or properties - see "Bestowed Existence")? Are intuitions the objects of the mental act of Intuition? Perhaps intuition is the mind's way of interacting directly with Platonic ideals or Phenomenological "essences"? By "directly" I mean without the intellectual mediation of a manipulated symbol system, and without the benefits of inference, observation, experience, or reason.

Kant thought that both (Euclidean) space and time are intuited. In other words, he thought that the senses interact with our (transcendental) intuitions to produce synthetic a-priori knowledge. The raw data obtained by our senses -our sensa or sensory experience - presuppose intuition. One could argue that intuition is independent of our senses. Thus, these intuitions (call them "eidetic intuitions") would not be the result of sensory data, or of calculation, or of the processing and manipulation of same. Kant's "Erscheiung" (Sic!) - the "phenomenon", or "appearance" of an object to the senses - is actually a kind of sense-intuition later processed by the categories of substance and cause. As opposed to the phenomenon, the "nuomenon" (thing in itself) is not subject to these categories.

Descartes' "I (think therefore I) am" is an immediate and indubitable innate intuition from which his metaphysical system is derived. Descartes' work in this respect is reminiscent of Gnosticism in which the intuition of the mystery of the self leads to revelation.

Bergson described a kind of instinctual empathic intuition which penetrates objects and persons, identifies with them and, in this way, derives knowledge about the absolutes - "duration" (the essence of all living things) and "élan vital" (the creative life force). He wrote: "(Intuition is an) instinct that has become disinterested, self-conscious, capable of reflecting upon its object and of enlarging it indefinitely." Thus, to him, science (the use of symbols by our intelligence to describe reality) is the falsification of reality. Only art, based on intuition, unhindered by mediating thought, not warped by symbols - provides one with access to reality.

Spinoza's and Bergson's intuited knowledge of the world as an interconnected whole is also an "eidetic intuition".

Spinoza thought that intuitive knowledge is superior to both empirical (sense) knowledge and scientific (reasoning) knowledge. It unites the mind with the Infinite Being and reveals to it an orderly, holistic, Universe.

Friedrich Schleiermacher and Rudolf Otto discussed the religious experience of the "numinous" (God, or the spiritual power) as a kind of intuitive, pre-lingual, and immediate feeling.

Croce distinguished "concept" (representation or classification) from "intuition" (expression of the individuality of an objet d'art). Aesthetic interest is intuitive. Art, according to Croce and Collingwood, should be mainly concerned with expression (i.e., with intuition) as an end unto itself, unconcerned with other ends (e.g., expressing certain states of mind).

Eidetic intuitions are also similar to "paramartha satya" (the "ultimate truth") in the Madhyamika school of Buddhist thought. The ultimate truth cannot be expressed verbally and is beyond empirical (and illusory) phenomena. Eastern thought (e.g. Zen Buddhism) uses intuition (or experience) to study reality in a non-dualistic manner.

IB. *Emergent Intuitions*

A second type of intuition is the "emergent intuition". Subjectively, the intuiting person has the impression of a "shortcut" or even a "short circuiting" of his usually linear thought processes often based on trial and error. This type of intuition feels "magical", a quantum leap from premise to conclusion, the parsimonious selection of the useful and the workable from a myriad possibilities. Intuition, in other words, is rather like a dreamlike truncated thought process, the subjective equivalent of a wormhole in Cosmology. It is often preceded by periods of frustration, dead ends, failures, and blind alleys in one's work.

Artists - especially performing artists (like musicians) - often describe their interpretation of an artwork (e.g., a musical piece) in terms of this type of intuition. Many mathematicians and physicists (following a kind of Pythagorean tradition) use emergent intuitions in solving general nonlinear equations (by guessing the approximants) or partial differential equations.

Henri Poincaret insisted (in a presentation to the Psychological Society of Paris, 1901) that even simple mathematical operations require an "intuition of mathematical order" without which no creativity in mathematics is possible. He described how some of his creative work occurred to him out of the blue and without any preparation, the result of emergent intuitions.

These intuitions had "the characteristics of brevity, suddenness and immediate certainty... Most striking at first is this appearance of sudden illumination, a manifest sign of long, unconscious prior work. The role of this unconscious work in mathematical invention appears to me incontestable, and traces of it would be found in other cases where it is less evident."

Subjectively, emergent intuitions are indistinguishable from insights. Yet insight is more "cognitive" and structured and concerned with objective learning and knowledge. It is a novel reaction or solution, based on already acquired responses and skills, to new stimuli and challenges. Still, a strong emotional (e.g., aesthetic) correlate usually exists in both insight and emergent intuition.

Intuition and insight are strong elements in creativity, the human response to an ever changing environment. They are shock inducers and destabilizers. Their aim is to move the organism from one established equilibrium to the next and thus better prepare it to cope with new possibilities, challenges, and experiences. Both insight and intuition are in the realm of the unconscious, the simple, and the mentally disordered. Hence the great importance of obtaining insights and integrating them in psychoanalysis - an equilibrium altering therapy.

Kazimierz Dąbrowski's theory of positive disintegration (TPD) posits that angst (existentialist tension and anxiety) not only induces growth, but is a necessary condition for it. Disintegrative processes are desirable. The absence of positive disintegration results in a fixated state of "primary (not secondary) integration", without true individuality. One's developmental potential, especially one's overexcitabilities (abnormally strong reactions to stimuli) determine the potential for positive disintegration. Overexcitability (OE) is a heightened physiological experience of stimuli resulting from increased neuronal sensitivities.

Like Jordan Peterson, Dabrowski regards suffering – including the self-inflicted kind - as a key to both progress and healing. Personality shaping depends on socialization and on peer pressure (second factor). Strict unthinking and unwavering adherence creates robopaths (von Bertalanffy). Disintegartion requires countering social signalling and pressures which, I suggest, are mostly detected intuitively. Intuition, therefore, plays a key part in the regulation of these processes.

IC. *Ideal Intuitions*

The third type of intuition is the "ideal intuition". These are thoughts and feelings that precede any intellectual analysis and underlie it. Empathy may be such an intuitive mode applied to the minds of other people, yielding an intersubjective agreement. Moral ideals and rules may be such intuitions (see "Morality - a State of Mind?").

Mathematical and logical axioms and basic rules of inference ("necessary truths") may also turn out to be intuitions. These moral, mathematical, and logical self-evident conventions do not relate to the world. They are elements of the languages we use to describe the world (or of the codes that regulate our conduct in it). It follows that these a-priori languages and codes are nothing but the set of our embedded ideal intuitions. This is why we can be pretty certain that the language of mathematics is inadequate and insufficient to capture reality or even the laws of nature.

As the Rationalists realized, ideal intuitions (a class of undeniable, self-evident truths and principles) can be accessed by our intellect. Rationalism is concerned with intuitions - though only with those intuitions available to reason and intellect. Sometimes, the boundary between intuition and deductive reasoning is blurred as they both yield the same results. Moreover, intuitions can be combined to yield metaphysical or philosophical systems. Descartes applied ideal intuitions (e.g., reason) to his eidetic intuitions to yield his metaphysics. Husserl, Twardowski, even Bolzano did the same in developing the philosophical school of Phenomenology.

The a-priori nature of intuitions of the first and the third kind led thinkers, such as Adolf Lasson, to associate it with Mysticism. He called it an "intellectual vision" which leads to the "essence of things". Earlier philosophers and theologians labeled the methodical application of intuitions - the "science of the ultimates". Of course, this misses the strong emotional content of mystical experiences.

Confucius talked about fulfilling and seeking one's "human nature" (or "ren") as "the Way". This nature is not the result of learning or deliberation. It is innate. It is intuitive and, in turn, produces additional, clear intuitions ("yong") as to right and wrong, productive and destructive, good and evil. The "operation of the natural law" requires that there be no rigid codex, but only constant change guided by the central and harmonious intuition of life.

Intuition is a topic that concerned many philosophers throughout the ages.

IIA. *Locke*

But are intuitions really a-priori - or do they develop in response to a relatively stable reality and in interaction with it? Would we have had intuitions in a chaotic, capricious, and utterly unpredictable and disordered universe? Do intuitions emerge to counter-balance surprises?

Locke thought that intuition is a learned and cumulative response to sensation. The assumption of innate ideas is unnecessary. The mind is like a blank sheet of paper, filled gradually by experience - by the sum total of observations of external objects and of internal "reflections" (i.e., operations of the mind). Ideas (i.e., what the mind perceives in itself or in immediate objects) are triggered by the qualities of objects.

But, despite himself, Locke was also reduced to ideal (innate) intuitions. According to Locke, a colour, for instance, can be either an idea in the mind (i.e., ideal intuition) - or the quality of an object that causes this idea in the mind (i.e., that evokes the ideal intuition). Moreover, his "primary qualities" (qualities shared by all objects) come close to being eidetic intuitions.

Locke himself admits that there is no resemblance or correlation between the idea in the mind and the (secondary) qualities that provoked it. Berkeley demolished Locke's preposterous claim that there is such resemblance (or mapping) between PRIMARY qualities and the ideas that they provoke in the mind. It would seem therefore that Locke's "ideas in the mind" are in the mind irrespective and independent of the qualities that produce them. In other words, they are a-priori. Locke resorts to abstraction in order to repudiate it.

Locke himself talks about "intuitive knowledge". It is when the mind "perceives the agreement or disagreement of two ideas immediately by themselves, without the intervention of any other... the knowledge of our own being we have by intuition... the mind is presently filled with the clear light of it. It is on this intuition that depends all the certainty and evidence of all our knowledge... (Knowledge is the) perception of the connection of and agreement, or disagreement and repugnancy, of any of our ideas."

Knowledge is intuitive intellectual perception. Even when demonstrated (and few things, mainly ideas, can be intuited and demonstrated - relations within the physical realm cannot be grasped intuitively), each step in the demonstration is observed intuitionally. Locke's "sensitive knowledge" is also a form of intuition (known as "intuitive cognition" in the Middle Ages). It is the perceived certainty that there exist finite objects outside us. The knowledge of one's existence is an intuition as well. But both these intuitions are judgmental and rely on probabilities.

IIB. *Hume*

Hume denied the existence of innate ideas. According to him, all ideas are based either on sense impressions or on simpler ideas. But even Hume accepted that there are propositions known by the pure intellect (as opposed to propositions dependent on sensory input). These deal with the relations between ideas and they are (logically) necessarily true. Even though reason is used in order to prove them - they are independently true all the same because they merely reveal the meaning or information implicit in the definitions of their own terms. These propositions teach us nothing about the nature of things because they are, at bottom, self referential (equivalent to Kant's "analytic propositions").

IIC. *Kant*

According to Kant, our senses acquaint us with the particulars of things and thus provide us with intuitions. The faculty of understanding provided us with useful taxonomies of particulars ("concepts"). Yet, concepts without intuitions were as empty and futile as intuitions without concepts. Perceptions ("phenomena") are the composite of the sensations caused by the perceived objects and the mind's reactions to such sensations ("form"). These reactions are the product of intuition.

IID. *The Absolute Idealists*

Schelling suggested a featureless, undifferentiated, union of opposites as the Absolute Ideal. Intellectual intuition entails such a union of opposites (subject and object) and, thus, is immersed and assimilated by the Absolute and becomes as featureless and undifferentiated as the Absolute is.

Objective Idealists claimed that we can know ultimate (spiritual) reality by intuition (or thought) independent of the senses (the mystical argument). The mediation of words and symbol systems only distorts the "signal" and inhibits the effective application of one's intuition to the attainment of real, immutable, knowledge.

IIE. *The Phenomenologists*

The Phenomenological point of view is that every thing has an invariable and irreducible "essence" ("Eidos", as distinguished from contingent information about the thing). We can grasp this essence only intuitively ("Eidetic Reduction"). This process - of transcending the concrete and reaching for the essential - is independent of facts, concrete objects, or mental constructs. But it is not free from methodology ("free variation"), from factual knowledge, or from ideal intuitions. The Phenomenologist is forced to make the knowledge of facts his point of departure. He then applies a certain methodology (he varies the nature and specifications of the studied object to reveal its essence) which relies entirely on ideal intuitions (such as the rules of logic).

Phenomenology, in other words, is an Idealistic form of Rationalism. It applies reason to discover Platonic (Idealism) essences. Like Rationalism, it is not empirical (it is not based on sense data). Actually, it is anti-empirical - it "brackets" the concrete and the factual in its attempt to delve beyond appearances and into essences. It calls for the application of intuition (Anschauung) to discover essential insights (Wesenseinsichten).

"Phenomenon" in Phenomenology is that which is known by consciousness and in it. Phenomenologists regarded intuition as a "pure", direct, and primitive way of reducing clutter in reality. It is immediate and the basis of a higher level perception. A philosophical system built on intuition would, perforce, be non speculative. Hence, Phenomenology's emphasis on the study of consciousness (and intuition) rather than on the study of (deceiving) reality. It is through "Wesensschau" (the intuition of essences) that one reaches the invariant nature of things (by applying free variation techniques).

Jacobsen: Is this a large part of intuition and/or gut feelings if inclusive of the filtration, processing, and prefabrication, of information from physiology – the body – too? I do not necessarily mean extensive amounts of time – could be fractions of a second – from input to presentation to consciousness (conscious awareness).

Vaknin:

There is no question that input from the body is crucial to the formation of intuitions. The sensa (sensory inputs) are only one part of it. Autonomous reactions – such as heartbeat or perspiration – also figure into the equation. As we try to make sense of these corporeal data, we often come up with a heuristic or a narrative and most of the time we perceive the outcomes of these attempts as gut feelings or intuitions.

Jacobsen: When something *feels* wrong to an individual, how is this justifiable in considering the "something" as *wrong* in and of itself, or *wrong* in interpretation of an

individual (more likely than not a fallible individual)? Are there moments when these feelings of wrongness about something are themselves inaccurate - following more generally from part of the last question?

Vaknin:

Intuition is wrong as often as right. It is a shaky foundation for decision making. But it is a reliable signal that further research and investigation are called for.

Intuition should not be confused with either emotions or cognitions. They are an amalgam of both but they are a form of anxiety reaction, a variant of hypervigilance.

Jacobsen: When someone is trying to force-fit a relationship, a friendship, a marital situation, a professional arrangement, why is this a sign of inauthenticity, a fake?

Vaknin:

Authenticity consists of being yourself even when you adhere to social strictures, norms, and mores or when you are trying to meet expectations and obligations. Feeling good about your choice to conform and act responsibly, reliably, and predictably (ego syntony).

If the sum total of an engagement with others causes you acute discomfort (ego dystony or dissonance) – this is a sign that you are betraying yourself somehow and, therefore, being inauthentic.

Watch "Being is Slavery, Nothingness is Freedom (Sartre's "Being and Nothingness", FIRST LECTURE)"

https://www.youtube.com/watch?v=vxfRneEDN3w

Watch "Relationships Always Fail, Inauthentic (Sartre's "Being and Nothingness", SECOND LECTURE)" https://www.youtube.com/watch?v=xFvRcB1MOWM

Jacobsen: Grandiose claims are made all the time. Those claims too good to be true. Why are the "too good to be true" more likely to be false than true?

Vaknin:

Splitting is an infantile psychological defense mechanism: the baby divides the world into all good and all bad. Of course, this is counterfactual: there is good and bad, right and wrong, helpful and obstructive in everything and in everyone.

So, "too good to be true" is an outcome of splitting coupled with magical thinking (the delusion that your willpower or thoughts affect reality even without any commensurate action). It is the offspring of a pathology of impaired reality testing.

Jacobsen: Why are we prone to believing things people say far more often than not, when people lie all the time in little and big ways?

Vaknin:

This is known as the base rate fallacy. This cognitive distortion aims to resolve a cognitive dissonance: I know that people lie but I want to trust them all the time in order to feel safe.

It stems from the same pathological roots which involve grandiosity magical thinking: other people are all good and can be always trusted because I am all-powerful and immune to harm as well as all-knowing and so, I cannot be conned.

Trusting other people is the optimal strategy when you are the omniscient and omnipotent master of the Universe: investing in research and investigation would be wasteful.

Jacobsen: Should we make decisions immediately based on gut feelings and intuitions or over a reasonable amount of time making incremental, moderate changes/decisions based on increasing feedback from the processes colloquially called "gut feelings" and "intuitions"?

Vaknin:

We should definitely listen to gut feelings and intuitions. They are telling us that something has gone awry with the way we perceive reality. This alert bears careful investigation and research.

But I would not act on my intuition or gut feeling unless and until I have delved deeper into what it is that is nagging at me.

Jacobsen: How can intuitions and gut feelings, ultimately, save us from our conscious delusions?

Vaknin:

Intuitions and gut feelings are a poor guide in this sense because, as I said, as often as not, they turn out to have been wrong. Some intuitions are delusional!

Shoshanim: Thanks so much for the time and opportunity, Prof. Sam (Wise Gamgee).

Shoshanim's Shoshanim: I have an intuition that you actually mean it this time!

Return

Narcissism: The Future Religion (News Intervention)

Pathological narcissism develops as a set of complex psychological defenses against childhood abuse and trauma in all its forms, including not only "classical" maltreatment, but also idolizing the child, smothering it, parentifying it, or instrumentalizing it.

Whenever the child is not allowed to separate from the parental figures, form boundaries, and individuate (become an individual), a disorder of some kind ensues, secondary (pathological) narcissism being among the most prevalent.

In the narcissistic pathology, the child forms a paracosm ruled over by an imaginary friend who is everything the child is not: omniscient, omnipotent, perfect, brilliant, and omnipresent. In short: a godhead or divinity. The child worships the newfound ally and makes a human sacrifice to this Moloch: he offers to it his true self.

The child strikes a Faustian deal: he is endowed with a grandiose albeit fragile self-image and a fantastic self-perception, but, in return, he ceases to exist.

The narcissist outsources his ego boundary functions to the False Self and regulates his internal environment (for example: his sense of self-worth) via constant feedback from a multitude of interchangeable sources of narcissistic supply. His is a veritable hive mind.

Narcissism is the celebration, elevation, and glorification of a superior absence, a howling emptiness, the all-devouring void of a black hole with a galaxy of internal objects (introjects) swirling around it.

Narcissism is, therefore, a private religion which resembles very much primitive faiths and rites. It is a fantasy defense writ large and gone awry, having metamorphesized into a delusion. Reality testing is severely impaired and the narcissist mistakes inner representations of people with the external objects that gave rise to them.

As a growing number of people become increasingly more narcissistic and as our civilization rewards narcissism and veers towards it, the allure of the narcissism religion is growing exponentially.

It is beginning to be widely and counterfactually glamorized - even in academe - as a positive adaptation. Counterfactually because narcissism ineluctably and invariably devolves into self-defeat and self-destruction.

Narcissism is the first distributed or networked faith: every believer and practitioner (i.e., every narcissist) is a worshipper but also the god that he worships (has a godlike False Self). Every node is equipotent and self-sustaining as it seeks to consume narcissistic supply (attention, good or bad).

Like every religion before it, narcissism is fast becoming an organizing and hermeneutic (explanatory) principle. It imbues existence with meaning and direction. It is both prescriptive and proscriptive. Fueled by technologies like social media, it is spreading with more alacrity than any previous historical faith.

Pathological narcissism is also missionary: the narcissist attempts to convert potential sources of narcissistic supply and intimate partners to participate in his shared fantasy and to worship his grandiose deity, the False Self.

Everything abovesaid applies with equal rigor to narcissistic collectives. This is where the danger lurks: narcissism is aggressive and intolerant, dysempathic and exploitative. It is a death cult. It elevates objects above people. In a society of the spectacle, everyone is rendered a commodity. Materialism and consumerism are manifestations of narcissism as is malignant, ostentatious individualism.

Narcissism in collectives is indistinguishable from the individual sort: it is always adversarial and results in dismal self-defeat and self-destruction. Left unbridled and unconstrained and elevated ideologically, it can bring about Armageddon in more than one way.

The rise of narcissism is inexorable. It is comparable to climate change and to the shift in gender roles: there is no going back now. If I am right, it calls for major adaptations on multiple levels, individual, institutional, and collective:

(1) To harness the considerable energy of narcissism and channel it in socially acceptable ways (sublimate it). Prosocial and communal narcissism could spell a workable compromise, for example;

(2) To put in place checks, balances, and institutions to prevent the more destructive, insidious, and pernicious outcomes and aspects of narcissism; and

(3) To prepare the general populace to accept narcissism as a part of the landscape and Zeitgeist. This latter goal is best accomplished via technologies that would provide outlets to conforming, positive healthy narcissism and at the same time isolate users from an increasingly more narcissistic reality as much as possible. Social media and the metaverse as harbingers of these twin tasks. Atomization and self-sufficiency as well as the disintegration of social institutions are mere symptoms of this tectonic shift in what it means to be human.

Return

Freedom of Will: Illusion or Reality? (News Intervention)

Scott Douglas Jacobsen: We will likely encounter moments of repetition in this session, in question and response.

What is free will? What are the ways in which "will" has been defined?

Prof. Shmuel "Sam" Vaknin:

Free will is a useful fiction, akin to god or the afterlife: only agents with free will can be held morally responsible.

Free will comprises three conditions:

1. The ability to choose and act otherwise;
2. Having control over one's choices and actions;
3. That the choice or act are rationally motivated.

The very concept of free will is founded on convenient delusions such as time or causation. Whereas teleology is prohibited in all sciences (we do not attribute purposeful actions to objects and animals, for example), it mysteriously permeates philosophy and more specifically the field of ethics.

Jacobsen: What are the ways in which "freedom" or "free" have been defined?

Vaknin:

Both the external world and our internal one serve as constraints. We cannot choose or act contrary to Nature or to our individual nature. What we call "change" is merely a transition between different constrained systems. So, ostensibly, free will is a myth, there is no such thing.

But this (nomological) determinism is merely optical (compatibilism).

First: there are always other options. If someone puts a gun to your head, you are still possessed of free will: you can choose to die (in Judaism, one is instructed to choose death over certain transgressions).

But, much more importantly, in complex systems the number of probable pathways is so enormous that for all practical purposes we can never specify all or even most of them (chaos theory, quantum mechanics). So, these systems, as far as we are concerned appear to be either random (libertarianism) or subject to free will (agency).

Jacobsen: What definitions of "free", "will", and "free will"/"freedom of the will", simply exist in the realm of fantasy, magical thinking?

Vaknin:

Free will is a conscious, introspected experience of the degrees of freedom in systems (such as the brain or society). It reflects the fact that our ability to know the world is limited by our finitude and mortality. Our descriptions of reality – including psychological reality – will always be subject to uncertainty, indeterminacy, and apparent randomness.

This is a terrifying realization which produces anxiety (angst in existentialism). It implies an external locus of control (our lives are determined from the outside by forces and processes we will, in principle, never fathom).

We defend against such helplessness and lack of autonomy and agency by deceiving ourselves into believing that we are exempt from the laws of nature and can alter the ineluctable course of events.

But this is a useful bit of self-deception and should be perpetuated, for two reasons:

1. Owing to our inability to secure all the information about reality, free will feels real!
2. The concept of free will guarantees the acceptance of moral responsibility and the reactions to it: desert, blame, guilt, and restorative justice.

Jacobsen: Apart from simplistic considerations of semi-dismissal, as in it is fantasy or magical thinking, is free will a complex illusion of human perception and cognition, even a non-conscious mental trick bundled in the languages – everything: semiotics, semantics, syntax, etc. - used to speak about it, a mistake of intuition of sorts?

Vaknin:

The BELIEF in the freedom to choose and do otherwise – regardless of whether such liberty is merely an illusion – is the foundation of human civilization, its core.

Free will is an article of FAITH. It is not a fact or a hypothesis or a theory. It has no truth value (it is not true or false). It has no ontological status, only an epistemological one.

Jacobsen: What forms of free will, if it's to exist at all (or, indeed, not), would fit the modern scientific universes of discourse for plausibility?

Vaknin:

None., Modern science is dichotomous: determinism vs. randomness (probability). In both approaches, there is no place for free will (the intelligibility problem). If the universe is preordained and predestined (by god) then, of course, individual agency is counterfactual. If, on the other hand, events are random, there can be no will, choice, or even action, all of which imply intentionality.

Some would say that Man converts the random into the structured, is an agent of increasing order in the universe. Humans, in this view, are AGENTS of determinism, the shapers of reality.

But this is just kicking the can down the road: we are still faced with randomness when human decisions and actions to increase order are undertaken.

Jacobsen: A bit of a longer question narrowed more within tighter philosophical and natural philosophical terms. In a prior session, you spoke on Kant, free will, nomic causation/causation by laws (of nature) versus causation resulting from free will, and a god. As has been phrased by others… "ultimately, of what is the will free?"

Vaknin:

Every single philosopher I ever heard of grappled with the question of free will and tried to square the circle.

Ultimately, it is just a question of frame of reference and level of description. The same substance can be described as 2 atoms of hydrogen and one of oxygen – or as wet, cold water. Both descriptions are valid statements about the reality of the substance - and yet they have nothing in common.

From a fine-grained point of view of the world, free will is a confabulation. But from a human being's perspective, free will is a very useful organizing and explanatory principle. It helps to make sense of life and provide one with self-efficacious guidance.

Jacobsen: Apart from the above mentioned considerations of the arguments, switching more to a personal voice, you have a ToE in Chronon Field Theory (CFT). Does free will exist in CFT?

Vaknin:

Moreso than in any other theory I am aware of. The Chronon Field Theory is all about Time as a field of potentialities. As some of these potentials materialize, they constitute input – but not to any deterministic process! They feed into other probable processes or events. "Choice" and "action" easily fit into this view of the world because our brains are just another such superposition.

Jacobsen: With everything, and the stance on free will, any final words of anxiety and discomfort if not anguish and torture?

Vaknin:

I don't do comfort. But thank you for giving me the opportunity. Every thinker whose work I have read has miserably failed in tackling the thorny topic of free will. Even the most rigorous amongst them made fools of themselves in plain view.

Don't go there. There is a thin line separating overthinking from inanity and overanalyzing from stupidity. Don't cross it.

Free will exists the same way Harry Potter and Sherlock Holmes most definitely exist. It is real. It is a force to reckon with. It shapes our minds and lives. It exerts a huge influence on multiple spheres. What more do we need to know?

Shoshanim: Thank you, Doc.

Lily's Lily: You are very welcome, survivor!

Return

Physics or Metaphysics? (Good Men's Project)

Scott Douglas Jacobsen: What would define a comprehensive physics?

Prof. Sam Vaknin: Ostensibly, physics is the science of studying reality. But, in reality, physics is a form of mysticism, it is where alchemy used to be a few centuries ago.

In alchemy, there was a preoccupation with language and a belief in a universal, invariant truth which would endow the practitioner with godlike powers. All alchemists believed that it was only a question of time before we attain this truth.

Similarly, physics is a self-contained, self-referential language. There are debates on how to use this language and on how to interpret its elements. But there is a broad agreement on its grammar and syntax.

Jacobsen: What would define a complete metaphysics?

Vaknin: Metaphysics deals with concepts that underlie reality.

Jacobsen: What would relate these two universes of discourse in the aforementioned definitions?

Vaknin: Physicists still believe that physics is asymptotic to the truth, that we are making progress towards an objective, invariant, immutable, indisputable verity. This is, of course, mysticism, not science.

Scientific theories are not about reality but about other scientific theories and about themselves, a discourse that spans generations and contrasts with previous ways of thinking even as it generates falsifiable testable hypotheses.

Theories are allegories, metaphors, analogies, glorified literature using a highly structured language known as mathematics. Scientific theories are descriptive, predictive, and wrong: after all, all past theories have been falsified.

Physics is an extension of metaphysics. We must revert to philosophy and metaphysics, our roots.

All scientific theories are fundamentally metaphysical. Examples: evolution is founded on teleology (the accepted truth that organisms wish to survive) and SRT (special relativity theory) emanates from the separateness of observers from the observed (which was proven wrong on the micro level).

The philosophy of science is a fancy rebranding of metaphysics. Its main tenet, falsifiability, is tautological (we can falsify only scientific theories which are the only theories that are falsifiable).

There is an age-old confusion between language and truth. For example: the solutions to an equation (language elements) are considered to be true and real. The very reliance on language is metaphysical because it assumes that language correlates with reality or can be perfectly mapped onto it.

But how many of our assumptions about language (such as axioms in mathematics) are real or true? We can study language only with a meta-language and this results in an infinite regression. So, there is no way to prove or to ascertain the validity or the relevance of a language. It takes a leap of faith.

Science is, therefore, a faith-based system that is helpful to survival (akin to religion). The core percepts are metaphysical, non-provable, they require a leap of faith. Physicists arbitrarily assume the validity and power of mathematics and the existence of reality - both are metaphysical assumptions which are unprovable, axiomatic, and not derivable.

I am a believer in physics, but I am not a naïve believer: it works, so I believe in it, but I am aware of my own irrationality. Reason is not primary, faith is.

Jacobsen: What was metaphysics in the past?

Vaknin: What we today call science. The study of both the essence of the world and of what makes it tick.

Jacobsen: What has been the origin and evolution of physics into the present?

Vaknin: There were two major revolutions in the history of physics and its divorce from metaphysics: Descartes' and Bohr's.

At some point in time, we started to believe that observer and observed are two separate, unrelated systems. In the twentieth century, we gave up on any pretension and attempt to capture the quiddity of the world or even to merely describe it. Instead, we settled on an instrumental version of physics: if it works, it is futile to inquire why and how it works. Quantum mechanics is a prime example of this blindfolded approach.

Jacobsen: How is physics beginning to turn into, or make a circumlocution back to, metaphysics, and into an evolution of "uber-metaphysics" - even mysticism? What are the dangers - let's say - to clarity of concepts and thought in turns, some of them, to mysticism now?

Vaknin: The minute you let language dictate your view of reality (because it is "self-efficacious"), you abandon the latter. The formalism rules and the procedures for manipulating its symbols become the laws of physics or of nature.

The problem with this kind of detour is that, as Godel has observed, formal-logical systems are incomplete or inconsistent and give rise to "hallucinations" (witness the recent debacle with artificial intelligence).

So, we end up further away from a true understanding of reality as we descend into arcane solipsistic sophistry.

Jacobsen: How is physics, in some sense, like a highly formalized structure of literature?

Vaknin: I don't think that it is like literature. Physics is not merely descriptive. It doesn't confine itself to taxonomy of the codification of experience. It aspires to decipher reality even as it translates into technology: tools to alter our environments, near and far.

Jacobsen: All scientific theories in the past have been proven wrong via experiment or come to inconsistent findings with Nature and the predictions of the theory. What will happen to the current set of theories, most likely?

Vaknin: The same fate awaits the current crop of dominant theories.

Jacobsen: If physics, currently, is rootless or physicists - as a category - have 'forgotten' their foundations in metaphysics as physics being a derivation from metaphysics, what is a necessary bridge to bring the roots back to soil for physicists - and for the structured narrative knowledge pool called physics to become crisp again?

Vaknin: Philosophy and logic. These should become mandatory studies. These disciplines are indispensable in the evolution of critical thinking and the generation of testable hypotheses.

Jacobsen: Thank you for the opportunity and your time, Prof. Vaknin.

Vaknin: Pleasure, as always.

Return

Censorship, East and West (Good Men's Project)

Scott Douglas Jacobsen: What defines censorship, or, more properly, characterizes censorship?

Prof. Sam Vaknin:

Censorship is any suppression of speech that is motivated by an ideology or by the perception of risk avoidance. It is intended to prevent challenges to the interests of an existing establishment or system or to safeguard secrets and national security interests.

Jacobsen: What have been the methods—and as two common placeholder spheres of influence concepts—of censorship in Eastern cultures and in Western cultures?

Vaknin:

Censorship in authoritarian regimes, most of which are indeed in the east or global south, is overt and institutionalized. The red lines are promulgated publicly and punishments for transgressions are enshrined in criminal law.

In the West, censorship is far more pernicious: it is stealthy, self-imposed, and adheres to standards of political correctness that reflect the interests and concerns of the identity politics of vocal victimhood groups.

Worst of all: the very existence of censorship is denied in the West as public intellectuals, the mainstream media, and societal and legal institutions uphold the counterfactual myth of "free speech".

Censorship reflects the breakdown of trust in society and the need to use violence, both verbal and physical, to prevent the utter disintegration of the social fabric and the institutions that preserve the privileges of the elites.

Jacobsen: How have those forms of censorship evolved into the present?

Vaknin:

The sociologists Bradley Keith Campbell and Jason Manning posited that have transitioned from the age of dignity and reputation to the age of victimhood. This is not just about identity politics: as multiple studies have demonstrated in the past 3 years, victimhood is a profitable proposition and a way to reallocate scarce economic resources coercively.

Additionally, we are in the throes of more than one century of unprecedented existential risks (from nuclear weapons and world wars to climate change and invasive surveillance).

The confluence of these two toxic trends has rendered speech a dangerous luxury. Speech acts are deemed subversive, offensive, or malicious, even life-threatening, both on the collective and on the individual level.

Jacobsen: What have been the forms of censorship most tragic to intellectual progress and scientific discovery?

Vaknin:

By far, political correctness. It has stifled legitimate scientific inquiry, stymied public discourse, and penalized free thinkers of all stripes. It is comparable only to the Inquisition or to McCarthyism.

Jacobsen: What have been the common forms of censorship against you?

Vaknin:

Ironically, my sister, Sima Gil-Vaknin, served as the Chief Censor of the Israeli Defense Force (IDF), so I know a thing or two about the inner workings and the psychological underpinning of censorship.

Over the decades of my intellectual efforts, I have been subjected to every form of censorship in more than 10 countries. My videos are shadowbanned (deranked) on YouTube. My articles have been deemed "hateful speech" and deleted from various platforms, including, most recently LinkedIn. I have been sued multiply and have received graphic death threats more times than I can count.

Jacobsen: Why are these tactics used against public personalities?

Vaknin:

Naming and shaming. Cancelling. Mobbing. Violence (Salman Rushdie, Jamal Khashoggi, to mention but two). Verbal abuse. Smear campaigns. All tried and true methods originally perfected by narcissists and psychopaths.

Jacobsen: Is censorship targeted against misunderstood or ill-understood individuals on the extreme ends of intelligence and creativity, i.e., geniuses, more often than cognitively average people if taking a per capita rate into account?

Vaknin:

I wouldn't say that. On the contrary: censorship targets the masses, the media, your average student or teacher, small to medium size businesses. In short: censorship targets constituencies whose vested interests in the current power structure are not great and who, therefore, are more open to evolutionary and even revolutionary ideas.

Jacobsen: What are ways for geniuses to protect themselves from the onslaughts of idiots? Leonardo Da Vinci devised some apparent techniques to keep certain aspects of his productions hidden in plain sight from sufficiently unintelligent people, as an example.

Vaknin:

This is by far the most serious problem: the inexorable rise of the idiocracy.

Why would women prefer men with an IQ lower than 120 to men with an IQ higher than 145? These are the results of a study published last year.

The answer is simple:

Our contemporary world is ruled by the feebleminded, dimwits are empowered by technology, and everything is dumbed down to foster mass consumption.

In such a world, lower intelligence is a positive adaptation which confers evolutionary advantages on its bearers - and on their spouses and offspring.

Women select for beta males because the current environment favors beta traits over alpha traits.

It is a paradigm shift of mind-bending proportions (for those in possession of a mind).

A study of nine million young adults over 40 years (conducted by Jean Twenge and her colleagues and published in the March 2012 issue of t*he Journal of Personality and Social Psychology*) has starkly demonstrated the deterioration from one generation to another. Youngsters are now focused on money, image, and fame and disparage values such as community, volunteerism, the environment, and knowledge acquisition. Other surveys have documented a rising level of illiteracy. As if to illustrate the imminence of these new Dark Ages, the Encyclopedia Britannica announced that it will cease the publication of its print edition after 244 years. Its surviving digital editions are a far cry from the print equivalent in terms of depth, length, and erudition.

The Stupid, the Trivial, and the Frivolous are everywhere: among the working classes, of course, but increasingly you can find them displacing the erstwhile elites, spawning hordes of mindless politicians, idiot business tycoons, narcissistic media personalities, gullible clergy, vacuous celebrities, illiterate bestselling authors, athletes with far more brawn than brain, repetitious pop singers, less than mediocre bureaucrats, bovine gatekeepers, and even ignorant and semi-literate academics. Their cacophony drowns the few voices of wisdom, expertise, and experience and their sheer number overwhelms all systems of governance and all mechanisms of decision-making. Rather than futilely fight back this tsunami, the well-educated, the erudite, and the intelligent choose to withdraw and seclude themselves in self-constructed, schizoid ivory towers, all bridges drawn.

Imbeciles are a menace to the continued existence not only of our civilization, but also of our species. We may end up being all Homo, no sapiens.

The percentage of stupid people in the general populace may not have changed. It may even have decreased. But in terms of absolute numbers, there are more Stupid heads now than the entire human population only a century ago. Modern medicine makes sure that the retarded and plain dim-witted live on to a ripe old age. That we are faced with the daunting prospect of idiocracy is the fault of the malignant transformation of the democratic ideal and the recent onslaught of the media, both old and new.

Start with democracy, the Stupid People's pernicious answer to meritocracy:

In the not-too-distant past dim-witted people had the right to vote once in a while and thus express their completely inconsequential opinion where it mattered least: in the ballot box. Alas, the inane idea of "one person (never mind how pinheaded, unqualified, or ignorant), one vote" has invaded and permeated hitherto hierarchical environments such as government, the workplace, and the military. With technology at their disposal, The Stupid repeatedly interfere with and disrupt the proper functioning of virtually every system.

Even the generation and transfer of knowledge have been "democratized" as crowdsourcing yielded enterprises such as Wikipedia, the "encyclopedia" that anyone can edit, add to, and delete from. Internet search engines rank results not according to the merits and authority of the content, but by the number of votes cast by ... you guessed it: mostly dense people (who now congregate on social networks). This widespread and much-lauded vandalism reflects the utter collapse and disintegration of the education system which turns out illiterate, nescient, and irrational graduates having annihilated its standards in order to lucratively embrace them as students in the first place.

The Stupid, dimly aware of their innate inferiority, are anti-elitist, anti-intellectual, and anti-excellence. But, while in the past these remained mere sentiments, today they have become an ethos, a code of conduct, a set of values and ideals. It is politically incorrect and impolite to claim any advantage and superiority. Egalitarianism is running amok. Everyone is equal: doctors and their patients; professors and their students; experts and laymen alike.

Continue with technology:

In an act of self-preservation, past civilizations had confined The Stupid to certain settlements, replete with their drinking establishments, entertainments, and sports arenas. There the "intellectually-challenged" could safely torment each other with their vulgarities and rampant, uninformed idiocy. The advent of radio, television, and, most egregiously, the Internet has changed all that: now stupid people have unmitigated access to the kind of technology that allows them to pollute the airwaves and the broadband with their inferior analytic capacity, low-brow output, trivial observations, monosyllabic exclamations, and harebrained queries. Thus, the New Media have transformed stupidity from a mental endemic to a viral pandemic. The wise and knowledgeable may broadcast while the Stupid merely narrowcast – but the Stupid have the upper hand, what with Google, Facebook, Twitter, Blogger, Amazon, and YouTube decimating the traditional print and electronic media.

This technological empowerment is the crux of the problem: there are no barriers to entry, no institutional filters, and no erudite and experienced intermediaries to hold back the avalanche of doltish balderdash, the tsunami of nonsense, and the flood of misinformation, factoids, and conspiracies that corrupt our intellectual space. "Discovery": separating the wheat from the chaff has become mission impossible. Commercial interests inevitably and invariably side with the brainless masses because of their superior aggregate purchasing power. The privatization of education is one manifestation of this creeping decadence. The mindless nature of television programming is another. The empty one-liners that comprise most "conversations" on social networks are its culmination. We are surrounded with clods, harassed by the lame-brained, criticized, censored, and ordered by simpletons. Welcome to the New Dark Ages.

Jacobsen: Thank you for the opportunity and your time, Sam.

Vaknin:

Thank you for having me, Scott. I appreciate your unwavering support.

Return

Mind, Reality, or Mere Language?

Polylogue on Reality and Language between Eytan Suchard, Shimon Vaknin, and Sam Vaknin

ES: Unless we are more than just biological machines, all physicists will be replaced. See: Sky News Australia interviews 'free-thinking' artificial intelligence - YouTube. However, our brain is not a deterministic machine due to quantum leeway in postsynaptic activations. That is why it is impossible to rule out the existence of an external entity that expresses itself through these degrees of freedom.

A healthy and well performing brain then serves as a vessel for such an expression. An external entity to the brain can reach insights beyond the usual neural computation that our theories predict. Physicists can only have hope through metaphysics, real one, not their crappy models.

SV: It is not an issue of ruling out the existence of such an entity - but of why assume its existence in the first place (parsimony, Occam's razor).

ES: 1) Because from the probabilistic non-local description of Nature, we infer there is no probability without a reference in relation to which measurement is probabilistic and probabilities sum to 1. As such, this reference is not probabilistic and is therefore not part of the publicly observed Nature. Therefore, we are not only the brain.

2) It is merely impossible to mathematically explain what is consciousness or how consciousness is "generated" by neural activations. Neural activations are publicly owned by all observers in the physical world. Pain and pleasure are not pulses per second and saying they are emergent from pulses per second, does not have any mathematical meaning.

Then you can argue that consciousness is just a language term but it is not to us as observers. The commonly shared information about neural activations has no interpretation as pain and pleasure. What can be said is that there is a correlation between neural activations and pain or pleasure, however, correlation is not causation and pain is not pulses per second or a combination of pulses per second as a very complex flow graph.

3) Empirically, if we can get information about future events and show that the publicly observed Nature is causal, then this information cannot be known only through the publicly observed Nature. At least two events in my history show exactly this. Large scale experiments can be and should be done.

4) Mathematically, we should be able to show chronon probabilities are in relation to a deterministic object as an embedding object. Note that this approach is diametrically opposed to Rafael Sorkin's Causal Sets. Causal Sets are inconsistent with non-local summation of probabilities to 1. You can argue that the existence of an embedding object is merely a mathematical construction like in Whitney's embedding theorem, so in such a case, we need

to show that there is no way to non-locally sum probabilities of events to 1 without such an embedding object. That would be a very deep theorem that would prove the existence of a Universal observer as an embedding object, possibly as a real object.

SV: Actually, I go a lot further than that. The psyche, perception, and consciousness are constructs that violate parsimony (Occam's razor) and, exactly like god, are unnecessary assumptions.

Experience, perception, and consciousness are not the outcomes of the brain's structure or functioning. They are merely self-referential language elements that have no place in proper science. In reality, there is only the brain, nothing else.

ES: Dismissing experiences as self-referential language does not mean they do not exist. "Only the brain" has quantum degrees of freedom in post synaptic activation and therefore local reference is wrong.

Experience of seeing color cannot be dismissed as self-referential language because it is a result of 3 receptors so to speak, and any symmetry in such a perception whether biological or artificial is a problem for a one-to-one determination of physical states and psych states as language or as not. If color was simply a result of a self-referential language, then why is there a degree of freedom between language labels and physical states (refer to my construction with robots R1, R2)? It does not make any sense.

The construction: Two A.I. robots R1, R2 with color receptors 1,2,3, are built instead of with the biological eye receptors Red, Green, and Blue. Unlike the asymmetry between Red and Blue that appears darker than red due to less receptors in our biological eye, we design 1, 3 to have the same response signal. Robot R1 accepts that color experience is undeniable, whether we call it illusion or figment of language or any other term and describes at least two possible but distinguishable experiences of robot R2. Either R2 experiences colors 1,2,3 just as R1 or R2 experiences them as R1 experiences 3,2,1. These two distinguishable descriptions, from R1's point of view, do not contradict the ontological color response signal. They break the one-to-one map between the ontological brain states and experience and therefore render the claim that experience is generated by the brain an untrue statement.

SV: "Color" is the name we give to a physical state. We should not confuse the name with the physical state.

"Experience of color" is the name we give to the process of naming the aforementioned physical state. We should not confuse or conflate epistemology with ontology.

ES: How do you know that color seeing is only a physical state? What is the proof? The problem is the dismissal of epistemology as a language artifact. In fact, all sciences are self-referential at the foundational level [1].

SV: Science is a language, I fully concur. Science is 100% epistemology.

ES: Also, consider the Gauge principle. If physical measurement can result from different underlying field states, then such states exist. The word result actually means correlation. Gauge fields are ghost fields. Consciousness is a gauge field so-to-speak.

SV: Again: fields are not "real". They are organizing principles. They make sense of observations (they are hermeneutic). And they are language elements. They are one way of looking at the world.

No one has the slightest idea what consciousness is, so, no one can say that the metaphor of "field" fits it best.

We can perfectly account for reality without "consciousness", so, exactly like "god", it is unnecessary and violates Occam's razor (parsimony).

We should not confuse observation with consciousness, of course. Nor is the act of observing dependent on a sentient or conscious observer. The interpretation of observations does depend on the existence of such an observer, though. But interpretation is again a mere exercise in language.

ES: All Gauge fields violate **Occam's** razor and indeed they are objects of a language.

The gauge principle is that if such a field can "exist" due to Lagrangian symmetry then it does "exist" although by the principle of parsimony, the Gauge field should be minimal.

If symmetry in a mathematical model allows for a gauge field to "exist" without contradicting the results of known measurements, then it does exist. The gauge principle has very far repercussions regarding chronon models which are apparently contrary to the principle of parsimony. For example, non-local summation of probability of an event to 1 can only be done on a deterministic geometric reference object, however, such a reference object can be understood as a mathematical construction rather than a physical object because physical measurement can only access chronon events.

By the Gauge principle, if such a geometric reference object can exist, then it does exist. Notice that this principle immediately rules out Causal Sets even without considering the problem of non-local summation to 1.

Another example is Whitney's theorem. Every manifold can be embedded in 2n dimensional Euclidean space and in a higher dimensional Euclidean space if the metric is needed to be preserved. The latter choice of embedding has an obvious advantage that it preserves the metric.

By the Gauge principle, such an embedding object is real and the balance with the principle of parsimony dictates that a minimal embedding, connected and continuous set must be chosen.

The gauge principle is indeed totally contrary to the principle of parsimony. The justification for the principle of parsimony is the avoidance of overfitting. A model too complex loses its prediction capability, however, symmetry within a model and the existence of Gauge fields need not reduce its predictive power and in some cases, such Gauge fields have a clear measurable outcome and are therefore dictated by empirical measurement results.

Scientific models are best when they balance between overfitting and over-generalization and thus underfitting and failing to predict the outcome of an experiment. Asking existential questions is not within the scope of such predictive models in general, unless the answer does have implications that can be measured.

By your worldview, there is no need for an entity beyond the brain that uses the probabilistic quantum degrees of freedom in the brain to influence decisions, to feel pain and pleasure and to experience colors, due to the principle of parsimony, however, by the Gauge principle, if such an entity can exist without contradicting physical measurements then it does exist and if it does exist then we are not just biochemical machines but we also have true free will at least in some decisions we make.

The Gauge principle requires symmetry to exist within a language description of a physical object.

With the current technology, e.g. Transformer Neural Networks and physical implementations, it is possible to build such an object and show a degree of freedom in its color perception.

SV: What I am saying is that "feeling", "pain", "pleasure", "color" etc. have no ontological status.

These are all mere epistemic elements – or even mere figments of language. They are not real.

So, there is no need – or possibility - to account for them in any way: not within a theory of the brain as an exclusive entity (materialism) and not with the introduction of any other entity.

Like "god", for example - pain, pleasure, colors, etc., are not legitimate objects of scientific discourse (though, of course, they do have a limited place in metaphysics).

Moreover:

Not everything that can exist does exist.

The existence of statements and theorems and theories ("gauge fields") is not the same as the existence of apples and space shuttles. It is not the same kind of existence:

https://samvak.tripod.com/bestowed.html

There is no way in principle to prove some statements, such as "god exists" "god does not exist", "subjects perceive color", and "subjects do not perceive color". These statements can never acquire a truth value. They are empty null sets, so to speak.

ES: 1) You say: "These are all mere epistemic elements – or even mere figments of language. They are not real".

They are very real to each one of us. Don't you feel pain? Don't you enjoy good music?

Denying your own experiences as figments of language does not make them go away.

If mathematical language cannot account for these experiences and therefore dismisses "experience" altogether, it only tells us that mathematics and scientism are limited to describe the common knowledge we call "the physical world" and on which we all agree. The "internal" world of yours which is your experiences is inaccessible to me even if your brain would be wired to mine. I would be able to get the same input but would not know what experience they correlate with, for you.

You write: "Like "god", for example - pain, pleasure, colors, etc., are not legitimate objects of scientific discourse (though, of course, they do have a limited place in metaphysics)"

Metaphysics does not equal leprosy.

The idea of probability is metaphysical and for Quantum probability to be a valid description of Nature, reference objects, which are not probabilistic, must exist at least locally and at least in relation to themselves, whatever that means.

In addition to that, if the best probabilistic description of Nature is also not local, e.g. requires summation of probability to 1 on a geometric reference object with non-zero volume of any degree or on an unbound graph, then this geometric reference object is deterministic and then the argument is if that object has a real existence or not. By the Gauge principle it does.

2) "Not everything that can exist does exist." - True.

The Gauge principle demands that a "Gauge Field" will be a symmetry that allows an unknown state to be correlated with physical measurements without contradictions. Our decisions, for example, can be attributed to an entity which decides on probabilities of postsynaptic activations as long as such intervention does not violate what we know about the physical world. Then the existence of such an entity is not dictated by Occam's Razor but by the Gauge principle.

From a physicist point of view, a universal entity can decide about results of experiments as long as its intervention does not violate what we know about the outcome of experiments. If such a universal entity can exist, then it does exist.

Spinor components are a bad example of physical gauge fields because spin 3/2 does have consistency problems with observation and the generalized Dirac equation does not limit in any way the representations of SU(2). Dirac's theory is therefore invalid.

Spin 2 has coupling problems even in Supergravity, although some are resolved: https://inspirehep.net/literature/8626

"Supergravity models generically result in an unrealistically large cosmological constant in four dimensions and that constant is difficult to remove, and so requires fine-tuning. This is still a problem today.

Quantization of the theory led to quantum field theory gauge anomalies rendering the theory inconsistent".

These are bad examples of physical Gauge fields that mainstream physics happily publishes tens of thousands of papers about, although there are charlatans that say that "there is no mainstream physics but charlatans", which in this case is indeed self-referential. Such a response was unfortunately posted in the comments to a YouTube video.

SV: Before I respond, I must understand why you keep insisting that "If such a universal entity can exist then it does exist." Contingency is never ontology even in metaphysics.

Lovejoy's 1936 principle of plenitude is Platonic and, later, Kantian. Leibnitz was its greatest proponent. It is known today as the principle of explanatory sufficiency.

It was Dirac who reintroduced the principle of plenitude into physics with his "magnetic monopoles".

But even the principle of plenitude applies only to probable entities WITHIN the universe (or Everett's multiverse). It has never been applied to an OBSERVER because nothing is OUTSIDE the universe. It usually applies to redundant or possible entities which are not actually used in the final output (example: degrees of freedom in gauge theories).

Observations (measurements) are the only way we know how to collapse the wave function.

Maybe I am missing something in your argument?

ES: Lovejoy's 1936 principle of plenitude resembles the Gauge principle.

The difference is the relation to measurement.

You ask: "I must understand why you keep insisting that "If such a universal entity can exist then it does exist.""

The reason is the correctness of probability and non-locality as a predictive description of Nature.

The reference to such probability must be deterministic and must exist at the same time.

The Gauss Bell lives in deterministic coordinates.

Since there is no deterministic measurement within the measurable universe, the conclusion is that such a reference object is not part of the observable universe.

We are not universal observers, but we cannot be local either due to QM. If we can be reference objects to measurement results, then we cannot only be brains because the brain is not deterministic and the argument that a reference to measurements in this commonly shared measurable world must be deterministic can only mean we are not only the brain.

There is still a problem of implication. One can argue that such a deterministic reference is nothing more than an average of probabilistic observables, although, averaging requires a reference object too and therefore such a claim has a consistency problem, unless the reference object can only be viewed as a mathematical construction.

As was mentioned in the AI robots R1, R2 experiment, the possibility of creating a robot with input symmetries, shows that observation is consistent with a none-one-to-one map between physical inputs and experiences if they do exist. So, if experience exists, it is beyond the observable Nature, but experience must exist as an observation of a reference object which is not the brain due to the previous arguments and by breaking a one-to-one map, it cannot be a result of the accessible observables, including the physical brain.

Not always Gauge fields are a blessing. There was a big expectation from Einstein that the Palatini action, which is identical to Einstein-Hilbert action, would be a great insight especially since spinor equations require tetrads because they are limited to an orthogonal reference frame.

However, it took a different approach, to leave the metric tensor as is and instead of using tetrads or Ashtekar variables, to consider the metric as of a reference manifold, like coordinates but as an entire geometric reference object, not as a physically accessible object. After adopting such a new approach, tetrads can indeed make a comeback.

Then in this framework, the idea was that time must be the engine of the model and that acceleration of that time in the sense of a generalized Reeb field (not limited to contact manifolds) will describe the possibility of non-geodesic curves and will predict the electric force. In (64) it became the electro-weak-strong action using indeed 5 fields, but unlike tetrads, time is a meaningful Geroch function while the other fields are Gauge fields. There is a redundancy in the system because this time can be accounted for by 3 vectors just as Ashtekar variables.

This redundancy is cancelled out in action (64) without using any ADM formalism or Ashtekar variables, and orthogonality is no longer needed, which renders the spin connections redundant. 4 out of the 5 scalar fields describe additional geometric information to the metric as foliations.

The same theory can be written with tetrads and generalized Reeb vectors of these tetrad fields but the Einstein-Hilbert action will be the same. On the other hand, action (64) in this case, does add geometric information as non-geodesic alignment of curves and thus of forces.

It is a far simpler approach than that of Abhay Ashtekar and it yields new results. Adding a summation constraint to the action of (64), e.g. that each chronon probability sums to 1, keeps the same action but then PP* is replaced by an event function and the integration of PP* becomes 1. That requires the only constant in the theory except for the speed of light to be with the units of 1/Length^2.

SV: I think the core difference between us is that I consider the claim that there is or could be anything outside the Universe or outside reality to be nonsensical.

Consequently, I would also argue with the way that you perceive the relationship between probability and determinism, for example.

We first must resolve this difference between our worldviews:

https://www.youtube.com/watch?v=flyEV60272o

https://www.youtube.com/watch?v=mAbVK0KbTMo

https://www.youtube.com/watch?v=ys6ln7I9XAo

ES: More precisely speaking, deterministic reference objects are not beyond the universe but beyond the directly measurable universe.

Sharon Shimon Vaknin and I concur that it does not make a difference for the subject if this experience is termed "illusion" or "unreal".

The creation of a symmetry in the commonly shared experience we call hardware, allows for more than one distinguishable experience from the observer side. Robot R1 describes at least one different experience from one's own while using oneself as a reference to doubt the possible distinguishable experiences of robot R2 and without any contradiction with the publicly shared/owned experience, which is neural activations as part of the physical world.

Sharon's view is that we do live in one universe but that the foundation of "ontology" is epistemological. In other words, consciousness is all there is. This idea settles the duality of matter and psych as both two manifestations of consciousness, one publicly owned and one privately owned - as was well described by Yeshayahu Leibowitz.

It also means that a "soul" is part of this one system although it does not have to be a derivative of the brain, which itself is a commonly shared experience, once we show an experience symmetry that does not violate distinguishable states within the commonly owned experience which is the "ontologic" hardware.

Such a symmetry means there is no one-to-one map between ontological states and psychic states and therefore the psych inevitably has its own existence within Sharon's view that there is nothing else but consciousness. With all the difficulty of defining consciousness, it has the characteristic of experience, including intentionality to experience pleasure and avoid pain.

Professor Yeshayahu Leibowitz:

https://www.vanleer.org.il/en/publication/mind-and-brain/

SV: My alarm at the conflation of physics and mysticism:
https://goodmenproject.com/featured-content/physics-metaphysics-mysticism-sam-vaknin-sjbn/

You may find this of interest, too:

https://www.narcissistic-abuse.com/psychophysics.html

ES: "There are physicists and mathematicians (like Penrose) who consider consciousness to be the "missing piece" – but not as dimension, more like another force that renders probabilistic nature deterministic."

Why not see non-local probabilistic models as a duality of a deterministic reference object and as events which are measurable on this deterministic object?

The axiomatic system of probability in mathematics is not equivalent to the meaning of probability in physics. In mathematics it is a measure theory, and it involves Lebesgue integration, sigma-algebras and events. In physics, it is a metaphysical model in which measurement events are described by the theory of probability.

The Laws of Nature are then a statistical recommendation which allows Roger Penrose's missing piece, however, why not to say that the missing piece is all that exists? Nature is not accessible not through the subject's experiences as Sharon Shimon correctly observed. That is why Shimon Sharon is correct.

Your description of the psychic linguistic energy conversions in the brain misses the probabilistic degrees of freedom in the brain. Such degrees of freedom do allow an entity external to the brain to be at work and by Shimon Sharon's method, this entity is the subject and is the only true existence.

The brain itself with all of its activities is a coherent commonly shared experience with privately shared minds. Again, you can see that my construction with colors 1,2,3 and deliberate hardware response symmetry between 1 and 3, poses a challenge to the causality between "the brain" as an object and the subject's internal world providing that you do accept that experience is the building block of consciousness.

I do not think experience can be ignored by dismissing it as an unreal figment of language.

The subjective experience is very real to every single person in the world.

The best way that the psychophysical problem has been presented IMHO is an early paper by Yeshayahu Leibowitz.

SV: I am a physicist. I have no need for "god" or "consciousness" or "experience".

"God" and "consciousness" are superfluous, ill-defined, and consequently non-sensical. In the best case, they are undecidable theorems. But they do not deserve to even be dignified this way.

I don't do mysticism. I regard it as a primitive stage that humanity has long transcended.

Metaphysics is another thing. It has its place and it should guide good science.

But "god" or "consciousness" have nothing to do with metaphysics. These are mystical propositions: language masquerading as reality.

Even by the standard of language, "god" and "consciousness" are deficient because they defy definition, lexical or other.

Discussing "god" and "consciousness" is a total waste of time.

Even if "consciousness" were a real thing, I cannot see why it would have a privileged position among other natural epiphenomena (emergent phenomena).

"God" I cannot discuss at all. It is out of the realm of any form of meaningful discourse that I am aware of or can conceive of. No language can apply to it. So, outside the realm of communication, "god" is unmitigated non-sense.

Finally, I know of no better way than the scientific method to approximate the "truth" however asymptotically.

Both "consciousness" and "god" are not amenable to the scientific method. More generally, language lends itself to scientific investigation but should not be conflated or confused with it. You cannot falsify language, for example.

Anything that is outside the remit of science is mere language. Of course, science itself is language - but it is never MERE language. It is checked by reality.

I am not interested in the study of mere language because it is self-referential. Real communication involves EXITING language to the real world (Wittgenstein).

ES: 1) Can you show that there is no quantum leeway in the brain that allows decisions to be made not by the brain?

2) Can you show that there is no quantum leeway in the universe that allows decisions to be made by a universal observer?

3) Your claims that such objects are not amenable can be empirically proven wrong by experiments, for example 50/50 events become 90/10 under questioning.

Here is a constructed AI robotic color symmetry that breaks the one-to-one map between physical and psychic states when experience is not labeled as "illusion" or "unreal" figment of language.

Psychophysical color experience theorem

The spectrum of colors as we experience it is correlated with RGB Red Green Blue with less cone receptors for blue and more for red cones and therefore blue appears to us as darker. This ontological property also introduces an asymmetry between the perception of red and blue in the epistemological sense.

Let us now study a claim of a colleague, Dr. Sam Vaknin that the psych, including the experience of seeing colors, is a physical process and that experience is nothing more than an artefact of a self- referential language.

His claim is that there is no need for any other terminology and by the principle of parsimony i.e. Occam's Razor, there is no reason to assume the existence of the psych other than the result of self-referential language. Let us also consider that in the most basic level, scientism is self- referential [1] and therefore dismissing experience as an artefact of a self-referential incoherence is not a valid argument.

Also, let us consider that dismissing experience as wrong mixture between ontology - which is the physical states accessible to measurement - and experience - which is epistemological although correlated with physical states – is at the very least questionable.

It will be shown that such an assumption that experience as language label of a hidden state is correlated with the physical states leads to a problem by construction. The conclusion is that experience as a language label of a hidden state, does not have to be correlated with physical states.

Trying to dismiss this assumption as a valid option due to a one-to-one correlation between the physical states of the brain and seeing color as an epistemological experience and therefore rendering the epistemological experience redundant is therefore wrong because the redundancy does not exist without a one-to-one correspondence between ontology and epistemology.

Claim, If the physical ontological process involved in color perception can be symmetrical, as a result of 3 artificial receptors response, and a cognitive machine which perceives the colors ontologically through physical processes can be said to be conscious as a hidden state, then the experience of seeing color, also as a hidden state, is not a result of any physical mechanism.

Notice that we identify experience with a property of consciousness both as hidden epistemological states and that we assumed that a cognitive machine which perceives colors can be conscious as epistemological hidden states, i.e. not accessible to measurement.

Proof

If the experience of seeing color is indeed a result of the structure of the brain, then an artificial robotic brain which is equipped with ontological vision and epistemological color experience can be constructed.

Unlike human vision, which is dictated by biochemical reactions, let us construct a color vision which is based on 3 color receptors as in the case of RGB but with 3 other different wavelengths $Color1 = Perception(R1, a1)$, $Color2 = Perception(R1, a2)$, $Color3 = Perception(R1, a3)$ with wavelengths $a1 > a2 > a3$ and $a1-a2 = a2-a3$ or $a1*a3 = a2*a2$ and such that the number of receptors of each color is the same, unlike in the biological brain.

This robot will therefore not perceive colors as we do and does not have to see the same number of different colors as we do. Now given that two such robots $R1$, $R2$ are conscious and have functionally identical color perception system, robot $R1$ wants to know if the epistemological color perception of robot $R2$ is as it perceives colors is like it does, Perception A: $Color1 = Perception(R1, a1)$, $Color2 = Perception(R1, a2)$, $Color3 = Perception(R1, a3)$ or Perception B: $Color1 = Perception(R1, a3)$, $Color2 = Perception(R1, a2)$, $Color3 = Perception(R1, a1)$ and thus $R1$ raises two possibilities of epistemological color experience in relation to its own epistemological perception despite the same ontological functionality of the artificial neural wiring.

Robot R1 will inevitably reach the conclusion that due to ontological color wavelength proximities and due to the ontological receptors response symmetry, which is artificially imposed, each one of the two epistemological perceptions is possible without contradictions to the correlation with the ontological signal.

But we have assumed by Sam's parsimony conjecture that color experience is a result language so how can language alone lead to two cognitively meaningful different epistemological states? If that was the case, R1 would not be able to assume at least two possibilities about the epistemological perception of R2 and there would be a one-to-one correspondence between the ontological physical machine and the epistemological experience. We reached a contradiction!

Where could problems arise? The assumptions of the theorem are

1) that an artificial ontological symmetric color response can be built. This question is purely technological but is not limited by asymmetries that exist in biological systems.
2) The second assumption was that robots can be epistemologically conscious.
3) The third assumption was that consciousness is a direct result of language alone. If this assumption is correct then since language is itself a result of the ontological neural wiring, there should not be two possible epistemological states correlated with the same ontological state.

As for now, any one of these 3 assumptions may not hold. Either no artificial symmetric color response system can be built, or robots cannot be epistemologically conscious, or epistemological consciousness does exist but is not a result of the machine alone.

The refutation of the first assumption is the hardest to achieve because the concentration of receptors can be controlled in the production process. In fact, as a good example, current cameras have twice the concentration of green receptors than red ones. These commercial cameras are adjusted to produce pictures that will look real to the human eyes.

References:

1. Dissertation: Dr. Rik Peels, VU University Amsterdam (the Netherlands) "SCIENTISM AND THE ARGUMENT FROM SELF-REFERENTIAL INCOHERENCE"

Shimon: In principle, despite the evident difficulties related to language, I reject the negation of the concepts of "experience" and "consciousness".

I find the denial of subjectivity and the arguments for reality or the universe which substantially transcend the limitations of knowledge unacceptable. These limitations are subjective and self-contained, a kind of bubble or solipsistic monad, enclosed and opaque to the subject (witness, observer, etc.)

Only the individual in his world, exercising rigorous and honest critical thinking, could gauge the limits of the derived and ultimate horizon of his awareness of reality. In fact, this awareness is reflexive, preoccupied with rendering a thorough account of its own boundaries and limitations.

You adhere to Occam's razor or parsimony as a minimal logical and epistemological threshold when it comes to the controlled deployment of language in its relation to reality. If I understood correctly, you are warning against an incautious and uncontrolled use of language as a practice with diminishing returns. In principle, I agree with this concern of yours.

But precisely because of this and due to your argument that these words when considered as stand-ins for actual ontological entities constitute "language masquerading as reality" (a naïve metaphysical concept akin to naïve realism), I reject concepts such as "energy", "spacetime", and "dimensions", except when we make use of them as mere theoretical constructs in the context of scientific thought and research. I call this "applied or critical metaphysics", as distinct from the classical or naïve variety.

But my argument is that Occam's razor is the default in logical thinking and should not constrain the derivation of every ontological or metaphysical necessity. It is a mere functional principle that serves the aesthetic and utilitarian conveniences of cognition.

You keep insisting that "reality" is sufficient, but then you add "physical" to it. Why is that? Uncompromising and consistent adherence to Occam's razor requires that we omit this descriptive of reality as well! How, therefore, should I understand "physicality": in the context of science? What is the meaning of "physicality" outside of physics?

I am well aware of your view that physical inquiry is not objective and does not deal either with reality or with the knowledge of reality. Physics therefore is not the equivalent of metaphysics and not the same as ontology. Physical inquiry is not the same as metaphysical inquiry.

Allow me to humbly propose this definition of "consciousness": the manifestation of reality's capacity to introspect, with itself as its own subject and to be aware of its existence.

The conceptual perception of the Universe as absolute in the sense that it constitutes the totality of the space of existence, an ontological axiom, is a metaphysical stance similar to Spinoza's philosophy which regarded reality as a totality (an infinite object) or an absolutely whole immanent unity.

My point of view is that the only universe in existence is the one given within the entirety of my subjective, self-explanatory, unambiguous consciousness. This universe is the space of all existence, though not absolutely, more as a default of the preference for a trivial certainty over the doubtful in principle. This implies the possible existence of a reality which is inaccessible to my knowledge. I call this approach "critical-reflexive solipsism".

We cannot deny the fact that we are imprisoned in a "solipsistic bubble" of sorts and that as far as each and every one of us, every "I", there is no other reality (except as a metaphysical speculation). Although our very capacity to conceive of a transcendental reality accessible to our minds is telling.

"The psychic reality of Man is the only thing that he recognizes with any certainty" (Y. Leibowitz). There is only the individual sphere of consciousness and only private languages. In my view, this is not a metaphysical statement, but an admission of the only reality we know of.

SV: Thank you both for your insights. I would like to respond further to some of the points made by my brother, Shimon.

I have always claimed that we have access only to one mind – our own. This is the intersubjectivity problem in the philosophy of mind. This is why we are forced to speculate about the states of mind of others (theory of mind, mentalization). There is no way to be sure that others – man or machine or animal or rock from outer space – have a mind at all.

I also insist that science is a self-referential language. Physics is not about "reality" or "truth". Theories in physics are about other theories in physics. Hence the pivotal role of mathematics – the most efficacious language ever.

Any reality that is inaccessible to our minds should be ignored. We cannot generate falsifiable hypotheses or meaningful statements and theorems with regards to such a "reality" beyond our ken. It is a nonsensical and wasteful pursuit. This is why I react dismissively and contemptuously to any attempt to discuss "god".

This is where parsimony comes in: it limits us to what we can accomplish by using the scientific method (aka the method of generating language). It is clear from your response that I failed to communicate my views clearly. Occam's razor or parsimony is a principle of language – not an ontological constraint. It is a rule on how to construct scientific theories which are the products of pure language!

This is why I kept disagreeing with Eytan whenever he attempted to make claims about reality by using his mind, thought experiments, or language.

But, after all, what is reality to my mind?

Reality is everything that exists whether accessible to our minds or not and whether amenable to being captured by language or not. This is not a metaphysical principle. It is a lexical definition and as such cannot be argued with.

I fully agree with both you: our minds and language itself limit our access to reality. We never have direct contact with the ontos – only with the epistemos.

But the fact that we are limited beings does not prove that there is no reality except the reality of our "consciousness". It doesn't even prove that our "consciousness" is real. It has nothing to do with reality or ontology. These are two parallel lines of thought that can never meet in principle.

Science is a faith-based activity. Axioms are its dogma. I am a believer and a practitioner. Occam's razor regulates my allowed and my prohibited communication (language). It is possible to communicate in science using other principles (plenitude or redundancy of degrees of freedom in gauge theories, for example or Newtonian vs. Hamiltonian vs. Lagrangian physics) – but these plenitude theories are always reducible to parsimonious theories without any loss of predictive or descriptive power. This is why I prefer to deploy parsimony to start with, even though I fully admit that it is an arbitrary and personal preference!!!

To summarize: my position is a hybrid of Heidegger's "thingness" and Lacan's "Real". I am not a Kantian by any means. I do not deny the role of our mind, nor do I deny the existence of language. But I reject the claim that the failures of language (the mind) and its limitations are somehow proof of some ontology or that there is no ontology except that of language (the mind).

ES: Quoting Shimon, "This universe is the space of all existence, though not absolutely, more as a default of the preference for a trivial certainty over the doubtful in principle. This implies the possible existence of a reality which is inaccessible to my knowledge. I call this approach "critical-reflexive solipsism" – it is indeed a parsimonious description of existence. It should be argued with SV that this claim renders color perception primordial, not an artifact of language to get rid of. The conclusion is that any symmetry in the commonly shared color processing, although a robotic-construction, cannot be ignored and that the rebuttal of a one-to-one map between psychic and physical states, does refute that the psych is a result of the brain. Due to Shimon's claim, the Psych's existence is inevitable. My view is that the ability to consider more than one option for psychic experience, which is correlated but not identical to hardware states, is in itself an indication that "experience" and "mind" cannot be a result of language limits and language failure and therefore cannot be cut out by the Occam's razor.

A second subject, in a more mathematical language bound description, is the probabilistic view of the shared experience we call ontology, as requiring a dual deterministic reference space to exist. As such, this dual space is not the observable Nature, although its existence is inferred from the probabilistic interpretation of the commonly shared experience, we call the physical world. It is a different route to show us that there is more than the shared experience we call the physical world, and such a space is still a parsimonious description of existence, as a whole, because the description of reality is inconsistent without the existence of a reference deterministic space, on which probabilities of observables non-locally sum to 1. In that aspect I totally agree with Sir Roger Penrose.

The principle of parsimony cannot be used to remove components of a descriptive language of reality if such a removal renders any possible description inconsistent. It is argued that by Shimon's claim, removal of the psych from the description is invalid and therefore the removal of any hardware symmetry as allowing more than one psychic state without contradiction, is also invalid.

Shimon: The theories within science thought up, created, developed, and crystallized by Man I regard as epistemological models, mere applied metaphysical systems in as far as they are embedded in this or that conceptual framework.

Any discussion of reality should be the domain of philosophy, not of science.

I do not claim that there is no reality outside of consciousness. I adopt a critical-solipsistic point of view as a default position since I can only judge by the extant evidence. There is only one reality that is knowable in principle and it is wholly subjective. I do not possess the capacity nor am I permitted to refute its postulated possible existence.

But, pay heed: it is impossible to refute the existence of a transcendental reality (non-subjective, independently existent). As a primary reflexive – in other words: a conscious – witness, any metaphysical claim or argument regarding the "objective" substantiality of this kind of reality is not falsifiable and, therefore, not scientific. It is a mere nonsensical speculation, intuition, or belief.

ES: This is not claimed, what is claimed is that probabilistic non-local models of Nature are dual. They are observables with probabilities that sum to 1 on either a sub-set of a reference object or on an entire reference object. Such a reference object is not directly accessible to measurement. This description of the world, we commonly experience, is the only consistent description of non-local Quantum Theories. It is a functional description that already shows that there is a problem with our current understanding of the observable universe as all that there is.

Regardless of any functional physical model, the very existence of ourselves is mystical. Questions of why, may never have an answer within the scope of physics, which is functional to achieve new technologies.

Eytan Suchard https://www.linkedin.com/in/eytan-suchard-4b447633/

Shimon Vaknin https://www.youtube.com/@MetaSphere1116

Sam Vaknin http://www.narcissistic-abuse.com/culture.html

Return

Psychology of Modern Warfare

Scott Douglas Jacobsen: Welcome back, Dr. Vaknin! I returned from Ukrainian territories visiting several cities in rapid succession over two weeks in late November and early December. I have war on the mind. Which makes me think about the mind in war, what is the nature of war?

Dr. Sam Vaknin:

Welcome back in one piece!

War brings out the best in us and the worst in us.

Throughout the ages, war has been perceived as the epitome and quintessence of masculinity (even when women, like the Amazons, had been doing the soldiering): valor, heroism, courage (overcoming fear), selflessness, altruism, self-sacrifice for the greater good, and protectiveness over the weak and the meek.

But violent conflict leads to negative identity formation: defining oneself in opposition to the Other by dehumanizing, objectifying, and demonizing the enemy.

Most wars are cast as morality plays (good vs, evil). They amount to role playing in an adversarial rule-based game (as revealed when veterans on both sides meet after the war is over, acting all chummy and convivial).

Winning a war validates the triumphant party: it is proof of a divine blessing and of having been chosen (akin to the Protestant work ethic which regards success in business as proof positive of God's favor). The Nazi SS had Gott mit uns carved on their daggers and belt buckles!

Finally, war mediates the tension between individual and collective via the concept of self-sacrifice (special ops are the middle ground).

Jacobsen: What happens to human psychology around war at a distance?

Vaknin: On the one hand, there is the pornography of extreme, gory battle. War is thus perceived as the ultimate reality TV, a video game come alive, or a horror film incarnate. There is vicarious gratification in witnessing all this safely, from the comfort of one's living room, having been spared the atrocities. A smug sensation of accomplishment, of having gotten away with it.

Distant wars also legitimize aggressive and entitled virtue signaling and competitive morality, a noxious self-aggrandizing and ostentatious form of self-imputed altruism.

There are, of course, those who empathize with the dying and the wounded and the suffering and do their best to help without seeking the attendant accolades of the professional do-gooder.

Jacobsen: What happens to human psychology in war up close?

Vaknin: From personal experience, it is a grind. There is no clear end or horizon to it all. It feels like it could last forever.

PTSD is very common and so is a mounting and all-consuming paranoia, a sense of extreme isolation and ubiquitous threat. It is as if war is a giant gaslighting experience where the very fabric of reality is torn asunder.

In many wars, there is little movement or accomplishments. The scene is frozen, surreal. Gruesome death and mutilation are constant companions.

There is an acute fear of abandonment, of getting lost and an extreme dependency on others, an external locus of control.

War regresses its participants to infancy. Primitive psychological defense mechanisms take over: splitting, alloplastic defenses, defiance, acting out/crazymaking, moral collapse, magical or superstitious thinking.

Jacobsen: What separates the psychology of a bystander in war versus a combatant in war?

Vaknin: Civilians in war are instantly and all-pervasively traumatized: they react with a form of trauma bonding or Stockholm Syndrome. They perceive soldiers – even soldiers on their side! – as looming, inexorable hotheaded, trigger-happy, demented, and reckless threats who are hellbent on endangering all and sundry. It is as if they are caught in the crossfire between two rival criminal gangs. They are wary of both parties of combatants and this radical loss of the ability to trust and to feel safe (no "secure base") yields terror, emotional dysregulation, and self-destructive acting out in some – or a freeze response in others.

Jacobsen: When it comes to politics and its psychology before, during, and after war, what characterizes the minds of the political class citizen - from high to low status - in each of these phases of war?

Vaknin: All politicians regard war as a legitimate and integral part of the toolbox of human affairs – and justly so: it is. Hostilities are always in the background of diplomacy. Violent conflict is ineluctable, inexorable, and periodic. In many cases, warfare is considered a superior form of geopolitical signaling and the only efficacious way to securing goals. Politicians are, therefore, fatalists: they are resigned to war, inured to it, comprehend it as a force of nature and the reification of "being human".

Jacobsen: When it comes to politics and its psychology before, during, and after war, what characterizes the minds of the non-political class citizen - from high to low status - in each of these phases of war?

Vaknin: Vociferous protestations aside, people love a good war: it is a prime variant of dramatic entertainment, a kind of exalted sport. They exult in it. This state of mind comprises extreme anxiety and fear, of course. Every experience is rendered sharper, more crisp, and memorable. In clinical terms, war is a psychotic fantasy, a mass psychegenic illness of sorts.

Jacobsen: What factors of human psychology increase the odds of war and decrease the odds of war?

Vaknin: Nothing decreases the odds of war. It is a myth that economic prosperity and democracy are bulwarks against the eruption of violent conflict. Conversely, literally everything in human psychology predisposes us to aggression. Even empathy makes us choose sides and aggress against the abuser on behalf of the victim-du-jour. War is, therefore, the natural state of the human mind: it caters to numerous deepset psychological needs. It cleanses, establishes a new equilibrium, and catalyses the replacement of the old with the new, for better or for worse.

Jacobsen: What are the positives and negatives of war in the advancement of human civilization?

Vaknin: War is a cultural-social activity that facilitates intimacy, bonding and cooperation, technological innovation, and the emergence of a cathartic new social or political order each and every time. It is a rite of passage, a redemptive ritual, an engine of progress, and a demarcator of eras.

Jacobsen: What happens to the mass psychology of a citizenry - of a society - of the original provoking power, the aggressor, and the defender, in the long term from war, after war?

Vaknin: Humans who are exposed to repeated violence – in wars, in prison, even in hospitals – grow insensitive to it. They dehumanize and brutalize both the Other and themselves. They are suspended in a post-traumatic state, replete with infantile psychological defenses, dissociation, cognitive distortions (such as grandiosity), and emotional numbing.

Jacobsen: Given the above, what can be the coda - the summative principles - of human psychology at war to comprehend individuals and humanity vis-a-vis war?

Vaknin: Like climate change, War is a human phenomenon. Rather than confront it self-delusionally, we better accept it and adapt to it. It is not going away, no matter what we do. So, why waste our scarce resources on its elimination?

Jacobsen: Thank you for the opportunity and your time, Sam.

Vaknin: Thank you for enduring me yet again. You are a brave man, indeed.

Return

The Future of Innovation

Scott Douglas Jacobsen: Today's topic: the next era of invention; what is the next era of invention? The previous eras relied upon unusually bright, innovative, and persistent, persons, solo: Legitimate geniuses. We have moved more into a world of invention emphasizing teamwork and dollars alongside *some* coordination with narrow artificial intelligence or specified algorithms, programs.

Prof. Sam Vaknin: Mankind have always alternated between teamwork and the individual genius. I think that we should focus on the raw materials (inputs) and the outputs of innovation rather than on who and how we bring it about.

We are transitioning from the age of monetized attention to the age of reality engineering.

Cities amounted to the first make-belief, virtual reality. Urbanization and population growth led to the rise of the creative genius (auteur), and the emergence of the concept of the original (due to the need to be seen and noticed in the multitude).

Intellectual property followed 300 years ago when mechanical reproduction blurred the line between original and copy and dramatically reduced the marginal cost of copies.

The Work of Art in the Age of Mechanical Reproduction" (1935), by Walter Benjamin, is an essay of cultural criticism which proposes and explains that mechanical reproduction devalues the aura (uniqueness) of an objet d'art.

Since then, identity has become a big business: patents, copyrights, brands, and blockchain NFTs. Distributed ledgers as well as centralised records vouch for one's identity and guarantee it.

The nonrivalrous zero marginal cost of digital goods has shifted the focus from manufacturing of tangibles to the manipulation of abstract symbols, the commodification of attention, and the emerging conundrum of discoverability.

Both individual creators and commercial enterprises reacted by interpellating potential consumers via propaganda and targeted advertising and by turning a profit via the aggregation of big data (targeting the demographics of attention).

These trends engendered self-sufficient disintermediated atomization - attention has been diverted to asocial online pursuits - and yielded an impaired reality testing (fantasy paracosms, virtual and augmented reality, and, soon, the metaverse).

The next frontiers are reality-like (pseudoreal) "real estate" and commodified but idiosyncratic menu-driven reality (the aforementioned metaverse).

Collaborative virtual realities will supplant physical ones and reality substitutes (sex dolls, intimacy apps) will proliferate. Tech behemoths, such as Facebook, Google, Apple, and Amazon will try to control the way we perceive reality and the immersive universes that we inhabit.

IRL AI will displace people as friends, advisors, interlocutors, lovers, and service providers. Users will construct online simulations and inhabit them. But this turn of events will also force the introduction of mandatory digital identities, hopefully based on blockchain rather than government regulation.

Jacobsen: What marks something as genuinely inventive rather than simply an update to some technology?

Vaknin: Truly innovative inventions profoundly change the way we live, communicate, work, make love, and interact. By this standard, neither the automobile nor the smartphone are veritable innovations: the former is a mere mechanized horse and the latter a derivative of the phone. But Bell's telephone and the telegraph are examples of paradigm-shifting, reality-altering inventions.

Jacobsen: More fundamentally, what is the basic principle of invention, its nature?

Vaknin: Most groundbreaking inventions generate their own markets, fostering needs in consumers that they were unaware of. They also recombine the familiar (e.g., previous technologies) in ways that produce alien, unprecedented, and strange products or services. Finally, true inventions become indispensable in short order: it is hard to imagine a life without them and we pity our predecessors for having been deprived of their existence.

Schumpeter seemed to have captured the unsettling nature of innovation: unpredictable, unknown, unruly, troublesome, and ominous. Innovation often changes the inner dynamics of organizations and their internal power structure. It poses new demands on scarce resources. It provokes resistance and unrest. If mismanaged - it can spell doom rather than boom.

Yet, the truth is that no one knows why people innovate. The process of innovation has never been studied thoroughly - nor are the effects of innovation fully understood.

Jacobsen: What do you see as the most significant biotechnology invention in the history of the biological world?

Vaknin: Possibly CRISPR, the revolutionary gene editing technology. Sometimes, advances in speed and quantity do constitute a quantum leap.

Jacobsen: What has been the most worldview-shattering invention in human history?

Vaknin: The harnessing of fire, the ability to reignite it at will.

Jacobsen: How does the psychology of an inventive person work?

Vaknin: The typical inventor is solutions-oriented. S/he perceives a lack, deficiency, or lacuna and sets out to remedy it. Inventors are also possessed of a synoptic-panoramic view, able to discern the connective tissue that binds apparently disparate phenomena. Finally, a true inventor is able to transition seamlessly from the theoretical to practical, from the drawing board to testing, and thence to prototype.

Creative people are feared and hated, ostracized and punished, unless they are willing to clown themselves or dumb down and conform to the biases, prejudices, and errors of the masses.

High IQ does not translate into success in the absence of perseverance, agreeableness, industriousness, stability (self-regulation), humility, a capacity for teamwork (minimal empathy and respect for others), robust mental health, a social support network, and luck. Many geniuses are homeless or incarcerated and all but forgotten.

The reality testing of inventors is impaired: they perceive the world differently (possibly a sign of autism). Coupled with recklessness, a sense of fearless godlike immunity, it leads to exploratory behavior.

Originality, novelty, difference: synoptic connectivity appears schizotypal or even psychotic (Schizotypy). Eysenck linked psychoticism to creativity. Indeed, the creative burst is often disorganized initially (inspiration, intuition, dreams). Attention multitasking generates unexpected insights and synergies.

Impatience, grandiosity or contempt and condescension charcaterize inventors: convinced of their superiority, they tend to block out "noise" and ignore criticism. Lability and dysregulation are sources of inspiration. Proclivity for change, thrill-seeking, and risky conduct result in innovation.

These are the reasons that most innovators endure inordinate hardships in life, their resilience and perseverance tested to the breaking point.

Jacobsen: With the advent of some software capable of mimicking human capacities more, and performing in superhuman capacities - at least on paper in computational power, how is this changing the interaction of human beings with software to invent in more precise and creative ways?

Vaknin: We tend to mythologize the process of invention, to render it mystical and uniquely human. The truth is that it is an emergent artefact (epiphenomenon), the ineluctable outcome of complexity. At this stage, we are feeding computer models with humungous reams of raw data in the hope that irreducible interactions between the umpteen pieces of information will yield innovative insights and discoveries. The next phase will involve fine-tuning the inputs so as to allow artificial intelligence to work on its own and to seek data as well as outputs autonomously. At that stage, we would still be able to define the research agenda, but not for long.

Jacobsen: In line with Alan Turing's views, who I agree with more than the 'moderns' in Western technology communities, *when* engineered computational systems match our "feeble powers," how will this change the world of invention?

Vaknin: We will be rendered obsolete. We would still maintain a parasitic, atomized, technologically self-sufficient kind of existence for a while, but then, like everything superfluous in Nature, we will wane and fade away. Hence my prediction of a Luddite counter-revolution which would seek to physically demolish or ban certain technologies, maybe justly so.

Jacobsen: How might the style of invention, or even the definition of invention itself, change with the precision and breadth future computation, and simulation, will bring to everything in our lives? Where, there might be the capacity of a constant roll of mini-invention increasingly in every facet of human life, similar to the infusion of - what we consider - ordinary technologies now.

Vaknin: The overwhelming vast majority of people are incapable of making use of the full set of features made available even by current technologies, let alone of innovating. I foresee "innovation engineers" whose job would be to cajole artificial intelligence codes and models into new discoveries. But innovation would become the domain of machines, not humans.

Jacobsen: How long until the technological world or the biological world make human beings, as an environmentally engineered (evolved) structure, neither entirely relevant to the business of the Earth nor the dominant conscious information processors on the planet?

Vaknin: I would be surprised if this would take longer than 50 years. With the exception of physical jobs like plumbing, AI would be perfectly capable of replacing and displacing us and doing a better job of it.

Jacobsen: Thank you for the opportunity and your time, and the happy final note, Sam.

Vaknin: You are welcome. Always delighted to spread doom!

Return

About the Author

Sam Vaknin (http://samvak.tripod.com) is the author of Malignant Self-Love: Narcissism Revisited and After the Rain - How the West Lost the East, as well as many other books and ebooks about topics in psychology, relationships, philosophy, economics, and international affairs.

He was the Editor-in-Chief of Global Politician and served as a columnist for Central Europe Review, PopMatters, eBookWeb , and Bellaonline, and as a United Press International (UPI) Senior Business Correspondent. He was the editor of mental health and Central East Europe categories in The Open Directory and Suite101.

Visit Sam's Web site at http://www.narcissistic-abuse.com

Work on Narcissism

Sam Vaknin is the author of Malignant Self Love: Narcissism Revisited, the pioneering work about narcissistic abuse, now in its 10th, DSM-V compatible revision

Sam Vaknin's work is quoted in well over 1000 scholarly publications and in over 3000 books (full list here). His Narcissists, Psychopaths, and Abuse YouTube channel and other channels garnered more than 35 million views and 155,000 subscribers.

His Web site "Malignant Self Love - Narcissism Revisited" was, for many years, an Open Directory Cool Site and is a Psych-UK recommended Site.

Sam Vaknin is a professor of psychology, but he is *not a mental health practitioner,* though he is certified in psychological counseling techniques by Brainbench.

Sam Vaknin served as the editor of Mental Health Disorders categories in the Open Directory Project and on Mentalhelp.net. He maintains his own Websites about Narcissistic Personality Disorder (NPD) and about relationships with abusive narcissists and psychopaths here and in HealthyPlace.

You can find his work on many other Web sites: Mental Health Matters, Mental Health Sanctuary, Mental Health Today, Kathi's Mental Health Review and others.

Sam Vaknin wrote a column for Bellaonline on Narcissism and Abusive Relationships and was a frequent contributor to Websites such as Self-growth.com and Bizymoms (as an expert on personality disorders).

Sam Vaknin served as the author of the Personality Disorders topic, Narcissistic Personality Disorder topic, the Verbal and Emotional Abuse topic, and the Spousal Abuse and Domestic Violence topic, all four on Suite101. He is the moderator of the Narcissistic Abuse Study List, the Toxic Relationships Study List, and other mailing lists with a total of c. 20,000 members. He also publishes a bi-weekly Abusive Relationships Newsletter.

THE AUTHOR

Shmuel (Sam) Vaknin

Curriculum Vitae

Born in 1961 in Qiryat-Yam, Israel

Served in the Israeli Defence Force (1979-1982) in training and education units

Full proficiency in Hebrew and in English

Education

1970 to 1978

Completed nine semesters in the Technion – Israel Institute of Technology, Haifa

1982 to 1983

Ph.D. in Physics and Philosophy (dissertation: "Time Asymmetry Revisited") – California Miramar University (formerly: Pacific Western University), California, USA

1982 to 1985

Graduate of numerous courses in Finance Theory and International Trading in the UK and USA.

Certified E-Commerce Concepts Analyst by Brainbench

Certified Financial Analyst by Brainbench

Certified in Psychological Counselling Techniques by Brainbench

Business Experience

1979 to 1983

Commentator in Yedioth Aharonot, Ma'ariv, and Bamakhane. Published sci-fi short fiction in Fantasy 2000.

Founder and co-owner of a chain of computerized information kiosks in Tel-Aviv, Israel.

1982 to 1985

Senior positions with the Nessim D. Gaon Group of Companies in Geneva, Paris and New-York (NOGA and APROFIM SA):

– Chief Analyst of Edible Commodities in the Group's Headquarters

– Manager of the Research and Analysis Division

– Manager of the Data Processing Division

– Project Manager of the Nigerian Computerized Census

– Vice President in charge of RND and Advanced Technologies

– Vice President in charge of Sovereign Debt Financing

1985 to 1986

Represented Canadian Venture Capital Funds in Israel

1986 to 1987

General Manager of IPE Ltd. in London. The firm financed international multi-lateral countertrade and leasing transactions.

1988 to 1990

Co-founder and Director of "Mikbats-Tesuah", a portfolio management firm based in Tel-Aviv.

Activities included large-scale portfolio management, underwriting, forex trading and general financial advisory services.

1990 to Present

Freelance consultant to many of Israel's Blue-Chip firms, mainly on issues related to the capital markets in Israel, Canada, the UK and the USA.

Consultant to foreign RND ventures and to Governments on macro-economic matters.

Freelance journalist in various media in the United States.

1990 to 1995

President of the Israel chapter of the Professors World Peace Academy (PWPA) and (briefly) Israel representative of the "Washington Times".

1993 to 1994

Co-owner and Director of many business enterprises:

– The Omega and Energy Air-conditioning Concern

– AVP Financial Consultants

– Handiman Legal Services – Total annual turnover of the group: 10 million USD.

Co-owner, Director and Finance Manager of COSTI Ltd. – Israel's largest computerized information vendor and developer. Raised funds through a series of private placements locally in the USA, Canada and London.

1993 to 1996

Publisher and Editor of a Capital Markets Newsletter distributed by subscription only to dozens of subscribers countrywide.

Tried and incarcerated for 11 months for his role in an attempted takeover of Israel's Agriculture Bank involving securities fraud.

Managed the Internet and International News Department of an Israeli mass media group, "Ha-Tikshoret and Namer".

Assistant in the Law Faculty in Tel-Aviv University (to Prof. S.G. Shoham)

1996 to 1999

Financial consultant to leading businesses in Macedonia, Russia and the Czech Republic.

Economic commentator in "Nova Makedonija", "Dnevnik", "Makedonija Denes", "Izvestia", "Argumenti i Fakti", "The Middle East Times", "The New Presence", "Central Europe Review", and other periodicals, and in the economic programs on various channels of Macedonian Television.

Chief Lecturer in courses in Macedonia organized by the Agency of Privatization, by the Stock Exchange, and by the Ministry of Trade.

1999 to 2002
Economic Advisor to the Government of the Republic of Macedonia and to the Ministry of Finance.

2001 to 2003
Senior Business Correspondent for United Press International (UPI)

2005 to Present
Associate Editor and columnist, Global Politician

Founding Analyst, The Analyst Network

Contributing Writer, The American Chronicle Media Group

Expert, Self-growth and Bizymoms and contributor to Mental Health Matters

2007 to 2008
Columnist and analyst in "Nova Makedonija", "Fokus", and "Kapital" (Macedonian papers and newsweeklies)

2008 to 2011
Member of the Steering Committee for the Advancement of Healthcare in the Republic of Macedonia

Advisor to the Minister of Health of Macedonia

Seminars and lectures on economic issues in various forums in Macedonia

Contributor to CommentVision

2011 to Present
Editor in Chief of Global Politician and Investment Politics

Columnist in Dnevnik and Publika, Fokus, and Nova Makedonija (Macedonia)

Columnist in InfoPlus and Libertas

Member CFACT Board of Advisors

Contributor to Recovering the Self

Columnist in New York Daily Sun

Teaches at CIAPS (Commonwealth for International and Advanced Professional Studies)

Columnist in Brussels Morning

2017 to 2022
Visiting Professor of Psychology in Southern Federal University, Rostov-on-Don, Russia

Web and Journalistic Activities

Author of extensive Web sites in:

– Psychology ("Malignant Self-love: Narcissism Revisited") – an Open Directory Cool Site for 8
  years

– Philosophy ("Philosophical Musings")

– Economics and Geopolitics ("World in Conflict and Transition")

Owner of the Narcissistic Abuse Study List, the Toxic Relationships List, and the Abusive
Relationships Newsletter (more than 8000 members)

Owner of the Economies in Conflict and Transition Study List and the Links and Factoid Study List

Editor of mental health disorders and Central and Eastern Europe categories in various Web
directories (Open Directory, Search Europe, Mentalhelp.net)

Editor of the Personality Disorders, Narcissistic Personality Disorder, the Verbal and Emotional
Abuse, and the Spousal (Domestic) Abuse and Violence topics on Suite 101 and contributing author
on Bellaonline.

Columnist and commentator in "The New Presence", United Press International (UPI),
InternetContent, eBookWeb, PopMatters, Global Politician, The Analyst Network, Conservative
Voice, The American Chronicle Media Group, eBookNet.org, and "Central Europe Review".

Publications and Awards

"Managing Investment Portfolios in States of Uncertainty", Limon Publishers, Tel-Aviv, 1988

"The Gambling Industry", Limon Publishers, Tel-Aviv, 1990

"Requesting My Loved One: Short Stories", Miskal-Yedioth Aharonot, Tel-Aviv, 1997

"The Suffering of Being Kafka" (electronic book of Hebrew and English Short Fiction), Prague,
1998-2004

"The Macedonian Economy at a Crossroads – On the Way to a Healthier Economy" (dialogues with
Nikola Gruevski), Skopje, 1998

"The Exporter's Pocketbook" Ministry of Trade, Republic of Macedonia, Skopje, 1999

"Malignant Self-love: Narcissism Revisited", Narcissus Publications, Prague and Skopje, 1999-2015

The Narcissism, Psychopathy, and Abuse in Relationships Series (electronic books regarding
relationships with abusive narcissists and psychopaths), Prague, 1999-2015

"After the Rain – How the West Lost the East", Narcissus Publications in association with Central
Europe Review/CEENMI, Prague and Skopje, 2000

Personality Disorders Revisited (electronic book about personality disorders), Prague, 2007

More than 30 e-books about psychology, international affairs, business and economics, philosophy, short fiction, and reference

Winner of numerous awards, among them Israel's Council of Culture and Art Prize for Maiden Prose (1997), The Rotary Club Award for Social Studies (1976), and the Bilateral Relations Studies Award of the American Embassy in Israel (1978).

Hundreds of professional articles in all fields of finance and economics, and numerous articles dealing with geopolitical and political economic issues, published in both print and Web periodicals in many countries.

Many appearances in the electronic and print media on subjects in psychology, philosophy, and the sciences, and concerning economic matters.

Citations via Google Scholar page:

http://scholar.google.com/citations?user=Yj7C8wOP-10J

Write to Me:
samvaknin@gmail.com

narcissisticabuse-owner@yahoogroups.com

My Web Sites:
Economy/Politics:
http://ceeandbalkan.tripod.com/

Psychology:
http://www.narcissistic-abuse.com/

Philosophy:
http://philosophos.tripod.com/

Poetry:
http://samvak.tripod.com/contents.html

Fiction:
http://samvak.tripod.com/sipurim.html

Follow my work on NARCISSISTS and PSYCHOPATHS

As well as commentaries on international affairs and economics

My work in Psychology: Media Kit and Press Room

http://www.narcissistic-abuse.com/mediakit.html

Biography and Resume

http://www.narcissistic-abuse.com/cv.html

Be my friend on **Facebook**:

http://www.facebook.com/samvaknin

https://www.facebook.com/narcissismwithvaknin/ **(personal page)**

Subscribe to my **YouTube** channel (620+ videos about narcissists and psychopaths and abuse in relationships):

http://www.youtube.com/samvaknin

https://www.youtube.com/user/samvaknin/community (Community)

Follow me on **Instagram**:

https://www.instagram.com/narcissismwithvaknin/ (active)

https://www.instagram.com/vakninsamnarcissist/ (archive)

Read my **Blog**:

http://narcissistpsychopathabuse.blogspot.mk

http://narcissistpsychopathabuse.blogspot.com

Subscribe to my **other YouTube channel** (200+ videos about international affairs, economics, and philosophy):

http://www.youtube.com/vakninmusings

You may also join **Malignant Self-love: Narcissism Revisited on Facebook**:

http://www.facebook.com/pages/Malignant-Self-Love-Narcissism-Revisited/50634038043 or
https://www.facebook.com/NarcissusPublications

http://www.facebook.com/narcissistpsychopathabuse

Follow me on **Linkedin, Twitter, MySpace, Pinterest, Tumblr, Minds, and Ello**:

http://www.linkedin.com/in/samvaknin

http://www.twitter.com/samvaknin

http://www.myspace.com/samvaknin

http://pinterest.com/samvaknin/the-psychopathic-narcissist-and-his-world/

http://narcissistpsychopath-abuse.tumblr.com/

https://www.minds.com/samvaknin

https://ello.co/malignantselflove

https://ello.co/samvaknin

Subscribe to my **Scribd** page: dozens of books for download at no cost to you!

http://www.scribd.com/samvaknin

Zadanliran is following my work as well:

http://www.scribd.com/zadanliran

Additional Resources

Testimonials and Additional Resources

You can read hundreds of Readers' Reviews at the Barnes and Noble, and Amazon Web pages
dedicated to "Malignant Self-love" - HERE:

https://www.amazon.com/dp/1983208175 (Amazon US)

https://www.amazon.co.uk/dp/1983208175 (Amazon UK)

Participate in discussions about Abusive Relationships:

http://www.runboard.com/bnarcissisticabuserecovery

http://thepsychopath.freeforums.org/

Abusive Relationships Newsletters

http://groups.google.com/group/narcissisticabuse/

https://groups.google.com/g/narcissistic-personality-disorder

To purchase from Amazon use this link:

http://www.amazon.com/Malignant-Self-Love-Narcissism-Sam-Vaknin/dp/8023833847

II. ELECTRONIC BOOKS (e-Books)

From KINDLE (AMAZON)

Kindle Books about Narcissists, Psychopaths, and Abusive Relationships – use these links:

http://www.amazon.com/s/ref=ntt_athr_dp_sr_1?_encoding=UTF8&field-author=Sam%20Vaknin&search-alias=digital-text&sort=relevancerank (Amazon USA)

http://www.amazon.co.uk/s/ref=ntt_athr_dp_sr_1?_encoding=UTF8&field-author=Sam%20Vaknin&search-alias=digital-text&sort=relevancerank (Amazon UK)

BUY SIXTEEN e-books about toxic relationships with narcissists and psychopaths - and get the PDF versions of ALL 16 books plus a huge bonus pack FREE!

Use either of these links and send the proof of purchase via email to samvaknin@gmail.com to receive the PDFs and Bonus Pack:

https://www.amazon.com/dp/B07FK6316T (Amazon USA)

https://www.amazon.co.uk/dp/B07FK6316T (Amazon UK)

III. Cold Therapy Seminar on DVDs

http://www.narcissistic-abuse.com/ctcounsel.html

IV. Counselling with Sam Vaknin or Lidija Rangelovska (or both)

http://www.narcissistic-abuse.com/ctcounsel.html

Free excerpts from the EIGHTH, Revised Impression of "Malignant Self-love: Narcissism Revisited" are available as well as a **NEW EDITION of the Narcissism Book of Quotes**.

Use this link to download the files:

http://www.narcissistic-abuse.com/freebooks.html

Download Free Electronic Books on this link:

http://www.narcissistic-abuse.com/freebooks.html